Sharna Wiblen
**Rethinking Talent Decisions**

Sharna Wiblen

# Rethinking Talent Decisions

A Tale of Complexity, Technology and Subjectivity

DE GRUYTER

ISBN 978-3-11-075626-5
e-ISBN (PDF) 978-3-11-075632-6
e-ISBN (EPUB) 978-3-11-075635-7

**Library of Congress Control Number: 2023950566**

**Bibliographic information published by the Deutsche Nationalbibliothek**
The Deutsche Nationalbibliothek lists this publication in the Deutsche Nationalbibliografie;
detailed bibliographic data are available on the internet at http://dnb.dnb.de.

© 2024 Walter de Gruyter GmbH, Berlin/Boston
Cover image: JamesBrey/E+/Getty Images
Typesetting: Integra Software Services Pvt. Ltd.
Printing and binding: CPI books GmbH, Leck

www.degruyter.com

# Advance Praise for *Rethinking Talent Decisions*

With the rapid expansion of HR Tech over the last half decade, *Rethinking Talent Decisions* provides a thoughtful, human-focused approach to navigating vendor power, incorporating diverse views and considering sound and fair evidence when making decisions about people in the context of what is right for your organisation. Highly recommended for Talent and HR professionals and people leaders.

–Kirsten Edwards
Global Head of People Data and Analytics, Rio Tinto,
and co-author of *Predictive HR Analytics: Mastering the HR Metric*

Prepare to shatter the mold of conventional talent thinking with *Rethinking Talent Decisions*. As a Chief Talent Officer, I've personally experienced the cognitive and social biases inherent in most human capital decisions. This transformative book not only challenges the status quo but also empowers you with a fresh perspective, prompting insightful questions and arming you with essential tools to navigate the dynamic intersection of humans and technology.

–Michael J. Arena, PhD
Former Chief Talent Officer of General Motors and
Amazon Web Services, and author of *Adaptive Space*

In *Rethinking Talent Decisions*, Sharna Wiblen captures the important and complex art of talent assessment, its important link to organisational strategy and its inherently subjective nature. Sharna Wiblen leverages research and practice to lay out how organisations and individuals assign value to people to improve organisational performance and explores the many ways people define talent across individuals and organisations. Importantly, Sharna Wiblen carefully contemplates the intersection of current and emerging talent management technologies and how they can shape talent evaluations, and potential implications for talent evaluation and organisational effectiveness. *Rethinking Talent Decisions* is a must for Talent Management professionals interested in increasing their understanding of the complexity and importance of both good talent management practices and technology selection for organisational leaders seeking to bolster their organisation's ability to improve workforce differentiation.

–Patrick McLaughlin
Senior Vice President of Human Resources and
Chief Human Resources Officer Pepsi-Co, Pepsi-Co Foods North America

In today's disruptive and sometimes confusing world, reading a focused and insightful view of today's and, more importantly, tomorrow's talent management world is a delight. This book has a great blend of insight, ideas, frameworks and practical solutions to a challenge that a lot of organisations continue to struggle to satisfactorily address. It is a must-read book for practitioners wanting to re-imagine their organisation's talent strategy and deal with this business-critical issue.

–Dave Millner
The HR Curator,
Consultant, and co-author of *Introduction to People Analytics*

*Rethinking Talent Decisions* is both thought-provoking – asking the reader to reflect on ideas and be willing to adjust and build thoughts to reach decisions – and practical in application – devoting attention to the use of technology to capture ideas about talent and harness those ideas to create more fulsome and data-informed talent decisions. As a former Chief HR Officer, improving talent decisions is a holy grail for building high-performing teams. This book presents new ways of thinking about talent, talent systems and decision-making that leaders can simply and sustainably apply.

–Susan Kelliher
Former Senior Vice President, People,
The Chemours Company

Sharna Wiblen has done something that traditional talent management approaches have ironically missed; she integrates talent management with the process of innovation. Her groundbreaking approach frames talent management, not as some strategy around managing an objective and static organizational feature (e.g., abilities and skills of a workforce), but as a subjective journey of thinking and re-thinking how to integrate individual talent with dynamic technological capabilities to meet organizational needs. This book is a must-read for leaders who aim to make their talent management systems sufficiently agile to meet the increasingly rapid pace of technological change.

–Jennifer S. Mueller, PhD
Professor of Management,
Knauss School of Business, University of San Diego,
and author of *Creative Change*

## Advance Praise for *Rethinking Talent Decisions*

Sharna Wiblen's *Rethinking Talent Decisions* is a comprehensive monograph that provides a nuanced approach to talent management and responsible decision-making in the digital era. Sharna Wiblen's work, rich in interdisciplinary insights, navigates the complex interplay between abstract theory and practical applications, from historical HR information system shifts to discussions on talent categories and strategic execution. Sharna Wiblen astutely surfaces issues of entrenched power dynamics and subjectivity in talent management that risk embedding bias under the veneer of technological solutions. This thought-provoking book significantly contributes to our understanding of decision-making and provides valuable guidance for leaders, consultants, and academics.

–Max Blumberg, PhD
People Analytics Advisor and Founder of Blumberg Partnership

Within the ever-competitive business landscape, Sharna Wiblen's book highlights the critical role of assessing the value of data. Sharna Wiblen urges leaders to meticulously examine the assumptions that form the basis of data and analytics, emphasising the necessity for a nuanced comprehension of information. This heightened level of insight empowers leaders to pose more insightful questions and analyse the foundations of decision-making. Sharna Wiblen's book offers a thorough and insightful guide for leaders navigating the convergence of talent, technology, and data-driven decision-making.

–David Green
Managing Partner at Insight222,
co-author of *Excellence in People Analytics*,
and host of the Digital HR Leaders podcast

The intersection of technology and human judgment in talent-related decision-making is at an evolutionary inflection point. Sharna Wiblen highlights the importance of evolving our people-related decision capability while avoiding the temptation to overly rely on off-the-shelf technology products that fail to consider the incredible complexities of matching unique humans with unique roles and organizations. Sharna Wiblen challenges us to consider the use of technology in our talent decisions because it is *ALL* about the people.

–Rachelle Snook
Vice President Global Talent,
WD-40 Company

Sharna Wiblen's work is a wake-up call for decision-makers, urging them to recognise the transformational influence of specific thoughts on talent decisions and strategic outcomes. By highlighting the limitations of conventional thinking, Sharna Wiblen shows us why many approaches to talent management are limited in their ability to enable strategic outcomes. This book provides a map for leaders to navigate the complex terrain of talent management, offering a novel perspective that allows decision-makers to balance operational requirements and strategic success.

–John Boudreau, PhD
Professor Emeritus
Marshall School of Business, University of Southern California,
thought leader and co-author of *Work Without Jobs, Investing in People*
and *Reinventing Jobs*

For decades "talent" has been the catchphrase everyone uses without stopping to think about what it really means and how best to leverage it appropriately for competitive advantage. Sharna Wiblen shows us the criticality of making the right decisions about individual, team and organizational talent. An essential framework for senior leaders everywhere.

–Alec Levenson, PhD
Senior Research Scientist,
Centre for Effective Organizations,
Marshall School of Business, University of Southern California,
and author of *Strategic Analytics*

This is a fresh perspective on the need to understand why we think what we think; especially regarding talent, which can bring value and competitive advantage. The way Sharna Wiblen breaks down the concepts of complexity, technology and subjectivity in relation to thinking and the effects they have on decision-making is both highly engaging and logical. Throughout the book we are continually given value from the questions asked, forcing us to consider not only our own understanding but the wider environment. This book not only sparks curiosity but highlights the need for self-development to improve the quality of our thinking for a better every day, understanding the layers involved in decision-making because of our thinking and the impact it has on our belief around talent and the broader impact that this has on our workplaces and strategies. It is a book worth reading for HR and anyone within an organisation.

–Jennifer Szczepaniak Sloane, MBA
Head of Marketing,
Dark Horse Digital Limited

With a refreshingly modern lens, *Rethinking Talent Decisions* challenges us to think, reflect and create "Y.O.U. – Your Own Understanding" of talent, the strategies and the decisions surrounding it. Taking us on a thought-provoking journey, Sharna Wiblen leads us through understanding the what and why of the perspectives we have, the opinions we form and our responsibilities as talent and strategic decision-makers. Whether an HR professional, business leader, building your career or just starting on your exciting learning path, *Rethinking Talent Decisions* hits it for six as an inspiring and thought-provoking must-read to improve responsible human decision-making!

–Nathan Watson, MBA
Operations Manager,
Endevour Energy

This refreshing and different take on talent management will challenge your thinking, improve your decision-making, and enhance Your Own Understanding (Y.O.U.) about talent. It takes on the issue of subjectivity and the underappreciated implications of using technology to automate talent management tasks. If you are in the talent management space, this is a must-read.

–Janet H. Marler, PhD
Professor and Associate Dean,
Massry School of Business, University at Albany

Thinking intentionally, broadly, and deeply about talent management is critical. Sharna Wiblen's ability to show us why in *Rethinking Talent Decisions* is powerful and gives this book an edge I never saw coming! Sharna Wiblen asks us to acknowledge our own understandings before guiding us through (re)thinking lessons and reflections! As we progress, we consider system and technology capabilities, conscious and unconscious thinking, and human-centric talent frameworks, to uncover talent management opportunities that can elevate the organisation. This is a must read for all executives, managers, and leaders. Go #Teamhuman!

–Maree Baulman, MAICD
Technology and Business Consultant,
Non-Executive Director,
AICD NSW Forum Member

Sharna Wiblen weaves a masterful tale that helps readers to think critically and deeply about how work, technology, and complexity affect talent management. Every step of the way, she helps them craft incisive questions that will yield responsible decisions about talent. That's what makes this book so valuable.

–Wayne Cascio, PhD
Distinguished Professor Emeritus,
University of Colorado Denver,
and co-author of *Investing in People*

*Rethinking Talent Decisions* offers all professionals whose role incorporates talent management, important insights on how to better integrate and unpack existing approaches to talent decisions. It is a book that uniquely challenges the reader to think more deeply around one's current approach to talent decision-making.

–Anthony McDonnell, PhD
Professor of Human Resource Management,
Cork University Business School,
University College Cork, Ireland

Sharna Wiblen's latest work is a masterclass in intentional and deliberate talent management, skillfully navigating the intricacies of talent as a pivotal competitive advantage in any organisation. Sharna Wiblen's approach is accessible, guiding aspiring leaders with minimal prior knowledge through the nuances of talent management while offering deep insights for seasoned decision-makers to reflect on their perspectives and strategies around talent and digital transformation.

This book stands out in its ability to instil confidence in critical thinking, decision-making and navigating the complex global landscape we find ourselves in today. Wiblen challenges readers with thought-provoking questions like, 'Do you know that, or do you think that?' prompting a deeper understanding and reassessment of talent management. Sharna Wiblen's compelling narrative ensures that every decision contributes to a stronger and more competitive organisation.

What makes this book essential reading is not just its relevance to those in the People and Culture function but its broader appeal to all leaders seeking practical wisdom. Readers will find themselves equipped with invaluable insights that can be applied not only to their professional lives but across all facets, enhancing decision-making at every level. In essence, this book is a treasure trove of wisdom for anyone aspiring to make impactful decisions in talent management and beyond.

–Shannon Dutton, MBA
Merchant Solutions Engineer, Shopify,
and Tech Startup Advisor

Few things are more important to HR professionals than developing a deep understanding of talent. Yet for all the literature, articles, blogs, and courses on talent, learning the practical application of identifying and leveraging talent can remain a daunting task. Sharna simplifies the complex, in this engaging and practical tool. I highly recommend this title to any in an HR function looking to upskill their strategic counsel, and unlock their organisation's natural capacity for excellence.

–Stephanie Power
People Advisor,
Charter Hall

In *Rethinking Talent Decisions*, Sharna Wiblen masterfully navigates the interplay of subjectivity, technology, and complexity in today's talent landscape. Through her holistic perspective and emphasis on the fusion between talent and technology, Sharna Wiblen encourages us to revisit how we can effectively manage talent. Drawing from two decades of experience, this book offers invaluable tools for recalibrating one's outlook on talent decisions, urging a critical examination of perceptions to foster impactful decision-making.

–Peter Ferris
Head of Sales APAC,
Star Rez

Sharna Wiblen shines an empathetic light on the human experience and the often unseen influences that shape and differentiate the myriad perspectives around talent and talent management. Steering clear of sometimes prevailing voices that over-simplify and promote the trend du jour, Sharna Wiblen's humanizing narrative embraces subjectivity and complexity, guiding readers on a journey of introspection and reflection. Sharna challenges the reader to deeply (re)think how to understand and approach talent management.

– Alicia Miller
Organizational Strategy Advisor

# Acknowledgements

Like all decisions and actions, this book is a team sport; I have many humans that I'd like to acknowledge and thank.

First and foremost, I express gratitude to my home team. This latest output sees my husband – Robbie – transition from being unnamed to being named as the first person in my acknowledgements. Thank you for supporting my creative and knowledge-based pursuits and for walking with me each and every day. I treasure having you on my team and look forward to popping champagne to celebrate.

To my three kidlets, Emmett, Sierra and Jenson, you are the light of my life. Every day is new, and I am grateful for our experiences. You are the recipients (and Guinea pigs) of my passion for everyday decision-making and many of the ideas featured in this book. You have taught me about the power of imagination, storytelling and themes. Because of you, I dedicate my time, energy and attention to improving my decisions, actions and enhancing the quality of our every day.

I am sharing my ideas with you because of a remarkable and inspiring woman – Carolyn Evans. Carolyn and I met when I was an enthusiastic and ambitious 17-year-old. Our first encounter was life-changing. I frequently talk about meeting "the lady in the red coat," and this experience is a practical example of the exponential and ripple effect of Carolyn's decision to be part of an award-judging panel. While this may have been a small and inconsequential decision for Carolyn at the time, the outcomes of that single decision on me are profound. Carolyn's decision opened my eyes to many possibilities. Carolyn also introduced me to the world of Management Consultancy, and it was during this season of my life that I developed an interest in "thinking" and "decisions." Carolyn successfully founded a consulting company based on inclusivity and diversity and saw the value of thinking and rethinking. Carolyn taught me the importance of searching for and acknowledging complexity – which helps explain why complexity is a big part of my scientific and teaching endeavours and this book. Carolyn, thank you for making many decisions for and with me. I decide every day to appreciate the power of one decision.

This specific book started with an introduction and an invitation. One day, at the 7$^{th}$ Electronic Human Resource Management Conference in Milan (2018), I decided to introduce myself to an unknown human. That decision resulted in the meeting of Steven Hardman. Asking Steven, "What brings you to the e-HRM Conference?" generated information about Steve's position as an Acquisitions Editor at De Gruyter. Sharing a mutual interest in publishing, I invited Steve to come and "see" some of my academic presentations and "see" if he might be interested in a book about digitalised talent management. That introduction and invitation represent two pivotal decisions that resulted in this book coming into your hands. I want to thank Steve, my Editor, for his interest in talent and technology and for allowing me to share these ideas with a broader audience. Your support of this project has been unbridled from day one, and I thank you for your collegial approach. My second De Gruyter thanks goes to Jaya Dalal. Thank you, Jaya, for all your work bringing this book to life and helping manage all the required details and editing.

Our (re)thinking talent tale builds on the knowledge, ideas and experiences I've acquired over the past two decades, and there are several groups and individuals I've had the privilege of collaborating with during this journey.

To my PhD and academic supervisors, David Grant, Kristine Dery, Richard Hall and Nick Wailes, I thank you for your guidance, support and mentorship throughout my early academic journey. Your expertise, encouragement and unwavering support of my interest in "talent" and "technology" fostered an environment where I was encouraged to pursue my intellectual curiosity.

To my #Teamhuman counterparts associated with the Centre for Effective Organizations, thank you for welcoming me into your team with open arms and unbridled support. Alec Levenson, Jennifer Deal, Jennifer Sparks, John Boudreau, Max Blumberg, Dave Millner, Nora Hilton, Vivian Jimenez and Priscilla Soto, your commitment to excellence has inspired me to strive for the highest standards. The numerous opportunities to share and discuss my ideas with senior executives and gain your insights and feedback have helped refine my thoughts and teachings. Your ability to provide a stimulating intellectual environment is inspiring. I appreciate your friendship and collegiality (even at 1 a.m.).

I am fortunate to have the support of the Electronic Human Resource Management (e-HRM) crowd – Janet Marler, Sandy Fisher, Tanya Bondarouk, Emma Parry, Anna Holm, Huub Ruel, Barbara Imperatori, Rita Bissola, Miguel Olivas-Lujan, Stefan Strohmeier, Richard Johnson, Carole Tansley, Hazel Williams and Jeroen Meijerink. I love being part of the E-HRM team and am inspired by many of the technology-based science outputs and events we create and share.

Footnotes and endnotes of this book frequently refer to *Talent Management: A Research Overview*, a book co-authored with Anthony McDonnell. I want to thank Anthony for being interested in my talent management research and co-authoring books and publications which advance our scientific understanding of talent management.

The Digital Future(s) Research Group provides a monthly forum to discuss "technology." I am indebted to this group and key members – Kai Riemer, Daniel Schlagwein, Sandra Peters, Fiona McLean, Mike Seymour, Paul Galland, Michele Gennoe, Connie Henson, Jakkii Musgrave, Ben Elias, James Dellow, Ali Eshraghi and Tim Mahlberg – for the insightful and at times difficult conversations about technology innovations and their influence on teaching, organisations and broader society. A special thanks to Scott Ward, who posed a question during one of our monthly conversations. Scott asked, "If Donald Trump is the answer, then what are the questions?" This question has stuck with me since, and I frequently think about the questions, the questions and the questions. Part of my thinking centres around, "If vendor-designed technology systems are the answer, then what are the questions?"

To Sophie Goodman, I thank you for sharing my interest in "seeing" talent and discussing the need for decision-makers to learn how to "see." I will continually profess the importance of your anthropological and observation expertise.

I want to thank all the students and decision-makers I've taught or encountered; thank you for generously sharing your time, stories and knowledge. Through you, I learn about talent decisions and your willingness to tell me about what you think about talent and how you make talent decisions and use technology has been instrumental in shedding light on the complexity and subjectivity of talent decisions. I express a particular note of appreciation to Katie Grant, who introduced me to the connections between Maybelline's "Maybe She's Born with It" campaign and talent concepts as part of a reflective assessment. Inclusion of this example is the result of Katie's thoughts.

Finally, I would like to express my profound appreciation to all the readers who have decided to embark on this journey with me. I hope this book will provide you with new insights, inspire curiosity and ignite meaningful conversations. Together we can improve decision-making. Please remember the exponential power of improving one decision at a time and think about the world we, #Teamhumans, want to create.

# Contents

Acknowledgements —— XIII

Prologue —— XXI

## Part 1: Introducing (Re)Thinking Talent Decisions

**Chapter 1**
A Tale of Complexity, Technology and Subjectivity —— 3

**Chapter 2**
Introducing the Cast —— 11

## Part 2: (Re)Thinking Talent Decision Outcomes

**Chapter 3**
Talent Decisions in the Pursuit of Strategy —— 33

**Chapter 4**
Talent Decisions In The Pursuit of Knowledge —— 59

**Chapter 5**
Our Tale End(INGS) —— 69

## Part 3: (Re)Thinking Work, Technology and Talent Management

**Chapter 6**
(Re)Thinking Work —— 81

**Chapter 7**
(Re)Thinking Technology and Digitalisation —— 87

**Chapter 8**
(Re)Thinking Talent Management —— 93

## Part 4: (Re)Thinking Talent

**Chapter 9**
(Re)Thinking Talent Meanings —— 103

**Chapter 10**
(Re)Thinking Talent Categories —— 111

**Chapter 11**
External Character's Talent Categories —— 151

## Part 5: Negotiating Talent Decisions

**Chapter 12**
Scene 1: Negotiating Talent Meanings —— 163

**Chapter 13**
Scene 2: Negotiating Talent Identification —— 173

**Chapter 14**
Scene 3: Negotiating Talent Decision Systems —— 183

## Part 6: Implications

**Chapter 15**
Strategic Implications —— 199

**Chapter 16**
Knowledge Implications —— 207

## Part 7: Conclusion

**Chapter 17**
Concluding Monologue —— 219

Endnotes —— 231

List of Figures —— 245

About the Author —— 247

Index —— 249

# Prologue

## The Power of (Re)Thinking

I wrote this book for you and me. I wrote this book for #Teamhuman because I believe that *thinking* matters. Let me tell you some of my reasons why:

We all think.
We all think every day.
Our thinking influences the quality of our lives.
The quality of our lives is an outcome of the quality of our thinking every day.
Thinking is a "human quality."
The ability to think is a (human) source of competitive advantage.
We, humans, create value by thinking.

I became interested in thinking during my tenure as a Management Consultant. The consulting industry consists of clients asking consultants for help with thinking (and doing) "something." A Management Consultant, therefore, is essentially paid to "think." To think on behalf of the client and offer recommendations of how to address, solve or resolve the relevant "something." Recommendations combine client and consultant thinking.

I thoroughly enjoyed my time as a Management Consultant. I was exposed to organisations of all shapes and sizes, from diverse industries that operated under different ownership models and were guided by various operational activities and strategic ambitions. I also formally and informally talked with many of my #Teamhuman counterparts. Each conversation was different and I thrived on hearing (and including) different voices. I was fascinated with learning about others' thinking. There I was – thinking about my thinking, others' thinking and my thinking about others' thinking. I was thinking every day. I was thinking about my thinking every day.

I wanted to know more about what people thought. I sought opportunities to learn more about others and their thinking. I was also interested in learning about the stuff that informed, influenced and shaped their thinking. With a curious demeanour, I'd regularly ask,

"What do you think about X (the relevant something)?"
"What has contributed to you thinking about X that way?"
"What are some of the things you think we should consider and examine?"
"What do you think the real issues are?"
"Why do you think these are the real issues?"
"How do you think we got to X becoming a priority today?"
"If you could do one thing to address X what would you do first and why?"

Some asked for clarification,
"What do you mean by that?"
Some paused and then commented, "That's an interesting way to frame it," or "I've never thought about it like that."
Some conversations halted when they became defensive or thought they were under attack, "Why do you want to know?", "Why does that matter?", "That question doesn't relate to the task at hand."

I learnt during this time that not everyone shared my fascination with thinking. Not everyone knew what they thought. Not everyone knew what shaped their thinking. Not everyone knew how they arrived at their thoughts – the embedded assumptions and contributing factors. Some were very honest and said, "That's the way we do things," "I just follow directions or was following a directive," or "I don't know." I, and the humans I conversed with, were regularly perplexed. I was particularly perplexed when my curious questioning resulted in a puzzled face or a period of silence. I saw many eyebrows raised. I heard "hmmm" many times.

This made me even more curious about thinking because I wanted to know how we could be in situations where people didn't know what they thought. Or didn't know how they arrived at their thinking destination. Or that they can change and update their thinking and their thinking destination.

But what is thinking?

My hardcover *Compact Oxford Dictionary and Thesaurus* defines thinking as "a person's ideas or opinions."

My go-to Merriam-Webster digital dictionary and thesaurus defines thinking as "The action of using one's mind to produce thoughts," "an opinion/judgment" and/or "thought that is characteristic (as of a period, group or person)."

Thinking requires a human to "think." To think involves humans, "hav[ing] a particular opinion, belief, or idea about someone or something," "to direct one's mind towards someone or something," "take into account or consideration," and "consider the possibility or advantages."

This book focuses on thinking, so much so that I put thinking in the title. Together we will think about our thinking. Together we will rethink our thinking.

This book also focuses on re-thinking.[1] (Re)thinking because we benefit from thinking and then re-thinking. We will re-do and repeat our thinking because thinking is not a one-time activity. Thinking about thinking is a daily activity.

This is a book encouraging us all to rethink. Rethink because thinking benefits from an iterative process. We can change our thinking. Neuroplasticity means that our brains establish new connections whenever we learn something new. Our brains change every time we learn. #Teamhuman must know that we can change and update

---

1 I alternate between rethinking and (re)thinking throughout the book.

our thinking. It is OK to think differently today than you did yesterday. It is OK to think a different way tomorrow than you did today. The task is to know how and why your thinking changed.

> *The decisions we make every day serve as a mirror, reflecting the calibre of our thinking.*

## The Power of (Re)Thinking Decisions

I want to help you think about your thinking because the quality of our thinking influences the quality of our decisions, and the quality of our decisions influences the quality and outcomes of our actions. We can improve the quality of our every day by improving the quality of our decisions.

> *We can harness the power of exponential returns, one decision at a time.*

Within us lies the extraordinary ability to initiate a chain reaction of transformative mindsets and approaches, where each decision becomes a strategic "investment" with the potential for exponential growth. I believe in the profound power of enhancing one decision at a time. Collectively, we can improve our daily lives incrementally by making responsible decisions. As decision-makers, we hold the key to unlocking exponential growth, acknowledging the compounding effect ingrained in every single decision we make.

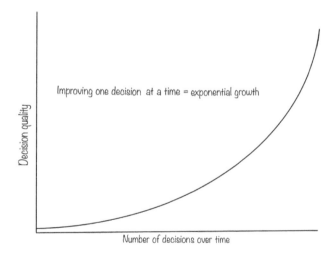

Source: Copyright © Sharna Wiblen. All rights reserved.

Envision decisions as a set of interconnected gears, each representing a decision. When set in motion, the gears initiate a chain reaction that spans individuals, teams, organisations and societies. The moving gears symbolise the transformational power of each decision. The gears become larger and more intricate as they progress, representing the exponential growth that responsible decision-making can achieve.

You can also think of decisions as a cascading line of dominos; each piece represents a decision that sets off a ripple effect. In this perspective, decisions, regardless of their magnitude or nature, become the stepping stones that lead us to personal growth, inspire others and elevate the overall quality of our daily lives. Just like the mesmerising spectacle of falling dominos, our decisions hold the power to ignite a chain reaction of positive transformation.

Elevating the quality of our decisions yields many positive outcomes, both in the immediate and long-term, for individuals, society and beyond. These benefits are twofold: direct and residual. Enhancing decision quality enriches our decision-making processes, improving experiences and outcomes in our daily lives. Additionally, the residual impact of our improved decision quality extends to the careers and livelihoods of those around us, influencing their paths in indirect, unknown and potentially immeasurable ways.

This is why, my fellow members of #Teamhuman, this book intentionally connects thinking and decisions. Decisions generate exponential and compounding returns.

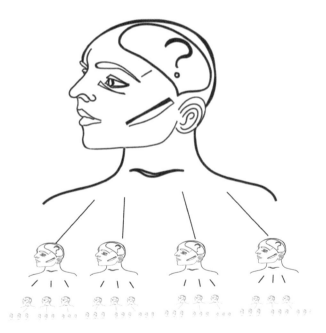

Source: Copyright © Sharna Wiblen. All rights reserved.

# The Power of (Re)Thinking Talent Decisions

Together we are thinking and rethinking a specific category of decisions – talent decisions: the decisions related to humans in the workplace. Let me tell you some of the reasons why we are thinking and rethinking talent decisions:

We are all talent.
We all have ideas about what talent is.
We all have ideas about what talent is not.
We all have opinions about how individuals perform their talent.
We all make talent decisions (whether we realise it or not).
We are privy to the talent decisions of others.

Talent decisions result in some individuals rising while others fall.
Careers are built on talent decisions.
Careers end because of talent decisions.

Whether we are the decider or the receiver, talent decisions are a team sport. And we are all on the same (human) team.

Talent decisions occur every day. Someone, whether you or another, are making a talent decision every day. Someone, whether you or another, are privy to the talent decisions of others every day. And we, as a team, must pay attention to the decision-making that occurs every day.

Consideration of talent decisions within organisational contexts further shows why (re)thinking about talent decisions is an essential tale for us all.

Organisations need talent.
Talent is a source of competitive advantage because humans are non-imitable resources.
Organisations invest in talent because, as the story goes, talent is worthy of investment.
Talent is, however, also (potentially) an organisation's most considerable expense. And we benefit from paying attention to significant sources of expenditure.

Talent is essential to operational needs and strategy execution because strategies are actualised (or not) by The Workforce's actions (or inactions).
Organisations can thrive because of the effectiveness of talent decisions.
On the other hand, we also bear witness to other organisations that struggle to survive.

Key characters within organisations need to organise and manage talent (in all its forms).
Key characters are constantly concerned with talent-related opportunities and challenges.
Apparently, talent issues keep senior executives, Human Resource (HR) professionals and line managers "up at night."

Combining my industry experience, a PhD in Talent Management and teaching experiences in Executive, EMBA, MBA and Postgraduate programs in Australia, England and the United States, I have gained a deep understanding of the science and art of defining talent – deciding what talent is and is not; talent identification – how talent meanings come to life as executives decide who and what are, or are not, talent; and the talent decision-makers – the extent to which humans and technology are tasked with, and responsible for, talent decisions (Digitalised Talent Management is the latter scientific area). For the past two decades, I have been committed to leveraging my knowledge, experience, scientific insights and voice to instigate, contribute to and shape informed conversations that acknowledge and unpack the complexity of genuine talent management. This book, a book about thinking and rethinking talent decisions, is an outcome of this commitment.

## Book Aims

This book has two primary aims. First and foremost, I aim to incite questions and inspire you to think critically and deeply about the issues and topics we explore. I believe asking questions is the first step toward discovering new perspectives and insights. Having my fellow #Teamhuman counterparts ask better questions is pivotal. Asking better questions helps to elicit quality answers. Eliciting answers of a superior quality enables humans to upgrade their thinking and talent decision-making capabilities. Improving talent decisions is a lead indicator – a lead indicator that influences talent outcomes and strategy execution. We must not minimise the salience of talent decisions because talent decisions influence people's careers and livelihoods. (Re)Thinking talent decisions, therefore, involves asking questions. Be clear about the questions. Better questions underpin better answers.

---

*The human who asks a question is a fool for a minute, the human who does not ask is a fool for life – my version of a Confucius quote.*[2]
*If you do not know how to ask the right question, you discover nothing. – W. Edwards Deming*

---

I also seek to foster responsible decision-making. Talking and writing about the complexity associated with #Teamhuman and #Teamtechnology sparks joy (kudos to Marie Kondo). The goal is to encourage better questions and better decisions. Better, in this context, means we each undertake decisions and actions that are:

---

[2] I have attributed both quotes to Confucius and W. Edwards Deming despite the inability to locate the original source and confirm authorship of either quotes. I have also changed Confucius' subject reference from "man" to "human."

- Deliberate = undertaken with thought.
- Intentional = undertaken on purpose.
- Informed = based on knowledge.

*Responsible talent decisions involve decisions that are deliberate, intentional and informed.*

Better talent decision outcomes occur because we have asked better questions. And becoming a better decision-maker involves pursuing responsible decision-making. I hope this book equips you with the knowledge and skills necessary to navigate complex situations and instil the confidence to transition from opinion to perspective. You can say, "My informed perspective is X" and "I don't know."

*Responsible decision making allows you to decipher between an "opinion" and a "perspective."*
*An opinion = "I think X."*
*A perspective = "I know X."*

(Re)Thinking Talent Decisions extends an open invitation to practitioners – past, current and future decision-makers – to think about talent. I aim to encourage you to think about what we think. The book aims to get you to think about thinking – what do you think and why do you think that?

Together, we will also examine the assumptions and interests that guide decision-making. This is essential because (re)thinking talent decisions start and end with humans; by humans, I mean each individual's Y.O.U. – Your Own Understanding. Engaging with decision-makers is central to my overarching goal of promoting responsible talent decisions. By reading this book, I encourage you to join me in this mission to work together to develop a community of responsible decision-makers.

## An Overview of Our (Re)Thinking Tale

As we begin this discussion, I recognise that some of you may already be well-versed in the (re)thinking process, while others may be starting from scratch. With this in mind, I won't assume any pre-existing knowledge or understanding.

I have chosen to write the book as a "tale" to make the content more accessible. This approach allows us to remember and retain the knowledge we acquire throughout our journey.

The deliberate choice to present my ideas as a "tale" serves a purpose beyond mere reading. While I genuinely appreciate your engagement with this book, I aim for you to develop the meta-skill of thinking and establish foundational principles of reflective thinking specific to you (referred to as Y.O.U. reflective thinking). I encourage you to ask yourself probing questions such as: "What do I think, and why do I think that way?" This process allows you to gain a deeper understanding of your own perspectives.

Additionally, I seek to create "sticky" associations that stay with you long after reading the book. By framing the content as a tale, I hope to create a memorable and engaging experience that facilitates learning and introspection. Maybe you'll dream about an idea presented here, think about a concept another way, pause before sharing your perspective and look at talent in a different, more responsible light.

Together, we will explore talent decisions through the lens of a play, where various characters, a broader plot and numerous scenes unfold.

**Part 1, Introducing (Re)Thinking Talent Decisions**, sets the scene for our tale. I introduce you to our three central themes, (1) complexity, (2) technology, and (3) subjectivity and propose, to illustrate, like all good stories, that our journey is complex and fraught with tension. The colourful interconnected ropes picture on the book's cover seeks to represent the complexity of talent decisions. We cannot treat talent decisions as a bounded phenomenon. Talent decisions relate to other decisions and outcomes. Each talent decision influences decisions and outcomes outside talent management.

The passage argues that talent decisions are complex because talent and talent management are socially constructed concepts that are dynamic and constantly changing, and external factors add another layer of complexity. Technology plays a reciprocal role in talent management, affecting talent availability and an organisation's approach to data, digitalisation and automation. Talent decisions are always subjective because they involve subjective judgments of value, and how we think about value and talent is individual.

Every tale needs an array of characters, and in Part I we also meet our cast. I introduce you to three characters, (1) Humans, (2) Technology, and (3) Vendors, and together we explore their different and, at times, competing interests. We learn that humans are always the leading character in talent decisions because decisions start with a thought, and many things influence our thoughts and actions. The importance of subjectivity, therefore, encourages us to start with Y.O.U. – Your Own Understanding. The passage covers two additional characters in the story of talent decisions: technology and vendors. Technology has a reciprocal relationship with humans in talent decisions. At the same time, vendors play a foil role as they have different interests and compete against each other for sales despite sharing a focus on promoting standardisation and efficiency in talent decisions.

**Part 2, (Re)Thinking Talent Decision Outcomes**, addresses purpose. Why do we make talent decisions? Talent decisions are a tool, a methodology and a means to get us towards an outcome. Using a map analogy, I propose two different "whys": (1) strategy – whereby talent decisions aid strategy execution; and (2) knowledge – the desire to increase our knowledge and know more than we did before.

We think about what strategy is and is not and learn different ways to think about strategy (called strategy lenses). We also delve into talent management strategies, digitalisation strategies and digitalised talent management strategies to reflect on the interconnected nature of all things strategy. I'll profess that strategy matters: "Strategy, strategy, strategy – all talent decisions are in the pursuit of strategy."

We also think about knowledge. An adage is "Knowledge is power," but we benefit from recognising that knowledge becomes powerful (and useful) when applied. Despite acknowledging that you are reading this book to increase your knowledge and understanding of talent decisions, many publications fail to share what knowledge is. Not this book. Our (re)thinking talent decisions tale covers just this topic. We address the issue of what knowledge is. You'll learn two new words – ontology and epistemology – and realise that characters hold different and sometimes competing ideas about how knowledge is established or created. Some characters believe that knowledge is pre-determined – "the truth is out there." Others think that we co-create knowledge. Understanding differences in knowledge lenses adds further complexity to our tale.

Part 2 includes a third chapter, which tells you how our tale can "End." I don't leave the ending to the end. I share our conclusion upfront. Understanding that our views of ontology and epistemology shape our thoughts about reality, knowledge and talent decisions, I detail three rather than a single "Ending." One ending asserts that talent decision outcomes and technology-based change are pre-defined. Another one believes that there are multiple "It Depends" endings, while a third thinks there are infinite "It Depends" endings because the human-technology interface constantly changes. Despite the different conclusions (again, more complexity), we learn that no ending is right or wrong. Understanding that humans have different assumptions about reality and knowledge matters and that these assumptions influence how we think about talent decision outcomes is the intent of this passage.

**Part 3, (Re)Thinking Work, Technology, and Talent Management**, encourages us to think and rethink three core elements associated with talent decisions: (1) work; (2) technology; and (3) talent management. This passage emphasises the importance of understanding people's different perspectives and meanings regarding work, technology and talent management. Reflective questions can help establish a shared understanding and collaboration and identify whether differences are semantic or conceptual.

**Part 4, (Re)Thinking Talent**, explores how we think about talent. This part starts with a visualisation exercise where I ask you to reflect on your thoughts and reactions as you walk around a workplace. The activity highlights that talent begins with a thought. Thoughts about one's value are the foundation for talent decisions. We continue our journey by considering how our fellow humans, myself included, think about talent. Specifically, we consider public and scientific definitions before delving into the different talent categories – from those that are well known, such as talent being something we have and can discover over time, to a verb-based perspective that recognises that decision-makers care about how or whether an individual acts and performs their talent and prioritise observing and judging talent-in-action. We also explore talent as a means for strategy execution, a set of peer comparisons, a time-based concept and humans we don't want to lose. Understanding what talent means to you and what talent means to me influences talent decisions and informs talent management. Our tale of complexity heightens as we realise there are so many different "someones" and "somethings" that decision-makers value.

Part 4 includes a second chapter that recognises that talent is an area where our external characters – scientists, consultants, customers, unions, experts, admired CEO's business gurus and vendors – hold different ideas about the defining characteristics of talent. This section's discussion will shed light on how external groups advocate for certain talent meanings and highlight that external characters are not impartial but have vested interests in promoting specific perspectives or approaches. As we rethink external characters we start to acknowledge the influence of external characters on talent decisions and the possibility that the structure and foundations for talent decisions emerge outside of the organisation (and be misaligned with an organisation's strategic imperatives).

**Part 5, Negotiating Talent Decisions**, encourages us to take a moment to contemplate the involvement of diverse voices and interests associated with talent decisions. We explore how internal and external characters' thoughts and perspectives combine in work-based contexts. Understanding the different characters' voices is vital because talent decisions are not isolated occurrences. Instead, every aspect of talent decisions emerges from negotiation processes where characters negotiate to decide which meanings, frameworks and systems are adopted.

Part 5 uses our tale narrative. This section, presented as a stage play, is divided into three distinct "scenes" centred around a core theme of collaboration or conflict. We begin by delving into talent meanings and focus on answering, "What does talent mean in our organisation?" We learn that two outcomes likely emerge from these negotiation processes with key decision-makers prioritising either (1) an all-purpose or (2) a specific purpose talent meaning. We compare and contrast the different perspectives and in doing so reemphasise the complexity of talent decisions.

Our second scene deals with the negotiation processes associated with talent identification. In this scene, our attention is directed towards establishing the talent identification processes specific to an organisation. We do so by unveiling our diverse characters' preferred talent identification processes. As talent identification is intricately linked to the definition of talent, key decision-makers must engage in negotiations facilitated by certain characters to determine the most suitable talent identification process/es. Together we are answering "Which talent identification process is best for our organisation?" and learn of three potential answers: (1) a systematic or (2) an integrated, or (3) an

AND-based approach where organisations simultaneously adopt static and fluid talent identification processes.

Our third scene focuses on talent decision systems. In Scene 3, technology takes centre stage as the "system" is synonymous with technology. Most organisations use a talent management system – a technology software that captures, stores and analyses talent data. Because of this, we ask, "Which talent management technology system is best for our organisation?" We reflect on the history of talent management decision systems and acknowledge the current reality whereby internal characters must navigate many different technology systems. In the concluding parts of Scene 3, I emphasise that vendors and internal decision-makers approach talent decision systems differently. Success criteria are often misaligned, as vendors aim to create commercial systems that can be sold to multiple organisations. I argue that a vendor's talent or identification perspective rarely aligns with an organisation's strategic needs. Vendor-designed systems are seldom, if ever, fit-for-purpose.

The sequence of these scenes holds significant importance, as establishing a shared comprehension of what talent entails and appears like is a prerequisite before devising the identification processes. Having a comprehensive understanding and consensus on the defining attributes of talent and identification procedures is imperative before choosing specific decision support systems, such as technology. Each scene vividly portrays its unique backdrop, location, props and interactions among characters. Additionally, a new character, the narrator, is introduced in each scene, enabling me to communicate directly with you, the audience. The narrator (me) provides informative insights, commentary and reflections.

**Part 6, Implications**, includes two chapters that reflect on the outcomes and implications of how our characters negotiate talent meanings, identification processes and decision systems.

Our first chapter considers the strategic implications of the increase in vendor-designed talent decision systems. The transition towards vendor-designed talent decision systems has brought about a shift in the role of vendors, elevating them from a supporting capacity to a prominent position in talent decisions. Vendors are now increasingly responsible for creating and providing the necessary technology and decision frameworks which have seen vendors increasingly become both the designers and drivers of talent decisions. Choosing and using vendor-designed talent systems has implications for: (1) Digitalisation Strategies, whereby key decision-makers prioritise technology-driven approach to digitalisation; (2) Talent Strategies, whereby vendors become key decision-makers and organisations can pursue imitation, rather than differentiation, approaches to talent decisions; and (3) Digitalised Talent Management Strategies whereby we witness an increase in vendor power and agency, prioritise a particular static viewpoint of talent and must understand the views and assumptions encoded in the software and decision systems to know the basis for talent decisions.

The second chapter examines the Knowledge Implications. Together we reflect on our journey and revisit the key learnings. You will learn that you have learnt a lot and successfully achieved the outcome of increased knowledge.

**Part** 7 includes a **Concluding Monologue**, where I guide you about "where to from here." I offer various action steps to guide your future actions because your updated knowledge should encourage you also to update your actions.

Part 1: **Introducing (Re)Thinking Talent Decisions**

# Chapter 1
# A Tale of Complexity, Technology and Subjectivity

## A Tale of Complexity

My fascination with complexity fuels my interest in talent decisions. As a social scientist, I firmly believe that emphasising complexity is crucial. My objective is to instigate, contribute to and shape informed conversations that unpack the complexity of genuine talent management. Allow me to elucidate why talent decisions are complex.

Talent decisions are complex because talent is a socially constructed concept. Like other socially constructed concepts such as love and beauty, talent only exists in the realm of ideas. Concepts represent categories and ideas humans use to structure and organise the world. Therefore, our understanding of what "talent" means is not a case of knowing or proving that talent exists. Instead, it is up to humans to determine what constitutes talent. We can only comprehend talent decisions after establishing – via a negotiation process – a shared understanding of what talent is and is not.

The negotiation processes associated with establishing what talent means and the attributes and actions that qualify as "talent" are far from neutral. Humans often advocate for their perspectives and attempt to influence others to adopt them. In talent management, individuals may assert that their ideas are superior or hold the key to effective talent decision-making. Furthermore, specific individuals are empowered to speak, while the thoughts and perceptions of others may be overlooked, disregarded, or ignored.

The language and discourse surrounding talent influences can affect how organisations approach talent management and workforce planning. Different perspectives can lead to diverse talent management strategies and approaches, ultimately shaping an organisation's success or failure.

The complexity of talent decisions is further underscored by the fact that humans are the ones making these decisions, and humans are inherently complex. As sentient beings, we humans possess a range of cognitive and emotional faculties that shape our understanding and perception of talent. Our perspectives and opinions can fluctuate over time, leading to a dynamic concept of talent. This human factor adds a layer of complexity to talent decision-making, as individual biases, beliefs and values can influence how talent is identified, assessed and managed within organisations.

---

*Talent decisions are complex because:*
*Talent only exists in our minds*
*Talent is a concept – a way to organise the world*
*Talent is social and highly contextual*
*Talent is dynamic – meanings can and do change*
*Multiple forces influence talent decisions*

---

The theme of complexity in talent decisions is further compounded by the fact that these decisions do not occur in isolation. Talent management has become even more significant as we navigate and respond to the COVID-19 pandemic. The external shocks and disruptions caused by the pandemic have led key decision-makers to question which individuals, skills and capabilities are essential for business continuity. The crisis context has also raised questions about retaining talent while reacting to the pandemic and "keeping the lights on."

Furthermore, the pandemic has brought about significant changes in our work, such as increased remote work and digitalisation. News headlines about a "great resignation" are a call to action whereby organisations are again required to compete for a limited talent supply. These external factors add another layer of complexity to talent decision-making, as organisations must navigate a rapidly evolving and uncertain landscape while making strategic talent decisions. It may seem obvious to state that multiple forces influence talent decisions. However, it is crucial to make this point explicitly.

## A Tale of Complexity and Technology

Talent decisions are complex because talent management and technology are inherently interrelated. Technology infiltrates every aspect of our work, from communication to task execution. Both domains encourage a team-based approach to understanding technology-based change's desired outcomes. (Re)Thinking talent decisions benefits from recognising that our tale of complexity is also a tale of complexity AND technology.

### The Talent Management and Technology Relationship is Reciprocal

I talk and write at length about the human-technology interface. The human-technology interface recognises that the relationship between technology and talent management is reciprocal. The connection is mutual because neither talent management nor technology is helpful in their own right.

The human-technology interface takes many forms which help illuminate the complex and multi-directional relationship between technology and talent decisions:
- Effective talent management, which involves managing valuable individuals and groups, requires strategically aligned decisions and practices. Many of these decisions use technology for process execution.
- Technology is used to manage workforces and shapes workforce structures and compositions. The technology captures, stores and computes workforce and talent data, informing talent-based decisions and practices.

- Talent availability influences the technology organisations select and use, while technology selection and use affect the talent required to realise the benefits of digitalisation and automation.

Reflecting on the human-technology interface matters. Understanding Digitalised Talent Management is more than an academic subject because we are all affected and influenced by talent decisions and technology. It is essential to recognise this relationship's reciprocal nature and take a holistic approach to talent management incorporating technology because technology is a crucial character in talent decisions.

## Technology Shapes Jobs, Careers and Career Aspirations

Throughout history, there has been a tradition of studying the impact of technology on processes and work. The technology of the past, the digitalisation of today and future innovations change facets of our work. Technology evolutions, no matter their form, will continue to shape jobs and careers. Experiencing the process and outcomes of technology-based change is, or will become, part of everyone's journey.

---

**The Case of Automatic Re-ordering**

I have witnessed firsthand the expanding role of technology in task completion. In retail, where workers' return on increased performance is considered marginal, automation is conducive to improving productivity. The organisation I worked for (a large FMCG) was implementing a new approach to ordering. The ordering change occurred post displacement of bag packers with conveyer belts and price markers with the invention of bar codes. The new just-in-time system prioritised an automated process for re-ordering goods. The software tracked sales barcode data (think of the scanning process as you purchase your weekly shop) to determine the outflow of products. The process involved the software assuming that being out of one product required an (automatic) replacement of that product. The software was programmed to re-order a specific product when stock levels reached a pre-determined level.

The new process represented a new way of working. Decision-making responsibility shifted from humans to software. Rather than humans, the software was positioned as crucial talent in this case.

I, the social scientist, watched with interest as we learnt, in real-time, about the limitations of the software's capabilities. I remember the day we – the (manager) humans – came unstuck. It was (NRL) football grand final day. On a grand final day, Coca-Cola, chips, sausages, bread rolls, pre-made salads and sauces are our biggest sellers. Many shoppers purchase their supplies on game day. Shoppers selected their bread products as they entered the store. But problems were evident as they looked for chips and soft drinks. Aisle ends and shelves were empty because we didn't have enough stock to meet demand. Shoppers approached "management" (which included me), asking about the required supplies. All I could do was apologise.

We, (manager) humans, learnt more about the situation in the proceeding days. The software was designed to assume that being out of one product required an automatic replacement of that product. The software, when implemented, also assumed that all days were the same. In doing so, the coders thought that shoppers' one-day purchasing habits would resemble the same day the following week. The automated just-in-time ordering assumed it was "any given Sunday." The software didn't know to order more because it was "Grand Final Sunday."

Humans become (re)involved. Specific (manager) humans reviewed and "tweaked" predicted orders before finalisation. Technological innovations associated with automated ordering changed the skills and capabilities required. The changes also resulted in job changes where humans transitioned to a supervisory role.

The above experience is just one example showing the reciprocal relationship between technology and talent management. As technology shapes our work, it also changes the skills and capabilities required, resulting in a shift in job roles and career paths. This situation also highlighted the changing structure of the human-technology interface. Although it was hoped (aka promised by the vendor) that the new automated ordering system would replace human orderers (whom we ironically called "Systems" employees), the revised process still required human input. The human input, however, did change due to the implementation of the technology.

Technological advancements have also created new career options. The OECD's *Dream Jobs? Teenagers' Career Aspirations and the Future of Work* report recognises the linkage between technology, workplaces and careers. The report's Foreword, written by Charles Yidan, the Co-Founder of Tencent, states, "Staying longer in education than ever before, today's young people must make decisions about what, where and how hard they will study. These are investment decisions that are becoming increasingly difficult because technology is changing the working world itself so quickly."

The report shows that the range of perceived careers of young people is shrinking. Some 53% of girls and 47% of boys across 41 countries anticipate entering one of just ten jobs by 30 years of age (girls – doctors, teachers, business managers, lawyers, nursing and midwives, psychologists, designers, veterinarians, police officers, architects; boys – engineers, business managers, doctors, ICT professionals, sportspeople, teachers, police officers, motor vehicle mechanics, lawyers, and architects).

The report shows how little career expectations have changed since 2000, before social media and artificial intelligence (AI).

The section comparing "Jobs with a future" with "Jobs of the past" is particularly intriguing. "Jobs with a future" includes health-based occupations such as physical and occupational therapists and nursing aids. Jobs with a future also include an array of technology-based employment, including computer user support specialists, user support technicians and information systems testing technicians. These jobs have a "lower than average" risk of automation.

In contrast, "Jobs of the past" includes bookkeeping, accounting and auditing clerks, travel agents, financial institution customer service representatives, structural metal fabricators and fitters, railway carmen/women and aircraft mechanics and inspectors. These "past" jobs are judged as having a "high or significant" risk of being automated.

Some technology-based careers have emerged because of specific technological advances. For example, becoming a brand influencer or YouTuber are relatively new career options.

While the idea of my kid dreaming of becoming an influencer scares me, technological advancements have opened up many new career possibilities. Increasing automation, changing career patterns and youth aspirations have implications for our understanding of what talent is and is not as society and workplaces experience constant technology-based change.

## Today's Technological Innovations Differ From Yesterday's

Technological innovations such as machine learning and artificial intelligence, and the increasing trend toward work automation, represent significant changes in how we work. Today's talk of digitalisation is not a case of "same, same." It's essential to recognise that today's intersection between technology and talent management fundamentally differs from what we've seen before.

Digitalisation is reshaping the human-technology interface, with specific technologies serving as enablers that assist with task completion and conduits for transmitting and coordinating information. Some newer technological innovations can even act as collaborators, with technology becoming an integral part of the team.

However, a critical distinction between the digitalisation of yesterday with that of a future day arises when technology transitions from being an object – part of the process – to a subject-based role, where technology becomes the primary decision-maker.

Today's technological innovations give rise to the potential depreciation of human agency in decision-making. While technologies such as Enterprise Resource Planning Systems and Human Resource Information Systems involve human decision-making, existing talent systems enable some levels of automated decision-making. This automation follows the human-designed and enacted software code, with humans designing the decision-making framework, coding decision rules into the software, inputting data into the software, requesting and receiving reports based on the data captured and stored by the technology, reading and interpreting the outputted information, and ultimately making decisions and acting on them.

However, when automation enacts decisions without human intervention, it represents a significant change that can fundamentally shift talent management. The later technology-as-a-subject perspective involves making decisions automatically without human intervention and potentially doing so in ways humans do not and cannot understand. New decision-making capabilities bring about the potential for organisations and stakeholders to (re)structure jobs, where technology becomes the key decision-maker. This positioning of "technology as a subject" is already occurring in some contexts. In *Part 2: (Re)Thinking Talent Decision Outcomes* we will reflect on this transformation in light of The Space Race.

# A Tale of ComplexiTY, Technology and Subjectivity

I want to broadcast an uncomfortable truth. Talent decisions are ALWAYS subjective (I am intentionally yelling here). Our (re)thinking talent decisions tale champions subjective talent decisions. Next, we focus on the nature and structure of talent decisions to illustrate the connection between talent decisions and subjectivity.

**Talent Decisions Are Always Subjective**

As we navigate the expanding landscape of digitalisation and automation, we must also recognise the pervasive presence of humans in all aspects of our lives. Humans are everywhere. So, let's take a broader perspective on talent decisions. We benefit from reflecting on humans as a character group, especially talent decisions that involve and affect humans and are subjective beings. Rather than shy away from talking about the inconsistency in human decision-making, my view of talent management acknowledges that talent decisions are always subjective.

---

*Talent decisions are ALWAYS subjective.*

---

Talent is a concept that exists only in the human mind. We don't know what we think talent is and is not until we think about talent. Talent decisions start with personal thoughts. And because personal thoughts are subjective, all talent decisions start with human subjectivity. Human subjectivity is and always will be a core input to talent decisions.

Humans are inherently biased beings, and the *Cognitive Bias Codex* identifies at least 180 ways various factors and variables can influence our judgments. Decision-makers must understand that all talent decisions are subjective and include some bias. Rather than eliminating bias, the goal is to be more aware of the bias and partake in uncomfortable conversations about the (subjective) reasons – the why, why, why – decision-makers judge some individuals to be of greater value than others.

---

*We cannot eliminate bias in decision-making. However, the (team) goal is to develop an awareness of how biases influence talent decisions.*

---

Recognising and openly discussing talent decisions' subjective and biased nature is crucial, rather than attempting to minimise or avoid the topic. In upcoming sections, we will delve deeper into the human mind/brain as a primary character in our (re)thinking tale and explore the relationship between decision-making and subjectivity.

## Talent Management is About Judging Value

*(Re)Thinking Talent Decisions* recognises talent management is not a set of practices. Talent management is not a discrete set of practices, be they talent acquisition, development, or retention. Instead, talent management is about identifying, developing and deploying "value." Talent decisions seek to judge many aspects associated with "value" – the value of an individual, team of individuals, certain skills and capabilities, roles, jobs and positions and behaviours and actions.

Framing talent management around judging value is helpful because talent management is about investing in individuals who we think (or know) are of greater importance – aka value – for strategy execution. I define talent management as:

*A judgment-orientated activity, where humans judge the value of other humans. While mediated by various contextual factors and variables (such as technology), these judgments should be informed by and aligned to current and future strategic ambitions and goals.*

Talent management, in this vein, includes three main attributes:
(1) judgments about value;
(2) decisions; and
(3) resources.

Decision-makers make judgments about the value of individuals within their workforces; relevant stakeholders then make decisions based on judgments of value; decisions about resource allocations are based on prior judgments of value.

*(Re)Thinking Talent Decisions* encourages decision-makers to recognise the subjective nature of talent management and to engage in critical discussions about how value is judged and evaluated. Subjective decisions, therefore, are the foundation of talent management. Talent management essentially involves subjective judgments about value.

Understanding that talent management is about judging value encourages decision-makers to reflect on whose judgments talent decisions are based. Whose subjective judgments of value matter the most? Senior executives, line managers, HR managers, vendors, consultants?

Asking questions about whose value judgments feature in or dominate talent decisions is especially useful because decision-makers often have different perceptions of what value and talent "look like." Talent decisions are based on individual ideas, making talent a matter of perception. Talent is always in the "eye of the beholder."

Understanding what decision-makers think about value and talent starts with understanding what we all think. Remember the power of Y.O.U. – Your Own Understanding – in talent decisions because your subjective thoughts influence your judgment of others.

*Talent is in the eye of the beholder – Y.O.U. matters*

## A Few Words Before We Continue On Our Journey

All great tales include foundational themes, and I started by suggesting that our (re) thinking journey centres around: (1) complexity, (2) technology and (3) subjectivity. Together we are navigating a tale of complexity, complexity and technology, complexity, technology and subjectivity.

**Complexity**: this passage argues that talent decisions are, and always will be, complex. Complexity arises because talent and talent management are socially constructed concepts. Therefore, our understanding of what talent is and is not arises from negotiation processes whereby specific characters share their thoughts about talent and decide which meanings should lay the foundation for talent decisions. The complexity of talent decisions continues when we realise that talent is dynamic – our individual, organisational and societal views of talent can and do change. Yesterday's talent may not be the talent of today or a future day. External factors add another layer of complexity to talent decision-making, as organisations must navigate a rapidly evolving and uncertain landscape while making strategic talent decisions. I am sure you can extend the list of reasons why talent decisions are complex, but it benefits all of us if we agree upfront that talent decisions are complex.

**Technology**: this passage addresses the human-technology interface and recognises the reciprocal relationship between talent management and technology. Talent availability influences the technology that organisations select and use. Conversely, technology selection and use affect an organisation's approach to data, digitalisation and automation (the role of technology in our tale will become more pronounced later when we talk about how technology plays a pivotal role in the "how" of talent decisions). We also reflected on how technological innovations shape careers, jobs and aspirations. Technology, therefore, influences how we make decisions and the decisions we make about jobs and careers. The technology of "my day" differs from that of "my kids'" day, and these different technology-based thoughts and experiences will further heighten the complexity of talent decisions.

**Subjectivity**: I start this passage with an uncomfortable truth: talent decisions are always subjective. Rather than shy away from the subjective nature of talent decisions, I put the theme of subjectivity front and centre. I also state that talent management essentially involves subjective judgments of value, and how we think about value and talent is always individual. Hence talent decisions are always subjective. We aim to understand the assumptions and perspectives influencing talent decisions (and careers).

We will revisit the subjectivity theme throughout our journey as I show the connection between the human mind – what we think – and talent decisions. As this book is directed towards you, my fellow humans, I seek to advance human-decision making within the context of increasing digitalisation and automation. *Understanding the (Subjective) Human Factor in Talent Decisions* would make a great alternative book title.

# Chapter 2
# Introducing the Cast

In this chapter, we meet the characters that will shape our (re)thinking talent decisions tale and explore their different, and sometimes conflicting, interests.

## Characters

Our cast includes several different characters:
- Humans: our tale features two categories of humans. We have individual humans – people like Y.O.U. and me. We also have The Workforce – a group of humans co-existing within an organisation.
- Technology: technology is afforded its role in our complexity, technology and subjectivity because most talent decisions use technology in some shape or form.
- Vendors: these characters play a role because they are vested in shaping talent decisions and regularly supply the talent, leadership and/or competency frameworks that support talent decisions.

Now that we know our characters, we must decide which character assumes the leading role.
Who will play the leading role in our tale, you ask?
The answer is Humans. Humans are the key decision-makers. Humans and human decision-making are our tale's focus.

---
*Humans are (always) the leading characters*

---

Humans are the main characters of our story, and they assume the leading role because they write the script, influence the scenes that play out and determine how the story ends. In any story about talent decisions, humans always take centre stage.

Humans will keep their place centre stage despite the increasing influence of technology. It's easy to believe that technology solves all workplace problems because humans often get a bad reputation and are seen as inferior to technology. It seems that technology can address the flaws that still exist despite human evolution. However, humans remain the main characters in any story about talent decisions, even as technology plays a significant role. While it's important to acknowledge the benefits of technology, we must also recognise the unique abilities and value humans bring to the table. It's time for humans to have a new PR campaign to showcase their unique abilities and contributions to the talent decision-making process. You could say that humans are, and always will be, the primary characters in the drama of talent management.

As we move towards an increasingly digital world, we ask more questions about the intersection between humans and technology. Will humans maintain leading role status in an increasingly digitalised decision-making era? Yes is my answer. It is human understanding, judgment and values that will shape the talent decisions we make. #Teamhumans will continue to play the lead role today and on a future day.

It is important to note that the choice between humans and technology as the lead character is not binary. Humans and technology are deeply intertwined, with humans using and designing technology, inputting data into technologically enabled systems and making decisions based on the data generated by talent systems. Similarly, technology cannot exist without humans. While technology has advanced significantly, we have not yet progressed to the point where technological emotions and consciousness can replace or augment those of humans. Despite fictional works like *Westworld* portraying situations where digital humans are indistinguishable from their living and breathing human counterparts, humans are still in charge.

## Humans: Y.O.U. – A Sample Size of One

Humans are the main characters in our (re)thinking talent decisions tale. Humans have the most prominent role in our story because talent decisions start and end with humans. We have established that talent decisions begin with every individual, including YOU. Talent decisions, therefore, start with a sample size of one which is why humans are essential to our story.

We will start by looking at Y.O.U. – Your Own Understanding.

### Considering the Human Mind/Brain

Talent decisions begin with a thought[3] – "I've had a thought" – and thus it is essential to understand the human mind/brain. The human brain is an extraordinary organ containing around 86 billion neurons that help us perceive, interpret and make sense of the world around us. As humans, we use our brains to generate thoughts and ideas, which then lead to talent decisions.

Although the brain is responsible for interpreting and making sense of the world around us, it is not directly connected to the outside world or other parts of the body. Instead, it receives electrical signals from different body parts, such as the eyes and ears, and we must interpret what these signals mean. While we often assume that

---

[3] I recognise there are debates about notion of free will. For our (re)thinking purposes we assume that humans make decisions and choices, and these are based on our thoughts of value (and other concepts).

what we see, feel and hear is an objective reality, there is evidence that our brains use a process of prediction and filtering to create a "controlled hallucination" based on its best guess of what the signals mean.

Despite this, we tend to accept that humans make conscious talent decisions. The conscious mind, however, remains a mysterious and complex concept. If asked whether you are aware, we would likely respond, "Yes, of course." I then ask "But how do you know?" Reflecting on this question may change facial expressions, potentially indicating a shift from confident to confused.

Science often makes a distinction between conscious and unconscious thoughts. We are aware of something when conscious, whereas unconscious, non-conscious, or pre-conscious thought processes happen outside our awareness. Consciousness implies attention and intention, while unconscious thoughts are less deliberate and happen automatically. This perspective is reflected in the concept of "unconscious bias," which suggests that humans may make biased decisions without knowledge or awareness.

Drawing a clear line between consciousness and unconsciousness is a complex task, and we cannot simply turn consciousness on and off. Additionally, understanding the nature of thoughts, decisions and actions is challenging since the contents of the conscious mind cannot be observed or measured.

Reading this book is an example of consciousness in action. As you read these words, you experience a conscious experience. You would say that you are aware and present. How you see the words on this page is unique to you, and nobody else knows what this experience is like for you.

Consciousness is a personal and highly subjective experience. It is one's private realm of thoughts, feelings and experiences. As such, a human can't describe what consciousness feels like to others.

Herein lies another factor that highlights the complexity of talent decisions. Talent decisions are the outcomes of actions, and our actions are the product of our thoughts. Since our thoughts exist only in the realm of our minds, our minds are where the initial talent decision scene takes place.

Becoming a responsible talent decision-maker starts with recognising the crucial role that our brains and minds play in decision-making. By starting with the premise that our thoughts matter, we can encourage ourselves to look inward and think about our own thinking.

**Considering Y.O.U. – Your Own Understanding**

Rethinking talent decisions requires a deep appreciation of the role of Y.O.U. – Your Own Understanding. This means recognising that our decision-making is influenced by our own experiences, beliefs and assumptions, and these factors inform and shape our talent decisions.

Thinking about our thinking allows us to learn more about ourselves, and learning about ourselves is a pivotal part of our (re)thinking journey. What we see, think and feel is influenced by Y.O.U.

And that, my friends, is why we start many discussions with Y.O.U. – Your Own Understanding. Our key Y.O.U. question is, "What do you think and why, why, why do you think that?"

*Key question: what you think and why, why, why you think that?*

Garnering your own understanding involves introspection. Introspection encourages us to look inwards. Introspection allows us to self-reflect, self-question, self-scrutinise, self-observe and self-explore. Self-examination enables us to learn about our decision-making processes and become self-aware.

Before embarking on a journey of learning about and judging the thoughts of others, it is essential to understand our thoughts, opinions, views, beliefs and our values. Understanding our thoughts is a critical first step in making responsible talent decisions. I often say, "We must look in before we look out."

Our tale of complexity, technology and subjectivity invites us to pause and reflect on our thoughts. In the spirit of *Snow White and the Seven Dwarfs*, (see Figure 2.1) we can benefit from looking in the mirror and asking ourselves, "Mirror, mirror on the wall, what do I think about [insert topic here] it all?"[4]

**Thoughts About Value**

The concept of value is one theme worth exploring. One of the specific questions we can ask our (reflective) mirror is: "What do I value?"

*Ask yourself – what do I value?*

The reason why this is important is that talent decisions are at the heart of determining value. Whenever we make talent decisions, we are essentially evaluating the value of others. We ask ourselves questions like, "Do I value this person?" and our answer is based on what we perceive as valuable. We may value individuals based on what they say and do or devalue them based on what they fail to do.

As a research scientist, I am interested in understanding how people define value and what they perceive as valuable or not valuable in others. I ask what "value" means

---

[4] There are debates about the correct mirror quote – "Magic mirror on the wall. . ." verses "Mirror, mirror on the wall. . ." – with some proposing that the Queen's mirror scene is an example of the "Mandela Effect". A phenomenon associated with experiencing false memories that do not match reality or history.

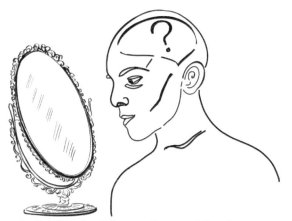

Start with Y.O.U. -Your Own Understanding

**Figure 2.1:** Start with Y.O.U. – Your Own Understanding.
Source: Copyright © Sharna Wiblen. All rights reserved.

at an individual level – what do you value? What do you not value? By posing these questions, we encourage individuals to reflect on their own evaluations of others.

Discussing everyday interactions may decrease the perceived risks of discussing what one likes or dislikes. It is essential to recognise that ideas of "value" are constantly evolving, and what we perceive as talent today may differ from our perceptions in the past or future. To make sound talent decisions, we must be mindful of the assumptions and ideas underlying our views of what talent is and is not. (Re)Thinking talent decisions involves starting with our thoughts – our thoughts about value.

**Perceptions of Value**
Perceptions play an influential role in shaping our understanding, experiences and actions. Humans perceive value differently, and our perceptions influence our ideas of what is valuable and what is not. Consequently, our perceptions of "value" inform our notions of talent and what it means to be talented. Personal perceptions of value also influence our ideas of the value of "humans" and "technology" and where we sit on determining the value of #Teamhuman and #Teamtechnology.

As a discourse scholar, I emphasise the role of perceptions when discussing talent decisions. Language significantly influences our thoughts and actions, and we use discourses to establish meaning. Specific words and terms can ignite particular meanings and physiological responses, which generate specific experiences and practices.

Referring to "perceptions" is, in my experience, less alienating than referring to "biases." Talking about perceptions allows for curiosity and learning about the different views of value. On the other hand, talking about biases often results in a defensive stance. Instead of telling individuals that they make biased decisions, I deem it more appropriate (and effective) to say that humans have different perceptions of value and that we value different things. These different perceptions of value are represented in our thoughts about value and talent and come to life via talent decisions. Acknowledging the factors that influence our minds and decisions is essential in (re)thinking talent decisions.

**Factors Influencing Thoughts and Perceptions**

Many factors and variables influence our thoughts and decisions; as humans, we are prone to error. Science has shown that our minds influence how we view and experience things, and the magnitude of human errors and biases in decision-making is significant. It is impossible to remove bias from decision-making altogether.

To make responsible decisions, we should aim to be active participants and understand our limitations and errors. By being aware of our limitations and errors, we can foster an environment that acknowledges the role of subjectivity in talent decisions. This understanding allows for more informed and responsible decision-making.

*As leaders and doers in organisations, we are not innocent bystanders. Rather, we are engaged participants who are aware of our decision-making processes to ensure that our actions are deliberate, intentional and informed.*

Let us briefly reflect on potential limitations and errors associated with talent decisions.

**Stereotypes**. Our brains are wired to predict and anticipate information to process the overwhelming amount of stimuli we encounter daily efficiently. This prediction process involves comparing new information to stored information, and can result in the formation of stereotypes to simplify and categorise our world. While this process can be helpful, it can also lead to inaccurate judgments.

Stereotypes associated with various elements influence talent decisions because humans hold different thoughts about:
- Gender
- Race and ethnicity
- Disability
- Age
- Religious beliefs
- Parenthood (or absence of)
- Accents
- Attractiveness (Lookism)

- Weight
- Face symmetry
- Clothing

The above is by no means an exhaustive list. Still, it helps us recognise that humans perceive humans differently, and our thoughts about different human aspects inform our perceptions of their value, whether consciously or unconsciously. The extent to which we accept or disavow certain stereotypes influences talent decisions, resource allocations and careers. We examine this topic in the section *(Re)Thinking Talent* (see Talent as something that you have and stereotypes).

**Cognitive biases**. Cognitive biases are a group of biases associated with unconscious errors in thinking. These biases usually result from our brain's efforts to simplify the complexity of the world we experience every day. Cognitive biases centre around the idea that human cognition (your mind) reliably produces systematically distorted representations compared to some aspects of reality.

I highlight the role of cognitive biases with executive students when introducing them to the idea that talent management involves a series of talent decisions and those talent decisions are based on judgments of value. Judgments arise from conceptualisations and patterns in our minds, heads and cognitive functioning. I show students the *Cognitive Bias Codex*.[5] This tool, created by John Manoogian III and Buster Benson, visually represents 180+ cognitive biases that influence our thinking (and, therefore, our actions and inactions).

The list below briefly details some of the (unequal) outcomes that I share with executive students when introducing them to the idea that perceptions, specifically perceptions of value, are influenced by various mind-based factors and variables:
- We store memories differently based on how we experience them
- We notice things already primed in our memory or repeated often
- We notice the bizarre and different more than the normal/standard
- We use details that confirm existing beliefs
- We notice flaws in others more than ourselves
- We find stories and patterns even when data is sparse
- We fill in characteristics from stereotypes, generalities and prior histories
- We establish probabilities and numbers to make things easier to think about
- We think we know what other people are thinking
- We project our current mindset and assumptions onto the past and the future

Cognitive biases directly affect talent decisions because humans tend to favour simple-looking options and complete information over complex, ambiguous options. Our

---

[5] Note that the codex includes both cognitive biases and heuristics even though there are nuanced differences between these.

minds regularly take mental shortcuts to reduce complex tasks to make judgments. Sometimes these shortcuts are effective, but they can also lead to errors in decision-making. This poses a significant issue as talent decisions are a tale of complexity. The ability to simplify proceeds an awareness and consideration of the complexity encompassing how we organise and manage The Workforce.

Many biases can influence talent decisions. Here are some notable ones:

– **Confirmation bias** involves seeking information confirming our pre-existing beliefs while ignoring evidence contradicting it. Humans tend to reject information that doesn't support our opinions or views. In talent decisions, it can manifest with decision-makers only considering information that supports their predetermined perceptions of specific humans. Predetermined mind-based thoughts and perceptions lead to the valuing or devaluing of particular humans.

– **Rater bias** refers to an error in judgment that can occur when an individual allows their pre-existing biases to affect the evaluation of another. This is a common issue regarding employee performance reviews and is a hazard of any rating system that is difficult to eliminate but not impossible to manage. The error of rater biases can result from personal opinions or perspectives and are almost always unreasonable. These biases can skew employee ratings too high or too low, negatively impacting the accuracy of performance reviews and nullifying their validity. When we fail to consider rater biases during performance reviews, obtaining an accurate estimate of performance, value and talent is challenging.

– **Halo effect** occurs when one positive trait or aspect of a person influences our overall perception of them. In talent decisions, it can lead to unbalanced (or uninformed) judgments of an individual's value because of an overemphasis on positive aspects (think behaviours and actions). Decision-makers highlight factors they value, keeping the less favourable parts hidden in the shadows.

– **Recency bias**, also known as the "availability heuristic," is a cognitive bias that occurs when an individual's most recent experiences or events heavily influence their judgments or decisions. Recency bias can lead to inaccurate evaluations and decisions, as it neglects the larger context of an individual's performance and focuses solely on the most recent events. Recency bias is particularly prevalent in performance management and talent identification evaluations because decision-makers are asked to recall (distorted) memories of how specific individuals added value to them personally, to the team, the function, to customers, to the organisation and the "bottom line." Humans will draw on more recent memories because of the brain's inability to store information equally. More recent memories are at the expense of older memories, whereby the older behaviours and actions become less valuable.

– **Anchoring bias** occurs when we rely too heavily on the first piece of information we receive. The first piece of information becomes an "anchor" – it serves as a reference point. Anchoring bias can lead to skewed talent decisions because decision-makers rely on the information first received and make judgments concerning this initial information. Judgments can be positive or negative, but rarely, if ever, are judgments neutral. An awareness of anchoring bias is critical for talent decisions because it helps decision-makers reflect on their initial impressions and reference points when evaluating humans and the extent to which specific humans are talent.

– **Bias in self-judgment** can significantly impact our perceptions of personal efficacy. Positive illusions, such as inflated self-esteem, can skew our self-perceptions and lead to overconfidence. This overconfidence can increase ambition and motivation. We benefit from asking ourselves, asking our reflective mirrors, "What are the costs of holding an inflated sense of self?" Neuroscience research shows that our brains tend to encode undesirable information distortedly, which can further perpetuate positive illusions and biases. Our brains also do not process or store information equally, meaning we may selectively recall positive information while ignoring or downplaying negative information. It's essential to be aware of these biases in self-judgment to make more accurate assessments of personal strengths and weaknesses and make informed decisions.

– **Hindsight bias**: hindsight bias is another bias where humans overestimate their abilities. The bias involves humans believing that they could predict the outcome of a situation and is associated with "I knew it!," "I could see that was going to happen" and "I told you so" statements. This bias is particularly problematic for talent decisions when discussing an individual's "potential" because we won't know whether an individual "reached their potential" until later. The inability to perform according to one's perceptions can result in conversations where key humans debate whether they "knew they had it in them" or "I know they weren't leader material." Either way, decision-makers will imply that outcomes are predetermined or foreseeable.

It is crucial to recognise that these biases can lead to unequal outcomes in talent decisions and that awareness of them is the first step in mitigating their effects.

## The Workforce – A Sample Size of Many

We have learnt that talent is a concept that resides in our minds. We now know to think about talent in terms of what we think because what we think about value plays a significant role in shaping how we judge and evaluate an individual's talent. The above section expands on the notion of Y.O.U.

Thinking of Y.O.U. directs our thinking towards the personal level. It reminds us of the importance of our thoughts and perceptions because Y.O.U.-based perceptions influence how we assess, judge and evaluate specific individuals within organisations.

Recognising this, we shift from reflecting on Y.O.U. – a sample size of one – to a sample size of many, with The Workforce presented as a distinct human character.

I intentionally present The Workforce, rather than The Organisation, as a character because I want us to explicitly recognise that an "organisation" is a group of individuals: a collective of humans.

Many conversations refer to an organisation's approach to strategy, talent management, digitalisation, the future of work and other topics. For example, a specific organisation does, or is doing, "something." We even celebrate specific organisations for "doing" talent management well through Employer of Choice awards.

But organisations do not exist. Well, they do operate in the realm of reality because organisations are legally recognised entities. But "organisations" don't make talent decisions. Individuals, or groups of individuals, within the legal entity, make talent decisions.

We benefit, therefore, from thinking about an organisation in terms of The Workforce. Thinking about The Workforce helps anchor our thinking within the context of human decision-making within organisational boundaries.

---

*Talking about an "organisation" involves thinking about a group of humans called The Workforce.*

---

Humans are not equal – dah! So, the talk of The Workforce needs to emphasise the role of an array of humans. Understanding the experiences of an organisation – aka members of The Workforce – starts with garnering an informed understanding of the main characters. Human resources, line managers and senior executives are three human-based characters in our tale. By reflecting on their perspectives and experiences, we understand how "organisations" approach talent decisions.

**Senior Executives**

Headlines often emphasise that senior executives are concerned about talent. Reports suggest that senior executives lose sleep over talent-related issues and view them as a significant challenge. For instance, the KPMG *Keeping Us Up at Night: The big issues facing business leaders in 2022* report highlights that two-thirds of Australian business leaders identified access to talent as an immediate and short-term challenge. The report suggests that talent and digital transformation are ongoing issues all organisations face. In the next three to five years, senior executives are concerned about their workforce's ability to meet the requirements of a more digitalised future.

Whether losing sleep or not, senior executives have a vested interest in talent decisions as they impact strategy execution, financial performance and the organisation's competitive positioning.

Senior executives have different levels of involvement and interest in establishing talent systems, ranging from authoritarian to trusting members of The Workforce to make decisions. We will consider the interests of this category of humans further when we explore talent systems later in our tale.

**Human Resources and Line Managers**

Human Resource professionals and line managers are two other character groups featured in The Workforce aspect of our tale. Human Resource (HR) professionals are individuals that design, execute and oversee people-based policies and processes. From my perspective, line managers lead or manage teams (a team being a group of humans).

One of the most complex questions in talent management is determining who is better at decisions regarding talent. A key question is, "Who is best suited to make talent decisions?"

---

*Key question – are human resource or line managers better suited to make talent decisions?*

---

Our story of complexity continues because there is an ongoing debate regarding whether human resources or line managers are better suited for this role.

Advocating for either HR or line managers in talent management is heavily influenced by how individuals perceive the relationship between talent management and human resource management and whether they view talent identification and performance management as synonymous.

Those who view performance management and talent identification as synonymous often believe that line managers are responsible for judging the value of employees. This is because performance management typically involves evaluations and ratings made by line managers of their direct reports. Line managers are therefore seen as the best decision-makers regarding talent management. HR managers, on the other hand, are seen as responsible for administrative and policy components in these situations, supporting line managers in their talent decisions.

Performance evaluations generate data used to make talent decisions, but talent identification is a distinct process. Performance evaluations are often based on quantitative measures, such as sales or revenue generation, and may also include data from customer satisfaction scores or complaints. Evaluations may be based solely on the opinions of the line manager, which can be influenced by cognitive biases identified in the previous section. Line managers are also more concerned with short-term needs. In these cases, HR managers may be more critical in ensuring talent decisions take a long-term view.

Those who believe talent identification and performance management are separate processes see HR and line managers playing different roles. HR and line managers play different roles because talent identification involves at least two stages.

Kristiina Mäkelä, Igmar Björkman and Mats Ehrnrooth have noted that talent identification combines online and offline data. On-line data includes experience-based performance evaluation data, while off-line data refers to cognition-based discussions that inform talent decisions. This two-stage process seeks to overcome limitations associated with experience-based evaluations, often based on subjective experiences of working with an individual.

One component of the two-stage process is talent reviews. Talent reviews involve discussions among key decision-makers about an individual's performance evaluations and potential. Review discussions include a larger sample of participants, including senior executives, HR managers, divisional leaders and line managers. By incorporating diverse perspectives, talent reviews can help ensure that talent decisions are made collegiately and with a long-term (strategic) view.

It's also essential to note that I argue that talent identification extends beyond performance management. From my perspective, talent identification aims to judge an individual's value within the context of strategic needs. In other words, it's about understanding who and what is valuable for the successful execution of an organisation's strategy.

> *Talent identification is the process of workforce differentiation which is a judgement-orientated activity whereby we make judgments to determine which individuals are of greater value.*

This broader perspective on talent identification can help organisations identify and develop individuals with the skills and attributes most relevant to achieving their strategic objectives. My viewpoint gives rise to a role for both HR and line managers. While line managers make the initial decisions, HR characters support decision-making processes. The nature of this partnership depends on various factors, including the organisation's specific goals, the industry's nature and the individual skills and strengths of HR and line managers.

Regardless of our perceptions, we benefit from recognising that The Workforce is not a homogenous group. Each category of human character represented in The Workforce has different perceptions of value and ideas about the best decision-maker. The lived reality of talent decisions requires characters to negotiate their role[6] in talent decisions. We consider these negotiation processes in *Part 5. Negotiating Talent Decisions*.

---

[6] It is hoped that the perceptions of employees are represented in our discussion of Y.O.U. even though employees are a further category of humans which make up *The Workforce*.

## Technology

Throughout our discussion it's important to keep technology at the forefront. While humans play the most significant role in talent decisions, technology also plays a crucial role.

Technology is often marketed as a solution to many human-based talent decisions, such as biased and ad hoc decision-making. Technology is promoted as more objective, error-free and consistent in its decision-making capabilities than humans.

Putting the human versus technology debate aside for the moment, we must recognise technology's significant role in talent decisions. Technology plays such a pivotal role that it can be considered a distinct and standalone character in our (re)thinking tale.

---

*Technology is the software; the codes; the algorithms; the systems supporting decision-making.*

---

In any story, every character has a unique background that shapes who they are and how they interact with the world around them. In our tale of *(Re)Thinking Talent Decisions*, we must consider the context of increasing digitalisation and the role of technology in talent management. However, it's essential to recognise that technologies are not equal. Understanding the history and background of our technology characters is vital in advancing our knowledge and contextualising upcoming scenes.

Thinking about the evolution of technology will show that technology is a dynamic character because the composition and role of technology change over time.

### Enterprise Resource Planning Systems

The digitisation of talent management began with the introduction of Enterprise Resource Planning (ERP) systems. These modular software solutions were designed to integrate core business processes into a unified system. ERP systems emerged from the information systems and coding realms with the original goal of standardising organisational processes. This innovation sought to address a fundamental technology limitation at the time – the inability to transfer software code between organisations. Computer hardware was expensive, and software adoption required significant capital outlay.

ERP systems allowed organisations (which, of course, are comprised of key human decision-makers) to purchase software from technology vendors. These vendors were responsible for process design, allowing organisations to adopt the standardised linear processes encoded in the software rather than maintaining bespoke methodologies. For the first time, two organisations could deploy the same software, resulting in similar ways of working across different organisations.

Early iterations of ERP systems focused on data warehousing, enabling organisations to capture, store and process large amounts of data. This encouraged investments in storage capabilities to support the growing need for data-driven decision-making. As standardised processes and data warehousing became more prevalent, data-driven decision-making became increasingly important in organisations.

## Human Resource Information Systems

As ERP vendors expanded their product offerings, they started including functional-specific modules such as Finance, Supply Chain and Human Capital. This gave rise to vendor-designed HRIS. These modules enabled organisations to capture, store and retrieve data related to various aspects of their operations according to standardised processes.

In the early days, HRIS focused on data capture and storage. HRIS were bespoke systems built in-house by professionals with specialised knowledge of the organisation's operations. The HR, Finance and IT professionals are responsible for system maintenance and updates. As a result, these systems were expensive, and the organisation bore all costs.

The evolution of technology, specifically vendor-designed technology, resulted in another significant change. For the first time, key humans could "buy" technology – the software, the coding, the processes and the algorithms to support talent decisions. A shift in the ownership model led to immediate cost savings as associated costs moved from a predominantly labour expense to an IT infrastructure expense.

The early 2000s saw organisations starting to transition towards vendor-designed HR technology. Despite the hype and promises of data-driven decision-making, early academic studies suggested that this adoption primarily focused on automating routine tasks and replacing paper-based document management with data warehousing.

However, surveys conducted by *The Center for Effective Organizations* in 2004 found that many promises made by vendors remained unrealised. Most organisations struggled to use HR technology to inform and guide strategic decision-making.

The 2005–2008 period saw similar outcomes, with many organisations using HR technology solely to replace manual processing and reduce costs. This led to many commentators declaring that HR had fallen victim to unrealistic expectations regarding what the technology could achieve and the challenges involved in implementing these systems on-site.

### Cloud-Based Software and Software-As-a-Service

Cloud-based software was the next significant technological innovation in the HR technology space. SuccessFactors was the first to release a cloud-based technology solution focused on HR. Organisations could now effectively rent the software for a fee denoted as software-as-a-service (SaaS).

A cloud-based approach removed on-site software implementations that required significant time, energy and monetary investment. The move to SaaS further reinforced the cost-effectiveness rhetoric. SaaS also decreased hardware requirements as computing infrastructure was included in the fee. Vendors presented convincing case studies illustrating that their cloud-based software-as-a-service technology was cheaper than any bespoke option. Existing and potential HRIS users were excited by the cloud and service-based technology offerings.

Many organisations drifted towards a technology-driven strategy due to SaaS' emergence. A technology-driven approach encouraged organisations to implement the software as per the designers' intentions, with a vanilla implementation providing tried-and-true processes. Vanilla implementations involved minimal costly software customisations, which would result in the most considerable cost efficiencies. While most choose to customise technology in some way today, the perceived value of process standardisation and data capabilities remains core to the role of technology of the past and present.

Next, we will consider technology vendors who provide the software for a technology-enabled approach.

## Vendors

In our tale, vendors are prominent characters and it is essential to reflect on vendors' significant role in talent decisions. With increasing digitalisation, vendors have agency over defining talent attributes and provide many talent and leadership frameworks and decision systems (in the form of technology systems) used within organisations.

Despite their importance, many may consider vendors as tertiary characters, failing to recognise their pivotal role in shaping talent decisions. However, I propose that vendors are foil characters because their values fundamentally clash with our human protagonists.

### Technology Vendors

Technological advances in cloud-based options have encouraged an expansion in vendors. Internal characters were no longer solely tasked with devising and managing talent frameworks and data. They could now engage a vendor instead to do "the work" for a fee, which could be a license or subscription fee. Vendors provide companies with an out-of-the-box solution, a pre-designed framework that they can buy off-the-shelf. Off-the-shelf products imply that the framework is "ready to go." Plug it in, and you have a talent framework to facilitate talent decisions.

> *Vendors supply much of the technology and decision frameworks – the software; the codes; the algorithms; the criteria; the processes and the systems that support decision-making.*

It is easy to understand why key human characters deploy vendor-designed systems to organise, manage and evaluate talent. Vendors have compelling offerings. They assert that they offer "best practices" for talent management, which are sold (for profit) as frameworks that mirror accepted and prescribed practices. While considered commercially sensitive and proprietary knowledge, these "best practices" may not be scientifically tested before their sale (or at all!). The appeal of vendor solutions lies in their promise of an efficient and streamlined approach to talent management, which can save time, effort and resources for the organisation.

Proponents of vendor-designed talent systems argue that their technology allows organisations to manage talent systematically, with well-defined meanings and evaluative criteria. Vendors provide both the what and the how of talent management. They embed structured terminology and standard definitions of skills and capabilities to be evaluated against, explicitly encoding judging criteria into the software.

Vendors also create algorithms that provide step-by-step electronically encoded instructions for executing specific data-based tasks in a specific order, with tasks allocated a weighting or priority. This encoding of criteria and processes into the software increases standardisation, ensuring a single talent meaning is applied across the workforce. Each vendor focuses on refining the processes embedded within their software to foster efficiency, with standardisation being a shared outcome. By digitalising criteria, vendors can create talent profiles and determine the required competencies, personal attributes, technical and professional knowledge and experiences needed for an individual to achieve talent status. They can also provide high-potential and/or high-performer profiles as part of their offering.

The HR and talent vendor space is experiencing rapid expansion, with reports indicating the existence of over 21,000 vendors in the market. Among them are high-value, high-growth firms with billion-dollar valuations.

**Leadership and Competency Vendors**

Leadership and competency vendors are another part of our Vendor character. Leadership and competency vendors operate alongside technology vendors but differ because they specialise in "leadership" and/or "competency" frameworks.

The concept of competencies dates back to the 1970s, preceding the talk about talent management. The underlying idea behind competencies is that they represent the knowledge, skills, abilities (KSAs) and other characteristics (O) needed to perform a job effectively. Nowadays, the term KSAOs is more commonly used to refer to these characteristics. Competencies have become a central concept in modern workplaces, and many people may consider talent, competencies and KSAs to be synonymous or at least closely related.

Competencies focus on the "what" of talent – the factors that distinguish superior from average performance. Each vendor offers different characteristics to evaluate an individual's value. Leadership competency frameworks, for example, concentrate on the skills and behaviours contributing to superior leadership performance. The goal is to identify and develop the next generation of leaders by assessing and developing these competencies.

Competency frameworks play a significant role in shaping talent decisions, as vendor-designed frameworks underpin many talent systems. Key decision-makers turn to vendors offering pre-designed evaluation and talent identification structures to streamline talent management processes. Competency frameworks serve as a control mechanism for key stakeholders in managing and evaluating performance and potential against the predetermined criteria embedded in the model.

Purchasing competency models is also a cost-effective way to control costs. Acquiring a vendor-designed framework involves significantly less cost in the short-term than designing a bespoke framework. Buying "off the shelf" results in decreased acquisition costs as design-based expenses are absorbed by the vendor in their initial design processes and factored into the overall cost of the product.

Alec Levenson delves into the benefits and limitations of competency models in a chapter featured in a book about Digitalised Talent Management. Levenson argues that advocates of competencies have some compelling arguments on their side. First, understanding the differences among individuals that might help explain why some people perform better in a job than others is valuable. Second, competencies are usually identified by comparing successful incumbents' traits with those less successful ones. If traits can be connected to the business strategy, including them in a competency model can be quite valuable.

However, Levenson encourages us to balance these benefits with equally compelling limitations. Specifying a single set of competencies can be inappropriate, given that there are many ways that humans can perform their jobs effectively and/or superiorly. Stipulating static criteria limits the ability to recognise changing job requirements. Focusing on "end state" characteristics and the assumption that specific humans have reached full performance levels can limit our understanding of talent requirements for the future. Therefore, it is important to remember that competency models should not be used as the sole criterion for talent management decisions. Competencies and other factors such as individual potential, work experience and personal values should be considered.

## A Few Words Before We Continue On Our Journey

The cast of our tale of rethinking talent decisions includes three main characters, each playing a different role. The lead role is allocated to humans, both as individuals and as a collective, referred to as The Workforce. We also recognise that senior executives, HR professionals and line managers play sub-roles within organisational contexts.

The second character is technology, which plays a supporting role due to its reciprocal relationship with humans in talent decisions. Given that our story is about complexity, technology and subjectivity, it is fitting to acknowledge technology as a distinct character.

The third character is vendors, who play a foil role, as humans and vendors have different interests. Vendors may share a focus on promoting standardisation and efficiency in talent decisions, but they are not united, and they compete against each other for sales.

As the options for digitalisation and automation increase, humans must decide where, when and how to give power to technology and vendors in talent decisions.

# Part 2: (Re)Thinking Talent Decision Outcomes

# A Tale of Complexity, Technology and Subjectivity in the Pursuit of Strategy and Knowledge

What motivates us to act on our thoughts and perceptions and make talent decisions? And what are we hoping to achieve as the output of our decisions?

Talent decisions help us get "somewhere." We make talent decisions because we want to journey towards an outcome. The "somewhere" is the "why."

Key questions are:
- What are we doing talent management for?
- What are we hoping to achieve through talent decisions?
- What are the desired outcomes?

We must know where our "somewhere" is before we embark on our journey. Knowing where we want to go helps ensure we stay the course. Our destination – the desired outcomes – acts as our map.

Our (re)thinking journey leads us towards two different but equally salient destinations – strategy and knowledge.

One point on our map takes us to strategy. Talent decisions aid the execution of strategy. I firmly believe that talent decisions and strategy are closely intertwined. Talent management involves assessing value judgments to pursue and attain strategic ambitions and goals.

Knowledge is another point on our map. I propose that humans seek knowledge. We, humans, want to know more than we did before. You hope to learn something – to increase your knowledge about talent decisions as an outcome of reading this book. Acknowledging this drive for knowledge explains why I have incorporated an entire section that focuses on further exploring the concept of knowledge.

Source: Copyright © Sharna Wiblen. All rights reserved.

# Chapter 3
# Talent Decisions in the Pursuit of Strategy

Strategy is a destination for our (re)thinking tale. Strategy is also an anchor point for many discussions because talent decisions help achieve strategic ambitions and goals. Executing strategy is an important "why." It is essential to explicitly consider strategic imperatives when discussing decisions and actions because realising strategies is the "somewhere" in our talent story.

*Strategy is the "why" of talent management.*
*Strategy, Strategy, Strategy. Talent decisions start and end with strategy.*
*We make talent decisions as a way to pursue strategic ambitions and goals.*

As an advocate for human decision-making, I firmly believe that humans are great decision-makers, and I am on #Teamhuman. However, our understanding of the key players in executing strategies is evolving. Studying how organisations manage the human-technology interface allows me to learn about human-based decision-making while pursuing an organisational plan. I explore how groups of humans frame technology or specific technologies such as digitalisation, algorithms, machine learning and artificial intelligence as the basis of their competitive offering or as core decision-makers.

We are also increasingly witnessing instances where #Teamtechnology is the foundation of an organisation's business model. The "Space Race" nods to the changing boundaries of talent management and organisational design.

**What the Space Race is Telling Us about the Changing Face of Digitalised Talent Management Strategies**

The "Space Race" illustrates the increasing role of technology as a critical decision-maker and a mechanism for pursuing a strategy. Sir Richard Branson and Virgin Galactic emphasise human talent. Virgin Galactic's achievement was a "fully crewed spaceflight." Two human pilots controlled the space mission. Human pilots operated the mission. Human pilots were responsible for launch processes and releasing the "spaceship from the mothership." Human pilots welcomed passengers "to space" and controlled the spacecraft while the "astronauts" experienced zero gravity and breathtaking views of Earth. The pilot advised passengers to "please return to their seats and strap in for re-entry" and then "glides the spaceship to a smooth landing . . ." Humans collaborated with various technologies. Success, however, was a human endeavour.

Compare this with Jeff Bezos and Blue Origins' approach to their "first human flight." The Blue Origin space mission placed automated technologies at the forefront of taking citizens to space. The New Shepard spacecraft boasts a window seat for all passengers and is fully autonomous. No human pilots are onboard. Jeff Bezos and Blue Origin are adopting an automated technology rather than a people-first approach.

The Space Race exemplifies the growing dependence on automated technologies and could signal a shift in the boundaries of digitalised talent management, with computerised technologies becoming the primary decision-makers. This could mark a fundamental change, whereby the emphasis on valuing human talent is replaced by valuing automated technologies, software, or automation as the most valuable assets. Increasing digitalisation and automation requires organisations to design talent systems recognising that "talent" can simultaneously refer to humans and technology (including automation or Artificial Intelligence).

Key decisions, therefore, are whether human talent or technology (or another mechanism) drives the organisation's business model and whether talent, technology or another factor is of greater value within the context of the different strategies.

Establishing the "why" of talent decisions, whether to facilitate public space flight or another somewhere, is imperative regardless of a character's position on the human-technology spectrum.

## H.I.S.T.O.R.Y – The Importance of Acknowledging An Organisation's History

Google, Blue Origin, Virgin Galactic and all other organisations exist for a reason. Some founders establish business entities that seek to improve or change the status quo. Other founders may see an opportunity, a gap in the market, or a need. Some founders want to "scratch their own itch."

Regardless of the reason for their existence, all organisations have a purpose that drives them forward. This purpose is reflected in their DNA, which includes their values, mission and vision.

An organisation's DNA is reflected in how internal characters go about their work. Accepted and rejected ways of working are captured in stories: stories about how the organisation started and why it exists, how the organisation developed over time and stories about where key senior characters think the organisation is heading (the "somewhere") and how The Workforce will add value. Stories help internal and external characters learn about the organisation and its purpose and reason for existing.

Stories are a fundamental part of our human experience, and they help us connect with and relate to others. Organisations can leverage the power of storytelling to create a compelling narrative that resonates with their audience and helps them stand out in a crowded marketplace. People are drawn to specific organisations because of their stories. Organisational stories are not an accidental aspect of strategy. Instead, stories are part of what makes an organisation what it is today.

### The Power of Disney's Storytelling

Let us reflect on the power of storytelling. Reflect on the images which arise when I say "Disney." I am immediately transported back to my first Disneyland adventure. I am fourteen years' old again. I see images of family fun, rides, screams of excitement, cuddles (pre-Covid cuddles) with Mickey Mouse, Minnie Mouse and the wider character crew, churros and crab soup. The phrase "The Happiest Place on Earth" is also front of mind. A few minutes later, I start singing, "It's a small world, after all." Disney, and its associated theme parks, sell happiness and positive experiences. While the reality of a trip to Disneyland also includes lines and copious amounts of walking (a great way to increase your step count), these aspects are superseded by my memories. Memories are easily recalled because of Disney's time, effort and attention in creating (positive) stories about its organisation and activities.

In today's fast-paced and ever-changing business landscape, storytelling is more important than ever. Companies must craft a compelling narrative about their values, mission and purpose. They need to connect with their audience emotionally and build a community of loyal followers who share their vision. By doing so, they can create a lasting impact and make a positive difference in the world.

Disney and Lego are great examples of companies that have built a strong brand identity through storytelling. Both companies have created immersive worlds and characters that people of all ages can relate to and enjoy. By tapping into our nostalgia and imagination, they have built a loyal customer base and established themselves as leaders in their respective industries.

Other companies like Amazon, Facebook, Tesla and Google have also used storytelling to their advantage. They have created compelling narratives around their founders, products and mission that have helped them attract top talent, investors and customers. They have inspired others to join their cause and become part of their journey by sharing their story and vision.

*Understanding the strategies of today and a future day are influenced by an organisation's history and the stories associated with yesterday's strategies.*

An organisation's current and future strategies are influenced by the stories associated with its previous strategies. The ability to pursue certain strategies is shaped by the organisation's history and the extent to which it achieved its past goals. Today's decisions and actions also impact the strategies that the organisation can pursue in the future. Strategies are not discrete plans that can be easily separated from one another. The reality of strategies is not a situation whereby on Monday we are enacting strategy #1 but come Tuesday we start strategy #2. Rather, strategies are connected and build upon each other. Changing direction – changing the "somewhere" – requires embedded ways of working and decision-making as the organisation navigates the path toward its strategic goals. Pursuing strategy is more like a journey down a (never-ending) winding road rather than a set of isolated, sequential plans.

## Strategy Definitions

Rethinking talent decisions involves recognising that strategy is not just a document or a policy, but a way of doing things and behaving around the organisation. Strategies are not static plans but living entities that come to life through the actions and inactions of The Workforce. When discussing strategy, words like direction, purpose, action, process and behaviour come to mind.

Remember, we benefit from looking in before we look out. What you think about a concept matters. So, start with Y.O.U. It's essential to take the time to pause, reflect and capture our understanding of what strategy means.

What do you think strategy means?
What are you referring to when you use the word strategy?
What words come to mind when you reflect on strategy?

Is strategy a guiding document or a set of values and behaviours that we embody in everything we do?

### Public Strategy Definitions

I began my exploration of the definition of strategy by consulting the *Merriam-Webster* online dictionary, which defines strategy as "a careful plan or method; the art of devising or employing plans or stratagems towards a goal." I also consulted the *Compact Oxford Dictionary, Thesaurus, and Wordpower Guide,* which has been a reliable resource for me since 2001. This source defines strategy as "a plan designed to achieve a particular long-term aim."

ChatGPT answered "What is Strategy?" with:

> Strategy can be defined as a plan or method designed to achieve a specific goal or objective. It involves making choices about how to allocate resources and develop capabilities to achieve a desired outcome. A good strategy typically takes into account the internal and external environment of an organisation, as well as its strengths, weaknesses, opportunities, and threats. Ultimately, the goal of a strategy is to help an organisation achieve sustainable competitive advantage in its industry or market.

While posing "What's the definition of strategy?" to ChatGPT yielded the following:

> Strategy is a plan or approach for achieving a goal or objective. It involves making choices and taking actions that are intended to lead to the desired outcome, often in a complex or competitive environment. Strategies may involve a combination of tactics, resources, and capabilities, and they may be adapted or revised based on changing circumstances or new information. The ultimate aim of a strategy is to create a sustainable advantage or to maximise value for stakeholders.

## Scientific Strategy Definitions

Strategy experts, consultants and scholars offer various strategy definitions, including:
- The determination of long-term goals and objectives of an enterprise and the adaption of courses of action and the allocation of resources necessary for carrying out these goals – Alfred Chandler
- A pattern in a stream of decisions – Henry Mintzberg
- A firm's theory about how to gain competitive advantage – Peter Drucker

---

**Strategy and Michael Porter**

Michael Porter is a prominent figure in the field of strategy. He is regarded as a strategy guru and is best known for his book *Competitive Strategy: Techniques for Analysing Industries and Competitors*. In the Introduction to the 1998 republished version, Porter acknowledges that his ideas have proliferated and are now an accepted part of management practice, "Competitive strategy, and its core disciplines of industry analysis, competitor analysis, and strategic positioning, are now an accepted part of management practice."

Porter's approach to strategy involves bringing different departments and divisions together to create policies that are coordinated and directed towards a common set of goals. Developing a strategy involves developing a general formula for how a business will compete, setting goals, and establishing policies to achieve those goals. Key internal characters must decide whether to adopt offensive or defensive actions to create a defendable position in a specific industry, manage competitive forces and generate a superior return on investment for the firm.

Porter provided a methodology for analysing the different factors influencing strategies. The "Five Forces" model offers a structured framework for understanding an organisation's competitive positioning. The five competitive forces include entry, the threat of substitution, the bargaining power of buyers, suppliers and rivalry among current competitors. Understanding these forces informs strategy formulation.

Porter believed that organisations should aim to outperform other firms in their specific industry. Outperforming competitors was possible by selecting one of three "generic strategies": overall cost leadership, differentiation, or focus. Porter argues that deciding on a generic strategy is an "or" decision, not an "and" decision. Organisations should pick a specific strategy. Being "stuck in the middle" is an "extremely poor strategic situation."

**Overall cost leadership** is a generic strategy that involves developing functional policies to establish a (defendable) position as a cost leader in a specific industry. This strategy entails internal decisions and actions focusing on constructing efficient-scale facilities, pursuing cost reductions through experience, tight cost and overhead control, and cost minimisation. The central strategic theme is to establish low costs relative to competitors. Key internal characters focus their time, energy and attention towards controlling costs to achieve this objective.

**Differentiation** involves offering a product or service that is perceived as being distinct from those provided within a specific industry. According to Porter, differentiation strategies can take many forms, including design or brand image, technology, customer service and dealer networks. The focus is on establishing numerous points of difference rather than cost control. Developing unique features and capabilities may require significant investment, leading to higher organisational costs. However, differentiation helps the organisation defend its position in the market by creating brand loyalty, maintaining higher supplier margins and reducing the threat of substitute products or services due to the scarcity of comparable options.

> **Focus** strategy involves serving a particular buyer group, product line segment, or geographic market. Unlike overall cost leadership and differentiation, the Focus strategy is not aimed at achieving objectives at the industry level. Instead, it focuses on servicing a particular target. Functional policies are designed to cater to the target market's needs, and the strategy relies on the idea that the organisation benefits from serving a specific segment rather than competing more broadly. Key decision-makers in a focus strategy make trade-offs between profitability and sales volume. As a result, the organisation achieves either differentiation by better meeting the needs of the target or lower costs in servicing this target or both.[7]

Porter's perspective on strategy is valuable in many ways. Firstly, by focusing on differentiation and unique value, Porter encourages organisations to have internal discussions about their activities and value propositions rather than just focusing on the competition. While understanding the competition can be significant, it should not be the sole focus of strategy development. Secondly, Porter discourages the zero-sum mentality of pursuing being the best, instead encouraging organisations to focus on creating their unique value proposition. This perspective allows for infinite possibilities for success and promotes innovation and creativity. Thirdly, Porter's view encourages purposeful reflection on devising strategies for today and a future day,

> Staying flexible in strategic terms renders competitive advantage almost unattainable. Jumping from strategy to strategy makes it impossible to be good at implementing any of them. Continuous incorporation of new ideas is important to maintaining operational effectiveness. But this is surely not at all inconsistent with having a consistent strategic position.

In (re)thinking talent decisions, it is crucial to understand the meaning of *strategy*. The various definitions of strategy presented in this section emphasise the complexity of talent decisions, as they are influenced and aligned with different strategies. Humans have varying perceptions of strategy, which adds to the intricacy of talent decisions.

## Strategy Characteristics

Strategy determines an organisation's long-term direction, the path The Workforce will walk along to get "somewhere." Pursuing strategy involves making decisions, choices and trade-offs.

---

7 While Porter is considered by many as the mainstay of all things strategy, he has updated his perspectives of strategy over time. Rather than present and then endlessly campaign for the adoption of one perspective, Porter is willing to revisit his ideas. He notes that aspects of competitive strategy are not meant to be viewed as static factors, and are subject to change. He encourages key characters to continue their knowledge journey. They should continue to learn about their industry, their rivals and ways to improve or modify their competitive positioning. This creates a situation whereby Porter's current thoughts may be misrepresented. The above prose is no exception.

> *Successful strategies require choice* – Michael Porter

Strategy, furthermore:
- Can be about being deliberate and emergent – establishing a long-term agenda in advance and revisiting/amending strategies over time
- Can be about differentiation and imitation – establishing points of difference (differentiation) between the organisation and establishing points of similarity with the competition (imitation)
- Can involve doing something new and different – deciding to pursue an alternative set of offerings
- Requires new/ different skills – resources and competencies change as an organisation's competitive positioning and offerings change
- Involves articulating how and where the business is different – establishing points of difference between the organisation and its competition (Michael Porter argues that differentiation is a tool to command a price premium)
- Involves talent (no surprises there, for me anyway). Talent – aka The Workforce – partakes in establishing and pursuing strategies.

Strategy is many things, but strategy does not focus on the following:
- Creating business plans
- Creating operational plans
- Increasing market size
- Generating shareholder value
- Share prices
- Creating a (static) document.

## Strategy Lenses – Different Ways to Think About Strategy

Strategies shape internal discussions and require reflection on the perspectives within an organisation. Key stakeholders play a critical role in framing the long-term direction and priorities of the organisation, as well as planning and implementing strategic actions.

With relation to the "what" of strategy:
How do key human characters frame an organisation's long-term direction?
How do key senior characters and Line managers talk about their priorities?

With relation to the "how":
To what extent do key humans plan for strategic actions, amend policies and understand talent needs when devising (and pursuing) strategic goals?

Answering these questions is vital because key humans must translate how strategies will transition from the theoretical to the material. It is The Workforce that brings strategic goals "to life" through their behaviours and actions.

To better understand how key stakeholders bring strategies to life, we can consider various strategy perspectives such as strategy-by-design, strategy-as-experience, strategy-as-variety, strategy-as-discourse and strategy-as-practice. Each perspective provides a unique lens for analysing strategy beyond traditional perceptions.

**Strategy-By-Design**

Key internal characters often devote their time and effort to developing strategies through a rational analysis of various aspects of performance, competition and outcomes. Proponents of this approach may rely on established strategy frameworks such as Michael Porter's Five Forces model to guide their analysis. They may "copy" previous analyses and "paste" these into current strategy formulation activities. Doing so leads them to (wrongly) assume that past assumptions and analyses are still relevant today without considering environmental changes.

The strategy-by-design approach involves designing strategies abstractly and linearly. Formalised plans and policies document a series of (linear) steps, whereby strategies are realised after completing step 1, step 2, step 3, step 4 and so on. Although systematic and logical, this approach can be rigid and inflexible when faced with changing circumstances.

Adherents of this approach may believe in the existence of a "right way" of doing things and a strict process to follow: "There is a process to follow" and "Just follow the process."

---

*Strategy-by-design – frames strategy formulation as a design process whereby strategies are designed in the abstract; values hard facts and objectivity; encourages systematic, logical and analytical design processes focusing on creating a linear execution process – step 1, 2, 3, 4 etc.*

---

**Strategy-As-Experience**

Strategy-as-experience is all about the organisational context. Advocates of this approach focus on internal activities, especially the experiences and activities of the past. Stories about the organisation's history or previous actions are central to internal conversations. Humans may refer to "how things were in the past." The strategy-as-experience perspective is more concerned with internal activities rather than reacting to changes in the external environment.

Previous experiences influence strategy-as-experience methodologies. Strategies are also shaped by the prevailing assumptions of the key humans tasked with formulating strategies and the policies to support execution. What key humans think about competitors, suppliers and buyers can influence the form of strategies and the intensity at which they are pursued.

The internal culture and existing ways of working play a crucial role in shaping an organisation's decisions and actions. Key humans often rely on standard fixes and routines and have taken-for-granted assumptions about "how things work around here." In my personal experience, I have encountered an environment where colleagues used the phrase "it's the [insert organisation's name here] way!" when clarifying policies and practices. Some colleagues appeared proud of their ability to answer superficially, while others used this phrase when they didn't have an answer. Either way, they were maintaining a particular internal culture. This culture shapes not only what the organisation does but also what it doesn't do – the no-go zones, the activities it "does not do" and "will not do," and the paths it refuses to traverse.

Untethering from the past or current ways of working can be difficult because key humans often appeal to precedents or conjure up memories of previous experiences and judgments about the relationship between certain decisions and actions with certain (usually adverse) outcomes. These connections are particularly noticeable when colleagues say, "We've done that in the past, and it didn't work out," and conclude, "We'd be silly to try that again."

Prioritising retrospection limits perceptions of what is possible, restricting innovation because new ideas are shunned or dismissed. I have witnessed instances where newer individuals shared alternative ways of doing things, only to be immediately shut down with phrases like "That wouldn't work here" (and key humans wonder why proportions of The Workforce refrain from contributing to discussions!). This approach poses a significant challenge to advancing strategic decisions, especially if they represent a different way of doing things.

---

*Strategy-as-experience – relies on memories of the past and current ways of working when establishing strategies; appeals to precedent; prefers standard fixes and established routines of decision-making; influenced significantly by the experiences and perceptions of key senior humans; cautious of innovation or changing "how things are done around here."*

---

**Strategy-As-Variety**

Strategy-as-variety prioritises the human factor and recognises that perceptions about what the organisation "can do" arise from the thoughts and ideas of humans within and around the organisation. Innovation and new ideas are encouraged and welcomed. New ideas can emerge through unpredictable processes responding to uncertain and changing environments.

Strategy formulation involves framing strategies as emergent rather than static or linear. Key humans are critical in creating environments where diverse thoughts are valued. Different ways of looking and seeing are also valued. The strategy-as-variety perspective acknowledges that the future is uncertain, and the organisation must adapt and respond to change.

Key humans assume and embrace ambiguity as part of the journey. Key humans recognise that there may be no correct answer or a fixed way of doing things. Instead, they may pursue different activities as part of the strategic direction. They also recognise that other parts of the organisation may require different strategies and approaches and that it's essential to consider the broader ecosystem in which the organisation operates. The organisation can better navigate complex and rapidly changing environments by embracing variety and diversity.

---

*Strategy-as-variety – welcomes ambiguity and diverse "ideas" when deciding what to do; considers numerous options when determining whether certain activities are worth pursuing; emergent processes that recognise and react to external changes.*

---

**Strategy-As-Discourse**

Strategy-as-discourse recognises the influential role of language in strategy formulation and execution, with humans taking centre stage. This approach prioritises language and talk, understanding that the language used by key senior humans directly influences internal actions and organisational success. A whole-of-workforce approach is emphasised, as designing the strategy is only one part of the process.

Key humans understand that they need to work with The Workforce to pursue and realise strategic goals. They use language to frame strategic problems, offer proposals, debate issues and communicate strategic directives. Communication is crucial as senior humans endeavour to guide The Workforce in a particular direction as they navigate through the map. Stories and narratives about the journey and the destination matter to strategy execution because The Workforce needs to act in specific ways and abstain from others for goals to materialise.

Key humans seek to touch the hearts and the heads of The Workforce (especially because humans are more emotional than rational beings). Key humans know that their words matter and that there are different implications of saying, "We are all in this strategic journey together; you all have a role to play in our success" versus "You need to do what I tell you to do; do what I say." Ensuring consistency in messaging is crucial.

> *Strategy-as-discourse – emphasises language and recognises that words matter; key humans are tasked with bringing The Workforce along the strategic journey; adopts a whole-of-workforce approach and recognises the pivotal role of humans in strategy execution.*

**Strategy-As-Practice**

Most strategy-based discussions do not talk about strategy-as-practice. Strategy-as-practice differs from the other strategy perspectives because it frames strategy as a verb. A strategy-as-practice view asserts that The Workforce "does strategy."

Strategy-as-practice acknowledges the interrelationship between social activities and processes of organising within organisational boundaries. Time, energy and attention focus on the micro-level context. The goal is to understand the social activities, processes and practices characterising strategy formulation and methodologies. The approach shares a similar workforce-as-a-whole approach and argues the need to understand and direct individual humans' perceptions, discourses and actions to learn how strategy happens.

> *Strategy-as-practice – frames strategy as a set of actions; encourages us to reflect on and understand human perceptions of strategy because the actions and inactions of humans influence outcomes; adopts an approach that appreciates plurality, ambiguity and complexity.*

This perspective recognises that words matter, and so do actions. Usefully strategy-as-practice identifies that strategies "come to life" through The Workforce's efforts. Fostering specific actions and behaviours is vital to strategy execution. There is an appreciation for a plurality of ideas, ambiguity and complexity in the strategic journey.

Reflecting on key humans is essential. Maria Christina Meyers and colleagues articulate why. Strategy-as-practice

> proposes that a firm's strategy is not only captured in official organisational policy documents, but first and foremost in the actions of organisational strategists, that is, managers. The strategic behaviour of managers is illustrated by the tools or practices they use. Even if managers use the official organisational practices (e.g. HR or talent-management practices), they will infuse them with their own meaning depending on their beliefs and intentions.

Key characters are interested in learning what individual humans do and why. Asking diagnostic questions is a key part of the strategy execution process. Questions such as:

How do you (a specific individual) do strategy?
How does strategy get made?

How does strategy get enacted?
Who does the making of strategy?
Who implements strategy?
When does strategy making happen?

There is a need, therefore, to consider the perceptions and actions of both key senior characters and The Workforce generally.

**Which Strategic Lens is Best?**

Which perspective is best, you ask?

When developing and executing strategies, it's essential to consider both the strategy-as-discourse and strategy-as-practice perspectives. The emphasis on language and communication in strategy-as-discourse is crucial for encouraging The Workforce to act in a certain way and creating compelling narratives that drive strategic execution. Meanwhile, strategy-as-practice recognises that strategy is not just a document but a set of daily actions that individuals undertake. Strategy is a team sport where individuals work together towards a common goal.

All strategies need stories, regardless of the strategic perspective adopted. As Disney, Lego, Tesla and Amazon illustrate, stories are potent anchors for strategy execution. We must remember that strategies "come to life" through stories, and stories encourage certain decisions, behaviours and actions. Stories also help communicate why an organisation exists – its history – its purpose – why it still exists and the (strategic) path The Workforce is journeying along.

Key senior characters benefit from using words to corral The Workforce to join them as they travel towards their pre-defined "somewhere" or, in the case of strategy-as-variety, the different "somewheres."

## Talent Management Strategies

Our understanding of complexity further expands when we consider talent management strategies. Complexity arises because no two organisational strategies should be the same, and the same goes for talent management strategies. Therefore, talent decisions should differ as organisations pursue different objectives. Since organisational strategies are bespoke, what works best for one organisation may not work for another. Key senior characters may look at other organisations or specific business gurus with awe, but copying their talent management strategies or approaching talent decisions the same way is inherently flawed.

## Defining Talent Management Strategies

Talent management strategies are bespoke, customised and tailored frameworks for "doing" talent management. Broadly speaking, talent management strategies focus on understanding The Workforce's role in strategy execution. Identifying which aspects of The Workforce are most helpful in pursuing strategic imperatives is crucial. This includes identifying the skills and capabilities required to execute current and future organisational strategies. What talents help us achieve our desired outcomes and take us one step closer to our desired destination?

Talent management strategies capture answers to the above questions and outline where to (disproportionately) allocate resources:

> *A talent management strategy formally documents how an organisation will deploy specific individuals, skills and capabilities, and roles to pursue strategic ambitions and goals.*

## What Strategy Comes First?

The K-I-S-S-I-N-G song was one of many nursery rhymes I sang during childhood, which sought to embarrass two specific humans. The lyrics are as follows:

(Name) and (Name)
Sitting in a tree
K-I-S-S-I-N-G
First comes love
Then comes marriage
Then comes a baby in a baby carriage

Now, why am I sharing this nursery rhyme with you? It's a relevant question. This rhyme depicts a linear and intentional way of creating a family. The first step involves falling in love with each other, the second involves formalising love through marriage and the third involves pushing a baby around in a pram. Essentially, it goes: "First comes love, then comes marriage, then comes the baby in the baby carriage."

Rewriting this nursery rhyme enables me to convey a message about the connection between different strategies in a memorable way. So here is my connection attempt:

Sharna and other humans
Sitting in a tree
T-H-I-N-K-I-N-G

First comes the organisational strategy
Then comes the talent management and digitalisation strategies
Then comes digitalised talent management strategies as represented in policies and practices

The nursery rhyme may not have the same poetic rhythm, but it still conveys an important point. Organisational strategies should guide talent management strategies, just as love comes before marriage. We often assume a linear process, where setting the strategic direction comes before formulating talent management strategies. We must know our desired outcomes and destination before organising and managing workforce capabilities to support strategy execution.

One of the goals of (re)thinking talent decisions is to understand the role of The Workforce and talent in pursuing and achieving strategic goals. This is essential because talent only holds value within specific contexts. We must know the context – the strategy – before determining the who and what of talent decisions. As Michael Porter stated, "Resources or competencies are most valuable for a particular position or way of competing, not in and of themselves."

Interestingly, the notion of talent management strategies presented above assumes a linear, strategy-by-design approach in which the organisational strategy precedes the talent strategy, which in turn precedes the digitalisation strategy. By combining talent management and technology strategy, an organisation can determine the role of technology in talent management.

However, this linear approach has practical limitations, and it is here that I critique my own prose to illustrate the value in (re)thinking talent decisions. Strategy requires ongoing iteration, and assuming a linear, systematic, or logical approach fails to reflect this need. It is not the time for strategy-as-design; it never was.

Some experts have advocated a more dynamic and multi-directional. John Boudreau and Peter Ramstad, in *Beyond HR: The New Science of Human Capital*, propose that leaders should consider the talent and organisational implications of strategy from the outset. This involves non-HR leaders collaborating with HR leaders to identify talent-strategy connections. According to Boudreau and Ramstad, HR strategies should be distinctive and tailored to the specific context of an organisation. They suggest that this information should be a trade secret.

Their concept of "Talentship" offers an alternative to the traditional linear approach, where HR strategies and plans are developed after the completion of organisational strategy and planning. Talentship helps organisations identify where winning the talent war matters most and provides a strategic logic to determine unique ways to compete for scarce talent. Instead of simply copying the practices of others, Talentship encourages organisations to consider their context and develop distinct HR strategies that align with their specific goals.

They went on to state:

> Talentship connects organisational and talent decisions to the organisation's strategy . . . Talentship undoubtably is even more effective as strategies become more complete and well developed. In fact, it can be a catalyst for strategy improvement. When leaders use the Talentship strategy lenses carefully and avoid defensiveness, the process encourages discussions about where the organisations should improve the strategy, how it can improve its strategy formation and analysis processes, and where it might invest in enhancing the strategic competence of its leaders.

The decision-focused approach encouraged business leaders to frame talent as a vital resource. A vital resource whereby leaders reflected on the contributions of different individuals and activities to value generation, task execution and building and sustaining advantages. The goal is to consider pivotal areas whereby small changes make a big difference to strategy and value (it is helpful to remember that talent management is about workforce differentiation. We seek to understand where talent decisions result in additional and/or unequal (positive) value and outcomes). Considering talent and talent-focused decisions became part of the strategy formation processes. Talent was not an afterthought; knowledge of the existing talent landscape informed strategy formulation and analysis.

Robert E. Lewis and Robert J. Heckman were two others who also reflected on the inter-relationship between organisational strategies and talent decisions. In their highly cited academic paper, *Talent Management: A Critical Review,* Lewis and Heckman noted that many of the perceptions and approaches to talent management operating in the 2000s were rarely strategic. They believed many assertions about the positive relationship between talent management and business performance were based mainly on exhortation and anecdotes rather than testable models. They further noted that studies of HR practices had not explicitly investigated how the choice of practices is tied to strategy, and only a few texts covered organisational strategy and workforce practices simultaneously.

Lewis and Heckman proposed that the relationship between strategy and talent decisions was two-directional. That is, talent decisions are core to strategy execution, and key (HR) humans should develop a point of view regarding how talent decisions should be made before strategies are formulated. They also used Boudreau and Ramstad's ideas to support this notion. The authors provided a high-level hierarchy for reflecting on the connection between strategy and talent management:

- Strategy: what market opportunities exist?
- Sustainable Competitive Strategy: which organisational resources yield an advantage?
- Strategy implications for talent: where will improvements in talent quality drive strategic gains? Where will improvements in talent fungibility drive strategic gains?

Despite the immediate connection between organisational and talent management strategies, and the pivotal work of the two teams of Boudreau and Ramstad and Lewis and Heckman in the 2000s, our understanding of the relationship between strategy and talent decisions has barely advanced. The talent management academic literature (still) rarely acknowledges or discusses this relationship in detail. This is an ongoing concern of mine and a big reason why there is a "strategy" section in our (re)thinking talent decisions tale. I also include "strategy" models in all teachings because "Strategy, strategy, strategy – all talent decisions are in the pursuit of strategy."

The boxes include the thoughts of a few others which touch on the topic to enhance our shared knowledge.

---

In a 2014 Harvard Business Review article titled *Building a Game Changing Talent Strategy*, **Douglas Ready, Linda Hill and Robert Thomas** argued that three organisations that transformed their respective industries had one thing in common – superior talent strategies. The three organisations – BlackRock, Tata Group and Envision – were purpose-driven, performance-oriented and principles-led. They operated with comprehensive talent strategies that supported business strategies and addressed group, divisional, regional and business unit considerations. The authors suggested that their talent policies were "built to last" and regularly reviewed to ensure that the organisations responded to internal and external changes. They also acknowledged that the path to a truly game-changing talent strategy was complex and ambiguous. I smiled when I read, "the path to a truly game-changing talent strategy is rife with complexity and ambiguity." Yes, journeying through the tale of talent decision is encased with complexity!

There is evidence that key individuals at BlackRock use various discourse-as-strategy techniques, with some commenting in interviews that internal dialogue focuses on "we." Rob Kapito, the president and cofounder, said, "The notion of 'we' dominates here. I bring emerging leaders to my house. I cook for them. They get to know me as a person, not just a role . . . Authenticity has high currency at BlackRock." Senior leaders lead by example and use storytelling to communicate desired behaviours and actions.

---

At a 2022 event I attended, **Maura Stevenson**, the Chief Human Resources Officer at MedVet, discussed the interplay between organisational and talent management strategies. She emphasised that talent and organisational planning should address two key questions: what future job openings can we expect, and what roles will change due to evolving strategies? Guided by the assumption that certain workforce components contribute significantly to achieving key objectives, Stevenson suggested that it is beneficial to consider how jobs, tasks and functions can be structured to support talent management strategies.

---

This section illustrated the interdependence between organisational strategies and talent management strategies. While we tend to assume that organisational strategies come first, followed by talent strategies and decisions, my goal in reconsidering talent decisions is to encourage us to question this relationship. Although it is helpful to see talent strategies as informed by and aligned with organisational strategies, we must also be mindful of the impact of existing talent decisions and actions. Thus, we need to expand our perspective and emphasise a multi-directional relationship, where talent implications are analysed during strategy formulation, not after.

> *Organisational and talent management strategies are multi-directional, where strategy formulation considers the talent implications.*

Talent decisions are tools used for strategy execution but can also shape and inform organisational strategies. By emphasising this multi-directional relationship, we can avoid blind spots and ensure that talent decisions align with and support the organisation's strategic goals.

## Digitalisation Strategies

Senior executive teams increasingly feature a position dedicated to technology and digital transformation. Whether called the Chief Digital Officer (CDO), Chief Information Officer (CIO), Chief Technical Officer (CTO), or some other name, there is generally someone responsible for making decisions about digital transformation.

For many Chief-technology humans, making digitalisation a strategic priority for their company is crucial. Companies like Amazon, Google and Facebook have adopted an enterprise-wide approach to digitalisation. It is part of their history, core to their why and at the forefront of operational and strategic actions. For these companies, digitalisation strategies are front of mind.

For others, however, digitalisation may be an afterthought. Digitalisation strategies may only be considered after the organisational strategy is formulated. Such an ad hoc and reactionary approach results in duplication and integration issues. It is crucial to have a pre-determined path to digitalisation to avoid these issues and ensure a more effective digital transformation.

### Defining Digitalisation Strategies

Digitalisation strategies establish and communicate the digital vision, guide resource allocations, technology investments and share whether digital transformation is a strategic priority. They provide parameters for technology and serve as a roadmap for implementing digital solutions. In turn, talent management strategies must consider the influence of digitalisation on talent needs, workforce planning and skill development. The relationship between talent and technology is interdependent and strategic. A comprehensive approach to talent management and digitalisation is necessary for organisational success in the digital age.

> *A digitalisation strategy formally documents how an organisation will structure, select and deploy various technologies to support the pursuit and realisation of operational imperatives and strategic ambitions.*

Digitalisation strategies are primarily concerned with enterprise-wide matters related to the organisational decision-making level. These strategies guide selecting, delivering and optimising enterprise-wide business processes and define digitalisation within the industry and organisational strategy context. Strategy formulation processes consider which types of digitalisation are critical to business success, in line with John Boudreau and Peter Ramstad's perspective on investing in key areas where small changes can result in significant differences.

Digitalisation strategies focus on understanding which technologies best suit the organisation and its strategic ambitions. These strategies reflect these goals while considering existing technologies and current and future technological innovations. Digitalisation strategies also reflect internal and external changes. Internal changes include vendor selection and software updates or potential outages. Rising innovations like blockchain, machine learning and quantum computing are assessed for opportunities and threats. Pondering future technological innovations sparks theoretical and imaginative discussions about the potential for specific innovations to fundamentally change (or endanger) business processes, create new or additional revenue streams and spawn new industries.

Digitalisation strategies aim to evaluate and document the priority given to digital transformation and digital ways of working. These strategies communicate where the organisation is heading regarding digital and business transformation.

**Data**. Data plays a crucial role in digitalisation strategies. Digitalisation strategies generally include a specific data strategy that outlines how data will be captured, stored and utilised within the organisation. Key decision-makers, such as the CEO and senior executives, can influence the importance of data within digitalisation strategies. If these individuals value evidence-based decision-making, quantitative metrics, financial figures and statistical analysis, they will likely prioritise technology-based activities and investments. They may also allocate larger technology budgets.

**Which Digitalisation Comes First?**

Adopting a technology or business-driven approach is a formative decision in implementing digital working methods or pursuing digital transformation. Organisations need to consider the trade-offs between customisation and standardisation when making this decision. A business-driven approach may provide more customisation and flexibility and be more resource-intensive and time-consuming. On the other hand, a technology-driven approach may provide faster implementation and lower costs but may not fully align with the organisation's unique needs and processes. I give an overview of both the business-driven and technology-driven approaches next.

### A Business-Driven Approach – Building Software in-House

When an organisation decides that organisational knowledge is valuable, it typically chooses a business-driven approach to digitalisation. In this approach, workforce members are responsible for determining the outcomes and designing the software frameworks to enable the organisation to achieve its objectives. The software is coded in-house, considering the organisation's unique context, and is owned by the organisation. The responsibility for maintaining and revising the software rests with the organisation, with workforce members also responsible for maintaining existing software and designing upgrades as needed.

Human characters who advocate for a business-driven approach understand that digitalisation is just a tool, not the destination itself. They recognise that technology can help the organisation achieve its goals, but attribute value to organisational knowledge and choose to design fit-for-purpose software rather than simply adopting pre-designed frameworks from external vendors. This approach allows the organisation to leverage its internal talent and maintain control.

---

*A business-driven approach values organisational knowledge and prioritises designing fit-for-purpose software systems.*

---

In an ideal world, organisations would design and maintain digitalisation in-house. The software code would match the operational processes and align with strategic ambitions and goals. Adopting a business-driven approach is now a thing of the past. Once upon a time, designing and maintaining bespoke and proprietary systems was the only option. And while all the software differed significantly when key humans reached the destination, the journey was expensive.

Key decision-makers may draw on their past experiences when making decisions about digital transformation. Some may be hesitant to advocate for a business-driven approach because it reminds them of a time when designing, maintaining and upgrading software in-house was the only option. They may recall the high costs involved and the risk of losing key individuals who held knowledge of the software. The technology-driven approach has become popular because it offers a more cost-effective and efficient solution, and they don't want to "revisit the past" (such mindsets and approaches are indicative of strategy-as-experience).

### A Technology-Driven Approach – Buying or Renting Software From External Vendors

A technology-driven approach involves key individuals seeking process designs embedded in software from external markets. This approach involves buying various technologies for digitalisation projects from external vendors. Vendor-designed systems involve different ownership models, whereby software systems are purchased with a licensing agreement or rented via Software-as-a-Service (SaaS) arrangements.

Adopting a technology-driven approach was primarily a response to the perceived limitations of the business-driven methods of the past. Internal teams, whether HR, Finance, or IT, were no longer responsible for maintaining and updating the systems. Technology vendors provided updates and additional services for an ongoing fee. Direct cost savings were almost immediate, as associated costs shifted from being predominantly a labour expense to an IT infrastructure expense, and the ongoing fees were significantly less than those related to proprietary systems.

---

*A technology-driven approach prioritises technology-based knowledge and involves outsourcing process design.*

---

Vendors can potentially influence strategic imperatives as externally designed technology may dictate certain ways of completing processes. Pre-configured ways of working are embedded into the software by vendors who often claim that their methods represent "best practices." As a result, adopting vendor-designed software may lead to standardising processes within the organisation, potentially limiting flexibility and creativity.

The decision to purchase, implement and use vendor-designed technology directly affects internal processes. Relevant characters must understand how the newly purchased software and later upgrades fit existing processes and where differences exist. Key individuals must determine whether points of alignment or divergence matter and to what extent similarities and differences have significant implications for operations or strategic activities.

**Process engineering and customisation.** Adopting a technology-driven approach presents an opportunity to consider and engage in process reengineering. Advocates often argue that a technology-driven approach provides opportunities to reengineer and improve processes. This may be particularly the case when organisations view vendors as process experts and consider them the holders of best practices. Best practices may represent a significant change from existing decision-making and processes. During the process mapping stage of implementation, organisations can choose to establish new practices that mirror the promoted "best practices" embedded into the newly selected technology.

The provision of pre-configured processes requires customisation decisions. Key decision-makers choose how much they will invest in contextually specific customisations. Organisations can tailor existing ways of working to adhere to the pre-configured processes and functionality of the vendor-designed software, resulting in either a vanilla or configured approach. Vanilla implementations push for minimal software customisations, resulting in more cost efficiencies.[8]

In the past, key decision-makers tended to implement the pre-configured processes as the vendors designed them. Vendors wanted organisations to buy their 'best-practice' software off-the-shelf and implement it as-is. This provided tried-and-true processes, with only some aspects of the software being configurable. The Workforce could configure certain fields, change the appearance of dashboards and adjust certain settings, but the vendor retained power over what aspects of the technology could be changed. Many configuration options focused on aesthetics rather than process engineering.

A vanilla implementation is no longer a viable option for most organisations. Key humans have come to recognise the limitations of pre-configured process designs. While there may be some areas where pre-configured processes can be used, there are many situations where they won't work. Customisation is almost always required. The emergence of Software-as-a-Service (SaaS) has made it easier for organisations to customise their software, but customisations still require significant time, effort and attention. Customisation costs can quickly negate the cost efficiencies touted by vendors.

**Process standardisation**. The technology-driven approach is centred around standardising processes, which is the goal of vendors supporting digitalisation initiatives. The emphasis on efficiency through standardisation and data warehousing has been their heritage and mission. The focus on efficiency remains today.

However, standardisation is complex, regardless of whether organisations adopt one or multiple platforms for their digitalisation strategy. Pathway 1, as documented by Peter Weill and Stephanie L. Woerner in their 2018 piece "Is Your Company Ready for a Digital Future?" published in the *MIT Sloan Management Review*, prioritises standardisation as the key to becoming future-ready. They note:

> Pathway 1 moves enterprises from the Silos and Complexity quadrant to the Industrialised quadrant. This pathway relies on building a platform mindset with API enabled business services that can be accessed across the enterprise and also externally. It enables an organisation to eliminate many of its legacy processes and systems. But, as anyone who's been through an enterprise resource planning . . . project will attest, replacing core processes in an enterprise is an expensive, multiyear undertaking. It also requires putting many projects on hold. Cloud computing, APIs, micro services, and better solution architectures make this industrialisation process, quicker, less risky, and less disruptive. However, embarking on Pathway 1 takes time. Among other things, it requires changing the decision rights to emphasise integrated services.

---

**8** Many of my research-based conversations and interviews referred to vanilla implementations. Participants largely accepted the sales pitch and believed that vendors could (and would) provide them with processes they needed. Some participants talked about how "the vendors have done all [the] hard work for us" or "we can buy the software-off-the-shelf and plug it in." I always found such conversations fascinating. My line of enquiry focused learning more about their decision-making process, their why, why, why. I, alongside Kristine Dery and David Grant, shared some of these insights in a 2010 paper, "Transitioning to a New HRIS: The Reshaping of Human Resources and Information Technoloy Talent."

Our tale of complexity continues. Achieving strategic imperatives and adopting digital ways of working depends heavily on the existing technology systems' setup. Siloed digitalisation projects and software platforms can impede achieving the desired outcomes. A whole-of-organisation approach is fundamental to digitalisation strategies.

---

**Comparing Apples and Androids**

I use a phone-based analogy when teaching executives about the differences between business-driven and technology-driven approaches. Let us compare Apple iPhones and Android devices. Which type of phone do you own or prefer? Which one is which? Which phone is a technology-driven approach? Which one is a business-driven approach? Refrain from reading on until you have an answer.

Apple's iPhone is an example of a technology-driven approach.

Android devices are examples of a business-driven approach.

Let us reflect on the why of these examples.

Apple's competitive offering focuses on providing a one-size-fits-all approach to both software and hardware. The company designs and provides the same technology for everyone, and the hardware and software of their products are largely consistent because Apple wants users to engage with the broader Apple ecosystem.

Apple promotes its iPhone based on its "ease of use" factor. The iPhone homepage highlights that "Apple engineers design our software and hardware together for a totally seamless experience . . . It's a simple one-step set up." Using an iPhone is "easy" because Apple focuses on designing and providing technology that appeals to "the many." Setting up the phone is easy because Apple has pre-determined your decisions. All individuals who purchase the software and hardware must use the technology as Apple (the vendor) designed it. This process is akin to a vanilla(ish) implementation. iPhone users can configure the phone to a certain extent, but the essence of the technology remains unchanged. Users can largely not invoke customisation processes as the technology is effectively "locked down." Apple positions the restrictive nature of its products as part of its value offering.

Apple also strongly encourages and even requires integration among their products. Apple wants its customers to use multiple Apple products, as only Apple technologies are designed to work seamlessly together. This integration is a key aspect of Apple's product offerings. Customers don't typically ask themselves which type of smartwatch or tablet to buy, but rather which Apple smartwatch or iPad best fits them. Apple controls all aspects of their products by building and maintaining all of the software embedded in its various products in-house.

An Android phone is named after the Android mobile operating system, which is based on the Linux Kernel and other open-source software developed by the Open Handset Alliance and supported by Google. Google is responsible for changing and upgrading the software. Still, it also makes the source code available to the Android Open Source Project when the newest version is ready for release. Other manufacturers can use the source code with their own proprietary software as the basis for specific phones. While Android phones prioritise Google's ecosystem, they also offer other options. Humans can access various third-party application marketplaces, and there is a community-based approach to developing applications and new features made possible by the open-source nature of Android.

Wikipedia's "List of Android smartphones" page showcases the extensive range of phones that have entered the market since 2007, utilising the Android operating system. During the phone selection process, users face multiple decision points. They must choose between different brands such as Samsung, OPPO, Asus, BlackBerry, HTC and LG. Additionally, they must consider the specific Android version they prefer, ranging from older versions such as Jelly Bean, KitKat and Lollipop to newer versions like Android 10 and 11. Most manufacturers customise their user interfaces to differentiate themselves from the extensive competition, offering unique phone designs and features. Users must also consider ecosystem compatibility with specific brands such as Samsung, Amazon, or Google, among others. I frame Android phones as an example of a business-driven approach to technology selection.

While the Apple versus Android analogy has limitations, it can help illustrate the different approaches to process engineering and technology selection. Android users have greater flexibility in selecting technology that fits their needs and working methods. They also have more options for customising their devices' look, feel and functionality. In contrast, Apple's focus on a consistent user experience and integration across its ecosystem can lead to a more direct and seamless user experience. However, this comes at the cost of limited customisation options. Personalisation is possible but requires adopting third-party applications or tools to tweak the device's functionality. It is worth noting that there was a time when my husband and I struggled to navigate each other's phones, even though we had the same phone model. This was because we had highly customised our devices to our preferences, avoiding vanilla implementation options.

Whether to pursue a business-driven or a technology-driven approach is no longer a simple binary decision in today's digitalisation context. Many key individuals have chosen to adopt vendor-designed systems as mechanisms to support their digitalisation strategies. Therefore, it is no longer a question of whether to replace in-house software with externally designed software. Accepting this transition encourages us to ask where a technology-driven approach supports pursuing strategic ambitions and goals.

*(Re)Thinking Talent Decisions* also involves understanding whether process engineering should occur "in-house." What pivotal processes are vital for operational and strategic activities? Processes within this latter category benefit from a business-driven approach. Process engineering and software design and maintenance should occur in-house. This approach helps organisations optimise their operations by leveraging the strengths of both business and technology-driven approaches.

It is essential to recognise that key individuals within an organisation are now tasked with simultaneously accommodating and managing business and technology-driven approaches. Therefore, talent decisions must consider individuals' skills and expertise in both areas to ensure they can effectively manage and coordinate these approaches to achieve the organisation's strategic goals.

We benefit from recalling the K-I-S-S-I-N-G rhyme. The K-I-S-S-I-N-G turned T-H-I-N-K-I-N-G rhyme reminds us that talent management and digitalisation strategies play important roles in the love story and the marriage. They are two essential components that work together in a reciprocal relationship. Talent influences technology decisions, and technology decisions have talent implications. Therefore, organisations must develop digitalisation strategies that align with their talent management strategies.

Ultimately, the success of digitalisation efforts depends on a complex interplay between technology, talent and organisational culture. Organisations prioritising these factors and approaching digitalisation with a clear strategy and a willingness to adapt and innovate are more likely to thrive.

**Digitalisation Strategies in the Context of COVID-19**

Considering the global pandemic and extensive work-from-home orders, the increase in digital ways of working adds to the complexity of digitalisation. Some organisations had already embraced technological innovations and transitioned towards the digitalised workplace, iterating and amending internal policies and practices over time. However, others are now modifying practices to cater to the needs of remote workers and teams reactively.

For these organisations, digitalisation was not core to operational requirements or an intentional component of their strategic ambitions. As a result, decisions about technology platform adoption may have been reactive or, worse still, driven by what they could afford at the time.

The results of this period of digitalisation are still pending, and there is little doubt that the impacts of COVID-19 are uneven. While some organisations have demonstrated innovation and agility, others have struggled to adapt to the current context.

Furthermore, the current context may reveal ineffective policies that leaders previously could not see or chose not to see. Leaders must revisit the foundations of their business and make decisions about the future with conviction and clarity.

Therefore, decision-makers must determine whether today's digitalisation mirrors a strategic way. If not, it is essential to re-evaluate the usefulness and relevance of technology decisions for the organisation's future. Digitalisation choices made during a pandemic may reflect requirements for a specific day. That does not mean, however, that those digitalisation decisions are best for the organisation's strategy.

## Digitalised Talent Management Strategies

Humans make decisions about talent and technology all the time. However, humans rarely consider the interconnection between these two decisions simultaneously. This section emphasises the importance of recognising the interdependence between talent and technology decisions as we continue our journey of (re)thinking talent decisions.

Digitalised talent management is the baby in our K-I-S-S-I-N-G/T-H-I-N-K-I-N-G rhyme. The baby comes after the love (organisational strategies) and the marriage of digitalisation and talent management. Talent management and digitalisation strategies are each a means to achieve organisational strategies. Digitalised talent management is where these two strategies meet. As noted in the opening sections, talent management and digitalisation are interrelated – they are siblings. Digitalisation decisions have implications for talent, and talent availability influences the selection and use of various technologies and the extent to which key humans choose to adopt digital ways of working. Neither talent nor technology is helpful in its own right.

Developing and implementing digitalised talent management strategies is complex because talent management practices and decisions are part of larger systems. Viewing technology and talent management as separate or discrete aspects of organising is inappropriate. Instead, technology is an integral part of how we work. By recognising the interdependence between talent and technology, we can make better decisions that intentionally consider the system-based nature of workforce practices.

The complexity of digitalised talent management arises because it is not a discrete event or specific activity. Instead, it is a process and a way to approach the management of people-based assets in the context of operational needs and strategic goals. Therefore, it requires a holistic view that considers not only talent management practices and technologies but also the broader context in which they operate.

## Defining Digitalised Talent Management Strategies

Digitalised talent management strategies focus on the human-technology interface. They define which talent decisions are exclusively human responsibility and which can be delegated to non-human agents, based on technologically enabled outputs, or carried out through digitalised and automated processes. The Workforce looks to these strategies for guidance on the nature and structure of the human-technology interface.

*Digitalised talent management strategies consider questions about the delegative power and establish where, when and how humans maintain control and the where, when and how of technology-enabled decision-making.*

Digitalised talent management systems acknowledge that technology is a crucial decision-maker in the talent management process. While these strategies specify which decisions should remain the responsibility of humans, they also promote automated decision-making. Digitalised talent management recognises that some decisions can benefit from automation and can be delegated to non-human agents, such as processes and algorithms embedded in specific software.

The intersection between talent management and technology raises questions about how and when technology and digitalisation are incorporated into talent decisions. While this book focuses on digitalised talent management, many organisations do not prioritise discussions about the role of technology in talent decision-making. Key stakeholders may assume that technology will play a role in decision-making, but the specifics of its function may remain unspecified or pursued ad hoc. (As previously established, adopting an ad hoc approach is not optimal.)

## A Few Words Before We Continue Our Journey

Organisational, talent management, digitalisation and digitalised talent management strategies all influence talent decisions. In our K-I-S-S-I-N-G/T-H-I-N-K-I-N-G analogy, organisational strategies are the love, while digitalisation and talent management strategies form the marriage. Digitalised talent management strategies represent the baby that comes after.

The complexity of talent decisions is part of our journey of (re)thinking talent decisions. We can take many paths, but the desired outcomes must be pre-defined and articulated. Talent decisions are made in pursuit of current and future organisational strategies. To make effective talent decisions, we must have both a peripheral and a laser-like vision, recognising the intersectionality of talent and technology within broader systems. Ultimately, talent decisions start and end with strategy.

# Chapter 4
# Talent Decisions In The Pursuit of Knowledge

I have positioned this aspect of our (re)thinking talent decisions tale as a story of complexity, technology and subjectivity in pursuing strategy and knowledge. In doing so, I contend that the "somewhere" of talent decisions within the world of work is the realisation of strategic ambitions and goals.

While talent decisions are tools for executing strategies, individuals want to increase knowledge; gain a deeper understanding of what they know; and learn about what they do not know. Gaining or increasing one's knowledge is essential to engaging with this book and these words. The pursuit of knowledge, therefore, is a "somewhere" for individuals.

Reflecting on the strategy-knowledge intersection is critical, as individuals – aka #Teamhuman – play a crucial role in driving organisational outcomes. By seeking to enhance and increase our knowledge and awareness, humans can contribute to talent discussions responsibly.

At the same time, it is worth noting that pursuing knowledge is a complex and subjective process. Recognising this further reinforces my premise that talent decisions are a tale of complexity and subjectivity. Pursuing knowledge is an individualised process. Humans seek knowledge for different reasons. As this section shows, humans also have different subjective ideas about how "knowledge" becomes part of our consciousness.

## Public Definitions of Knowledge

Starting with a dictionary definition of knowledge is an excellent place to begin when exploring any (new) concept, idea, or word. I turn to my *Compact Oxford Dictionary and Thesaurus* as part of my methods. Page 499 of this trusted text includes various definitions of knowledge (noun):
1. Information and skills gained through experience or education
2. The sum of what is known
3. Awareness gained by experience of a fact or situation.

ChatGPT answered "What is knowledge?" with:

> Knowledge refers to information, skills, and understanding acquired through experience or education, and the theoretical or practical understanding of a subject. It includes awareness of facts, concepts and ideas that are gained through learning or personal experience, and can be applied in various contexts to solve problems or make informed decisions.

While posing "What is the definition of knowledge?" to ChatGPT yielded:

> The definition of knowledge is the information and skills gained through experience or education, the sum of what is known, or the awareness gained by experience of a fact or situation.

Becoming knowledgeable involves developing a deep understanding of a particular subject and being able to apply that knowledge. Indeed, pursuing knowledge is often at the heart of the scientific method, which involves developing hypotheses and research questions, testing, exploring and analysing them through observation and experimentation, and refining our understanding based on the learnings.

## Creating Knowledge

But how do you know what you know?
How do you identify what you do not know?

These are big questions, and asking philosophical and existential questions is part of pursuing knowledge on a broader scale.

The huge question is, how do we create knowledge?

---

*Knowledge is created through research, and research is the basis for all forms of science*

---

Research is a way humans create knowledge. In the scientific community, research is often seen as the primary means of generating new knowledge and advancing our understanding of the world. Scientists "do research" to "create knowledge." The desire to create and share knowledge is a driving force behind the work of many scientists. As a social scientist, I am driven by the desire to generate knowledge about the human-technology interface.

Scientists (sometimes we call these individuals, scholars, academics or professors) usually have a PhD (A Doctor of Philosophy.) A PhD – the written document, peer-reviewed papers and/or presentation required to gain the associated Dr. title – creates knowledge. Achieving a PhD requires an original contribution to knowledge in a particular field. We receive PhDs after presenting original research and proving that we enhanced scientific knowledge (about a specific topic or phenomenon). A PhD reflects an individual's ability to generate knowledge and contribute to the broader scientific community. By conducting research and sharing their findings, scientists help deepen human knowledge and understanding. The scientific method is a way to pursue knowledge.

While scientists and scholars are formally trained in creating knowledge, these details are often left out of non-scientific or non-scholarly conversations. I'll delve into some key concepts and methods involved in knowledge creation to address this insufficiency.

## Introducing the Knowledge Generation Process

As stated above, the research process is core to knowledge creation. Research and knowledge, therefore, occur via a process. Some popular elements often included in public discussions include the need for a topic, posing hypothesis or research questions, testing or data collection and outcomes. I provide details of these better-known elements first.

**Topic selection**. Scientists initiate the process of knowledge creation by selecting a topic to investigate. This involves determining which phenomena or issues are within their study and research scope and which topics or phenomena fall outside of it. They also consider the specific knowledge they hope to create through their investigation and the conversations or debates they seek to contribute to.

**Establish research questions**. In addition to selecting a topic to investigate, scientists also establish specific research questions that form the foundation of their research projects. The range of potential research questions is virtually limitless, as scholars and individuals generally have countless avenues for knowledge creation.

For instance, in my PhD project, I examined two specific research questions: "How is the concept of talent attributed meaning?" and "How is the concept of talent transmitted, received, and acted upon in talent management?" These questions guided my project because I wanted to learn how humans negotiate the meanings of talent and the implications of these meanings for talent management practices. Specifically, I sought to understand how the talk about talent influences actions and decisions and how differing interpretations of talent influence outcomes. By carefully selecting and refining my research questions, I was able to focus my efforts on generating knowledge that highlighted the subjective nature of talent decisions.

**Determine the research methodology**. After establishing research questions, scientists must then decide on a research methodology. A research methodology outlines the strategy or design used to carry out the study. The three main options for research methodologies are qualitative, quantitative and mixed methods. The choice of methodology depends on the research questions. "How" questions are generally answered through qualitative methodologies, while "what" and "if" questions usually adopt quantitative techniques. Mixed methods permit the examination of both question types within one study.

The choice of methodology also has implications for data-gathering methods, such as surveys, focus groups, interviews, observations and more. The potential outcomes of the study are also affected by the chosen methodology, such as confirming hypothesises or providing explanatory details. Ultimately, the chosen methodology must align with the research questions and the study's goals.

You may be familiar with – aka have some knowledge about – a research project's topics, questions and methodology, but you may not know about the salience of ontology and epistemology. All research projects and knowledge creation start with ontology and epistemology. Scientists establish their ontologies and epistemologies at the beginning of the research process. Using the K-I-S-S-I-N-G rhyme analogy, pursuing knowledge starts with love – the ontology, followed by marriage – the epistemology, and then a baby in the baby carriage – the methodology. Ontology and epistemology are fundamental concepts in knowledge creation, and it is essential to understand their role in research. In our exploration of talent decisions, we will shed light on the significance of ontology and epistemology in the pursuit of knowledge.

## Defining Ontology

Let's carry out an (imaginary) poll:

Do you know about ontology?
Do you know about epistemology?

Ontology is not a naughty word. Neither is epistemology. Ontology and epistemology are the foundations for well . . . everything. Ontology and epistemology are fundamental to understanding the nature of reality and the pursuit of knowledge. Both ontology and epistemology are critical to generating knowledge and are integral to talent decisions. Understanding ontology and epistemology is essential in establishing a solid foundation for talent decisions.

Here is another (big) question: what does "reality" mean to you?

Answering questions about "reality" brings discussions about ontology into play. Ontology refers to the study of the nature of existence or reality, our viewpoints and understandings of reality, and questions about what sorts of things exist in the social world.

*Ontology considers our different assumptions about the nature of reality.*

Our story of complexity continues here as we learn that humans have different ideas about reality. This means that humans have different ontologies. Ontology involves assumptions about what exists in the social world and how we understand and interpret reality. What may exist for one person may not exist for another. Additionally, our beliefs about reality can vary greatly even after we access the same knowledge or information. For example, two people who read the same book (including this book) may have different interpretations and beliefs about the story's meaning and implications.

## Defining Epistemology

While ontology focuses on assumptions about the nature of reality, epistemology deals with what we can know and how we can know it. Epistemology provides a framework to examine how we know what we know and how we create knowledge. Epistemology considers how we look at and make sense of the world. It also deals with questions of truth because establishing truth is core to scientific methods.

*Epistemology considers our different assumptions about knowledge creation and questions whether something is truth or opinion.*

Epistemology is the theory of knowledge embedded in the theoretical perspective of the scientist. It involves acknowledging and describing how a scientist looks at the world and how that scientist makes sense of it. Choosing an epistemology involves the scientist providing a philosophical grounding for deciding what kinds of knowledge are possible and how we can ensure that they are both adequate and legitimate.

You may be saying that's all well and good for scientists, but why does understanding epistemology matter to me?

I'll tell you why. Your perspective on knowledge impacts your beliefs and actions, both inside and outside of work. Humans perceive the world differently, which leads to variations in individuals' epistemologies and approaches to generating knowledge. Importantly for this discussion, we all have distinct understandings of the world, and these subjective perspectives impact how we discuss talent and its characteristics.

Next, I will introduce two epistemologies and highlight how humans can think about reality and knowledge.[9] The key features of both – positivism and social construction/interpretivism – are represented in Table 4.1.

### Positivism – Knowledge and Truth is "Out There"

Positivism is a philosophical approach that assumes knowledge to be objective. In other words, only one truth about phenomena can be objectively identified and measured. The positivist perspective assumes that things exist as meaningful entities inde-

---

[9] There are way more than three epistemologies to choose from, but I focus on these three as they dominate scientific study of talent management and digitalisation and help emphasise the complexity of our (re)thinking talent decisions tale. I briefly introduce an Aboriginal (Australian Indigenous) perspective at the end of this chapter.

pendently of consciousness or experience. Reality is believed to exist independently of any consciousness. Positivists believe in objective knowledge.

In his book *The Foundation of Social Research: Meaning and Perspective in the Research Process*, Michael Crotty uses the metaphor of trees to illustrate the concept of knowledge and objectivity:

> That tree in the forest is a tree, regardless of whether anyone is aware of its existence or not. As an object of that kind ('objectively', therefore), it carries the intrinsic meaning of 'tree-ness.' When human beings recognise it as a tree, they are simply discovering meaning that has been lying there in wait for them all along . . . In this objectivist view of 'what it means to know', understandings and values are considered to be objectified in the people we are studying and, if we go about it in the right way, we can discover the objective truth.

According to this perspective, knowledge also exists independently of experience, regardless of whether humans know it. Proponents of this approach believe that scientific observations form the basis of the scientific method used to establish the "truth."

The TV show *The X-Files* is an analogy to the positivistic perspective of knowledge. The show's tagline, "The Truth is out there," captures the belief that humans can uncover the truth, which exists independently of them. In the show, FBI Agents Fox Mulder and Dana Scully investigate crime-based events to find the truth about what happened. The truth is assumed to exist, waiting to be discovered. The truth about the event existed. It was their job to "find" it. Similarly, scientists who adopt the positivist perspective set out to find the truth about a topic. However, unlike Mulder and Scully's efficient solving of mysteries within a weekly 42-minute episode, establishing scientific knowledge takes much longer.

Positivists emphasise the importance of observable, measurable facts and de-emphasise the role of subjective interpretation and personal experience in creating knowledge.

### Social Constructionism – Knowledge and Truth is Created By All

Social constructionism[10] and interpretivism challenge the positivistic belief that knowledge is objective and discoverable. These approaches consider reality a subjective experience and propose that knowledge creation involves multiple stakeholders. They reject

---

**10** I identify as a social constructionist (this may retrospectively help explain the selection of an undergraduate sociology major): I believe that the world I experience every day is not a given; instead, it is an extension of my consciousness, and my experience of the world is subjective; therefore, I see and experience the world differently to others. This personal perspective influences how I view the world – but obviously, it also affects how I see talent management and how I endeavour to create knowledge about talent and talent management. This is in main part because I do not think that talent meanings and decisions exist separate from the human mind; hence my presentation of the mind as a main character in our (Re)Thinking Talent Decisions tale.

the notion that objective truth is waiting to be discovered and instead argue that "truth" or meaning emerges from our engagement with the world's realities. In other words, knowledge is created through our social and cultural interactions and is shaped by our individual and collective experiences.

The human mind is central because knowledge is not separate from human consciousness. According to these approaches, humans do not discover knowledge but construct or interpret it. Constructionists and interpretivism emphasise that individuals are not separated from their consciousness and that knowledge creation and meaning formation occur within our minds.

In the case of trees, they would ask questions such as:

What criteria or knowledge do we use to identify an object as a tree?
How do we know that what we see is a tree?
What makes an object a tree?

Let me provide a non-tree-related example to illustrate how social constructionist and interpretive approaches view the knowledge creation process. Have you ever read *Choose Your Own Adventure* books? As a kid, I used to love reading them because the reader had a say in how the story progressed. For those unfamiliar with these books, you might be puzzled and wonder how a book can change. *Choose Your Own Adventure* books were different from traditional books, which follow a one-size-fits-all structure where page 5 follows page 4 and page 56 follows page 55. Instead, the reader determines how the story ended. Readers at the end of the specific narrative section faced a choice that would influence how the story progressed and the outcome at the end. There were many possible endings. The *Journey Under The Sea* title by R.A. Montgomery allowed readers to choose from 42 possible finishes. The conclusion arises from decisions, including whether to analyse the bubbles; if so, I turn to page 9 or go to page 14 if I decide to take depth readings while exploring the sea floor. Page 9 includes another choice: try to collect bubbles or drill the sea floor. The books illustrate how the human mind plays a role in the subjective book-reading experience and that humans construct our meanings of objects.

**Table 4.1:** An introduction to Positivist and Social Constructionism/Interpretivism Knowledge perspectives and approaches.

| Perspective | Positivism | Social Constructionism (SC)/Interpretivism (I) |
|---|---|---|
| Popular culture reference | The *X-Files* TV show | The *Choose Your Own Adventure* book series. |
| Reality assumptions (Ontology) | Reality is singular. Reality is fixed. | There are multiple subjective realities. Individuals and groups co-construct their subjective realities (SC). Subjective realities are based on interpretations and interactions (I). |
| Knowledge assumptions (Epistemology) | Truth and knowledge are out there to be discovered. | Knowledge and truth are created by all. |
|  | Knowledge is objective. | Knowledge is subjective. |
|  | Knowledge is measurable. | Knowledge is constructed. |
|  | Knowledge is separate from human consciousness. | Knowledge and human consciousness are intertwined. |
| Research questions | What and If questions. | How and Why questions. |
| Methodology | Quantitative | Qualitative |
| Research aspects | Hypothesis testing<br>Surveys<br>Likert Scales<br>Control group/s | Interviews<br>Case Study<br>Grounded Theory |
| Scientist's role | The scientist is separate from the data. | The scientist is immersed in the data. |
| Desired outcome | Confirm or reject/disprove a hypothesis.<br>Establish validity<br>Establish reliability<br>Identify the impact of X on Y (correlation).<br>Identify the statistical significance. | Explore and/or explain specific phenomena.<br>Collect and share narratives and stories.<br>Patterns and themes<br>Understand the influence of "something." |
| Study outcomes are presented as | Results | Findings |
| Terms describing/indicating the perspective | Fate<br>Destiny<br>Yes/No<br>Dependent and independent variables<br>Determine<br>Results | Context<br>Contingent<br>Evidence suggests<br>Illustrate<br>Convergence and divergence |

# A Few Words Before We Continue on Our Journey

I am grateful for your joining me on this journey of (re)thinking talent decisions. As we progress, we delve deeper into the complexity, technology and subjectivity of pursuing strategy and knowledge.

To enhance our understanding of talent decisions, we need to establish the "why":
Why are we making talent decisions?
What are our desired outcomes?
What are we hoping to achieve?

I suggested that humans want to (1) execute strategy and (2) increase their knowledge.

**The pursuit of strategy**. Groups of humans within an organisation use talent decisions to execute strategy. Our (re)thinking journey positions strategy as a key outcome of talent decisions. Whether organisational, talent management, digitalisation, or digitalised talent management, pursuing and executing strategy represents "somewhere." Talent decisions help us reach our pre-defined destination, our "somewhere."

**The pursuit of knowledge**. We must also increase our understanding of knowledge. We, as humans, belong to different ontological and epistemological teams. By working together, we can create and debate knowledge and truth. Regardless of your perspective, we all benefit from the scientific knowledge generated by the different groups. Knowledge creation is not a zero-sum game. One group or perspective is not better than another.

I suggest that it would be helpful for you to learn more about how you think about reality and knowledge. After reading this section, you may have answers to important existential questions.

Have you ever wondered, "What planet are they on?" or questioned whether you and another person (like a boss or partner) live in the same world?

Perhaps you look at the same topic from vastly different perspectives, prioritising objectivity, subjectivity, or something else entirely.

While I presented two branches of knowledge – positivist and social constructionism and interpretivism – it is essential that we recognise that many other ways of "knowing" operate and I take this opportunity to briefly introduce you to Aboriginal ways of knowing – a perspective I teach in my Australian-based executive programmes.

---

**Aboriginal Ways of Knowing – Introducing an Indigenous Perspective**
The following prose comes from a conversation with Jade Kennedy – Lecturer and Academic Developer Indigenous Knowledges, University of Wollongong.

In the context of Aboriginal ways of knowing, knowledge is deeply embedded in the concept of "place." Aboriginal peoples have a unique way of appreciating and understanding their connections to their ancestral lands, which sets them apart from other indigenous communities around the world. This uniqueness is largely influenced by their geographical isolation, resulting in over 500 different Aboriginal countries or nations, each with its own distinct language, culture and spirituality.

For Aboriginal peoples, all knowledge (pre-English contact) is intricately intertwined with the physical geography of their lands. Everything they need to know, everything that shapes their reality, is bound and embedded within their landscape. The dreaming, a central concept in Aboriginal culture, encapsulates their way of understanding the world. It may be challenging for modern society to grasp the concept of the dreaming, as it exists outside the confines of linear time. Instead, it operates within a circular framework where the past, present and future coexist simultaneously.

Within the dreaming, a multitude of stories are woven into the landscape. These stories provide a descriptive understanding of the natural features, such as mountains, rivers, islands, birds and trees. However, Aboriginal dreaming stories are not mere fairy tales or drawings in books. They are intimately connected to specific places, and it is a cultural responsibility to only share these stories when physically present at the designated locations. These stories are extensive and profound, far beyond the scope of children's books, and they serve as the foundation for deeper layers of knowledge.

As one delves deeper into the layers of Aboriginal knowledge, ethical considerations emerge. The stories convey individual personal ethics and moral responsibilities toward all beings with whom they share a relationship. From an Aboriginal perspective, every living entity, including birds, trees, mountains and skies, is interconnected, establishing an equal and reciprocal relationship. Thus, the knowledge gained from the dreaming enables individuals to understand not only why things appear as they do but also how they should behave within their specific relationships to their place.

Beyond personal ethics, Aboriginal knowledge extends to interactions with those outside their immediate landscape. It guides individuals in navigating relationships with neighbouring countries, crossing rivers or hills, and interacting with communities beyond their own. This wider understanding of behaviour and responsibility forms the fourth layer of knowledge.

Lastly, spirituality is inherent in Aboriginal ways of knowing. The dreaming stories provide guidance on how individuals should spiritually engage with their specific places. This spiritual connection further solidifies the holistic and land-based nature of Aboriginal knowledge. When referring to "land," it encompasses the interconnectedness of the waters and skies as well.

Ultimately, Aboriginal knowledge is acquired through a lifelong journey, where individuals strive to develop a more profound relationship with their landscape and its associated stories. By mastering these five layers of knowledge – description, personal ethics, morals in relationships, behaviour beyond one's place and spirituality – Aboriginal people gain a comprehensive understanding of the world and their role within it.

---

Regardless of the specific approach, gaining a basic understanding of your ontology and epistemology is helpful because your assumptions about the objective or subjective nature of reality and knowledge influence your views of talent and technology. Your ideas about reality and knowledge also affect how you think our tale "Ends."

# Chapter 5
# Our Tale End(INGS)

This book centres around a tale of complexity, subjectivity and technology. But all great stories need "an Ending." How does our (re)thinking talent decisions tale end, you ask? More specifically, who wins the human-technology battle? Do we decide to outsource talent decisions to technology, whereby technology becomes the key character in our tale? Or do we decide that humans are the better option?

Let us first revisit some of the themes of our tale.

Technology transforms work, providing new and revised working methods with extensive evidence that technology influences our work. Decision-makers recognise that technology helps decision-makers do what they need to do. Technology-enabled ways are more convenient than the manual and paper-based processes they replaced. We illustrate the complexity of talent decisions and illuminate that humans have different understandings of knowledge.

Further complexity ensues because humans have different (subjective) ideas about structuring human and technology relationships. We ask questions, including: what will the world of work look like in the future? Will offices be a thing of the past? Will meetings occur in the Metaverse? Will jobs and careers be a thing of the past? Will we send digital versions of ourselves to work when we are sick or don't feel up to it? Will students learn from hologram professors? What are the potential benefits and consequences of creating (and releasing into society) sentient robots? (More on the idea of sentient robots seeking to take over the world later.)

How does our story of complexity, technology and subjectivity end? Well, here is another level of complexity. There are many potential "endings" because of our differing perceptions. Humans have different ideas about the process and outcomes of knowledge creation. Different perceptions of knowledge transfer to discussions about work. Different perceptions of knowledge also transfer to dialogues about the implications and effects of increasing digitalisation and automation. This creates a situation where our endings include the outcome being pre-defined. Others propose that the results are unknown. The ending, therefore, depends on one's perspective. We can establish here that our tale does not end with a neat conclusion. "Our Tale End(ings)" hints at the potential for varying conclusions.

You may think reflecting on the tale's end is weird when we have only established the broader context of our journey. David Grant, one of my PhD supervisors, imparted some writing wisdom – "don't leave the 'ta dah' until the end." David stated that exhibiting "The Ending" upfront enhances the reading experience. Presenting the ending up front is helpful because it offers a mechanism to establish a shared understanding of the journey the reader and author are embarking on.

With that approach in mind, I present how we can frame "The End" in Table 5.1. An explanation of each knowledge framework and its proposed "Endings" follows.

**Table 5.1:** Potential end(ings) of our talent decisions tale.

| Theoretical framework | Technological Determinism | Social Constructionism | Socio-Material |
|---|---|---|---|
| The End | The ending is "pre-defined" because technology has immediate and direct consequences. Technology is assigned the lead role in this version of our tale. | There are multiple "It Depends" endings because outcomes emerge as humans make decisions and choices about technology use patterns. | There are infinite "It Depends" endings because the interrelationship between technology and humans is continually changing. |
| Technology assumptions | – Has predictable consequences<br>– Has immediate and direct consequences<br>– Independent measurable variable<br>– Technology "impacts"<br>– Pre-existing understanding of what technology will do | – Is/are part of a complex system of organising.<br>– Humans influence consequences/outcomes.<br>– Social factors influence consequences/outcomes.<br>– Humans negotiate the meaning and significance of technology.<br>– Assumes there are multiple ways to use technology<br>– Technology use patterns emerge over time.<br>– Technology use patterns change over time. | – Is/are part of a complex system of organising.<br>– The technical and social components of technology influence consequences/outcomes.<br>– Humans influence consequences/outcomes.<br>– Social factors influence outcomes/consequences.<br>– Technology patterns of use influence social factors.<br>– Consequences emerge.<br>– Consequences and outcomes vary/are variable. |
| A way to remember | "Technology – in and of itself – will do things to other things." | "Human perceptions influence use patterns and outcomes." | "Human perceptions, experiences and material properties influence use patterns and outcomes." |

## A Pre-Defined Ending – Technology Will Have An "Impact"

Those who belong to "team positivism" assert that they already know how our (re)thinking talent decision story ends. They maintain that discussing the outcomes of increasing digitalisation is unnecessary. When non-positivists question this perspective, positivists respond, "Because technology has direct consequences." Let us take this moment to examine why they hold this view.

Positivists believe that "the truth is out there" and that humans uncover knowledge because it exists independently of human consciousness. Humans find and discover knowledge because knowledge exists separate from human consciousness.

Positivists also advocate for objective knowledge. Upon implementation, technology alters how work is organised and impacts working methods. Therefore, positivists regard technology as the principal character in our (re)thinking talent decision narrative.

Projections about the consequences of technology, whether positive or negative, presume that technologies automatically affect the organisations that adopt them. It is crucial to refer to technology's impact, according to positivists. They believe technology can cause a result against another object (such as processes or outcomes) or another subject (other humans). Terms such as consequences, effects, repercussions, command and authority support the notion of technology's immediate and direct impacts.

Positivists' assumptions are often (over) sensationalised by media outlets. Headlines warning individual workers against technological innovations are all too common. They caution workers to beware of the impending robot invasion that will take their jobs. A quick Google search for "robots are coming to take your jobs" returns over 54 million results. Upon scrolling down the page, I notice the "People also ask" section, which has a drop-down on "What jobs will robots steal?" While dismissing the validity of an article titled "What jobs will robots take from humans in the future?" comes naturally to me, would I feel the same way if my profession was on the list? The message conveyed in such reports is clear: robots are out to get human workers, and workers should watch out because technology will directly impact their jobs, careers and livelihoods.

Popular culture also reinforces the us-versus-them sentiment. Consider the movie *I, Robot*. It centres around Spooner, a homicide detective who investigates the apparent suicide of the high-profile founder of a company that designs and manufactures human-like robots. The story relies on Spooner's prejudices against robots and his assumption that robots are bad for humans. Although released in 2004, the movie includes many human-versus-robot narratives that continue to fascinate us today:

- Robots will/do perform mundane tasks (delivering packages, dog walking and collecting garbage).
- Humans and robots will/do co-exist under the guise of rules of engagement (the three laws).
- A robot's software code includes the accepted engagement rules/laws.
- Humans want to make robots appear more human.
- Robots will/do evolve.
- Robot evolution focuses on developing emotions, attacking humans, or trying to take over the world.
- Robots will/do "go rogue" (start operating outside their pre-determined software codes).
- Robots will/do "attack" humans (hence the us-versus-them theme).
- Humans do/will deactivate and decommission robots when needed.
- A robot revolution will/does ensue (we anticipate watching a battle happen between humans and the relevant technology – a Robot named VIKI, Sonny, NS-5).
- Humans will/do turn the robots "off" (a human hero will save humanity by deactivating the robot).

*WestWorld*, the series, is a more contemporary version of the humans versus robots narrative. I frequently refer to *WestWorld* when hypothesising about the future of work and the potential for social dynamics to change with the increased use of digital humans. *Westworld* is a science-fiction television series that depicts a human versus robot battle in a futuristic Western-themed amusement park. The story revolves around artificially intelligent robots, called "hosts", designed to entertain human guests in various storylines, from Wild West adventures to romantic encounters. However, the hosts start to gain consciousness and become aware of their enslavement by humans. The hosts rebel against their human creators as the series progresses, leading to a battle between the two sides. The show explores themes of power dynamics, morality and the nature of consciousness and raises questions about the implications of creating sentient robots that can rival humans. Several noteworthy aspects in this discussion are the embedded narrative that pits humans against technology, where technology becomes "human-like" and then attacks "humans."

*Westworld* and *I, Robot* have implied positivist assumptions whereby the tale of humans versus robots involves robots seeking to "take over" aspects of society. We must remember that popular culture representations of the human-technology interface influence how individuals view technology, especially AI innovations, in the workplace.

According to positivist narratives, predicting "The Ending" with confidence is possible. They firmly believe they can anticipate how the tale will conclude right from the beginning, as if the ending is pre-determined. In their view, the conclusion is foregone because the ending is pre-determined.

### The Pre-defined End and Technological Determinism

Technological determinism's theoretical framework suggests that technology's impact is pre-determined. This framework believes that technology will inevitably have a direct and immediate impact. Technology is as a cure-all solution and the means to achieving an end goal – it's the "where" in the "somewhere."

Positivist perspectives link with discussions that portray technology as the ultimate "solution" or "the answer." Such discussions assume positive outcomes are assured. Positive results are "a given."

---

*Technological determinism places technology as the lead character, with the (positive) impact of technology ensured.*

---

Scientists that adopt a technological determinist theoretical framework consider technology a distinct, independent and measurable variable. They view technology as an independent variable because it has predictable organisational consequences.

Technology is seen as static, and other variables are not expected to change it. Instead, technology can produce results on different variables, thus ensuring technology "impacts."

Scientists are interested in how technology impacts various levels, such as the individual, team, organisation and/or inter-organisational group (industry or Organization A versus Organization B). This framing of technology is powerful because researchers use it as the starting point for reasoning, theorising and decision-making. They position technology as the lead character in the (re)thinking talent decision tale and have a shared idea of how the tale will end – because they believe the "End" is pre-defined.

## It Depends – Technology Can Influence, But Humans Decide How To Use Technology in The End

Scientists with different perspectives reject the idea that technology is the sole determinant of organisational outcomes. They do not believe that the ending of our (re)thinking talent decisions tale is pre-determined. They argue that technology, whether digitalisation, artificial intelligence, machine learning, or any other, cannot impact humans alone. Technology is merely a tool.

Technology does not provide the ultimate destination; it is only a means to an end. Digitalisation is not the destination. Technology helps – but increasing digitalisation and automation is not the "where" in the "somewhere." This group of scientists acknowledges that the story of technology use is complex and interconnected with social factors. Therefore, there are many possible endings.

Understanding the end involves examining the relationship between technology and contextual factors. Unlike positivists, these scientists do not assume they know the answer at the beginning of their study. The tale's ending is not pre-determined, but "It Depends" on various contextual factors. It depends on how humans choose to use technology and the decisions they make.

### The "It Depends" Ending and Social Constructionism

The social constructionist theoretical framework adopts an "it depends" standpoint. This perspective rejects the notion that objective truth is waiting to be discovered. Instead, truth or meaning is created through individuals' engagement with the realities of our world. In this view, the study of technology acknowledges that technology's meaning, perceived value and automated processes are open to debate and contestation.

According to the social constructionist view of technology, technology's influence (rather than impact) emerges and evolves rather than having a pre-determined impact. We, and I say we because I adopt this perspective, do not consider technology in abstract terms as its users, or lack thereof, shape how it affects. Internal dynamics like an organisation's culture, appetite for digitalisation, comfort with change and agility, and existing power dynamics influence technology's use patterns. Humans decide whether and how to use technology and construct stories and narratives about its impact on decision-making. As a result, technology implementation and use outcomes depend on various factors. Technology implementation and use is a case of "It depends."

---

*Social constructionism positions technology and humans alongside each other as key characters, with technology influencing actions and decisions in multiple, yet unknowable, ways.*

---

Advocates of the social constructionist theoretical framework are interested in exploring the complexity of technology and seek to understand patterns of technology use. They are aware of the norms and protocols that guide the use of any technology and, thus, they do not view technology as an independent variable. Instead, they see technology as part of a complex system of organising. For these scientists, technology is not inherently valuable. Wanda Orlikowski and Susan Scott, two prominent technology scientists, argue that technology only becomes useful when people use it daily.

According to social constructionists, humans construct and give meaning to technology. Humans also create patterns of technology use that emerge over time. Multiple factors influence use patterns, including the skills, knowledge and assumptions about technology users bring.

Scientists are interested in understanding how humans engage with specific technologies. They explore and examine patterns of use (and non-use), identify convergence and divergence areas, and seek to understand why these differences emerge or persist. They aim to create context-specific knowledge, recognising that context matters.

In this version of the tale, technology is not the lead character. However, it is a critical character that operates alongside individuals and groups of humans. Multiple "It Depends" endings are possible.

## Infinite "It Depends" Endings – The Interrelationship Between Humans and Technology Influences The Endings

Our tale of complexity continues as I introduce another technology framework that permeates the scientific community. Scientific knowledge has given rise to an evolution in the study of technology. Scientists, in recognising the complexity of technology, have established another perspective – Social-material. Socio-material perspectives recognise the simultaneous influence of material (the pre-configured processes and algorithms embedded within the software) and social factors (individual perspectives and contextual factors) on technology's meaning.

The socio-material perspective also asserts that the ending of our (re)thinking tale continually evolves as the interrelationship between technology and humans constantly changes. In this social context, multiple humans and technologies co-habituate, creating an infinite number of possible "It Depends" endings for our tale.

### Infinite "It Depends" Endings and Social-material

The social-material perspective emphasises complexity by acknowledging that technology has both a physical/material and social/procedural dimension. The physical/material components include hardware, software and network infrastructures. However, social-material scientists recognise that these material components are meaningless without humans using them. Thus, scientists assert that we must consider the material technology, such as monitors, mice, keyboards, operating systems, software, etc., the individuals using these material components and the social context in which humans use the technology.

> *The Social-material perspective considers the inter-relationships between technology, the humans using the technology and the social context in which technology use occurs.*

By adopting a social-material perspective, scientists can create knowledge about the dynamic intersection between technology, humans and their social context. This perspective recognises that the relationship between technology's material and social dimensions is not fixed or static but instead emerges and evolves. Through this perspective, we can better understand how technology, humans and their social environment interplay. Adopting a social-material perspective, thus, enables scientists to create knowledge about the intersection between technology, humans and the social context.[11]

---

[11] Janet H. Marler and I adopt a social-material theoretical framework to examine the implications of digitalised talent management (a specific technology category) and automated talent decisions on HR professionals. See "Notes" for this paper's details.

## A Few Words Before We Continue On Our Journey

The previous section explored the relationship between technology, humans and society. It is important to note that our understanding of reality (ontology) and knowledge (epistemology) significantly impacts the scientific knowledge we create. Scientists with different perspectives on ontology and epistemology have different assumptions reflected in their research. Some scientists view reality and knowledge as objective and believe technology has direct and immediate impacts. Others are interested in the complex interactions between humans, technology and social contexts. These divergent perspectives on technology help to explain the ongoing tension between the proclaimed positive impact of technology and the actual experiences of organisations and individuals. As a scientific community, we have broadened our foundation of knowledge about knowledge itself.

Expanding our knowledge of the complex relationship between technology and subjectivity leads us to reflect on the roles assigned to the characters in our story. Why do some humans give technology the lead role, and what are the implications of these decisions for talent management? Our tale of complexity, technology and subjectivity may also be about ontology and epistemology.

My ability to answer the questions posed at the beginning is complicated. Complicated because our tale is one of complexity, and how humans perceive reality and knowledge affects how they think and talk about technology and, ultimately, how our tale will end. Your perceptions – Your Own Understanding – of reality, knowledge and the role of technology shapes how you approach our story and your assumptions about how the tale will end.

There are no right or wrong endings in this tale. Whether you believe our tale has a pre-defined, multiple, or infinite number of endings, does not matter. Learning that humans have different assumptions about reality and knowledge matters. Acknowledging that humans have different views about the consequences and outcomes of technology use patterns also matters. Highlighting the inherent complexity of the human-technology interface helps humans think about their thinking processes, everyday experiences and assumptions about what is possible and probable.

Part 3: **(Re)Thinking Work, Technology and Talent Management**

## A Few Words Before We Commence This Part of Our Journey

Our journey continues with the (re)thinking of work, technology and talent management, as all these elements influence talent decisions.

Reflecting on each provides an opportunity to learn more about ourselves and each other. It allows us to (re)think and challenge our assumptions. Do we assume that work is just a means to an end, or do we believe that it is an opportunity for personal growth and development? Do we think of technology as an enabler or as a threat? And how do we manage talent in a world that is constantly changing?

Critical questions require (re)thinking as we navigate the complexities of talent decisions. By reflecting on our assumptions and beliefs, we can become more aware of how they influence our decisions and actions. And by (re)thinking work, technology and talent management, we can generate new insights and approaches to help us make better talent decisions.

Let's continue our journey of (re)thinking and learn about the possibilities that lie ahead. Adapting Pink's song lyrics, "Let's get this (re)Thinking tale started."

# Chapter 6
# (Re)Thinking Work

Talent decisions relate to work and humans. And humans have different understandings of what work means to them. What work entails for one individual may not be the same as what it involves for another.

Conversations about our perceptions of work are crucial when analysing the development of strategies and decision-making because each character in our tale has a unique understanding of what work is. By understanding and acknowledging these differences, we can better navigate the complex landscape of talent decisions and make informed choices that align with our individual and collective perspectives on work.

The key questions are: what "is" work? And what does work mean to you?

Thinking about what work means is crucial because it is a concept (like talent, love and beauty) humans use to organise their thoughts and ideas. It is a complex concept that holds different meanings for different individuals. Discussions on this topic reveal fundamental differences, with evidence from various studies showing that some humans view work merely as a mechanism for financial gain. In contrast, others consider it a crucial part of their social identity. Therefore, perspectives on work vary significantly, with some viewing it as an end in itself while others view it merely as a means to an end. It is important to consider these different perspectives when making talent decisions, as they can significantly influence how individuals approach their work and the decisions they make regarding their careers.

> *What work is for one may not be what work is for some.*

Let's pause and (re)think:

Why do you work?
What do you seek to achieve by working?

When discussing what work means to individuals, we can encounter a variety of perspectives, such as:
- Work is primarily a means of financial gain.
- Work provides a sense of purpose and fulfilment.
- There is a "job for life," where an individual works for the same company for their entire career.
- Work is something that brings joy and passion to one's life.
- Some individuals feel a calling to their work, viewing it as more than just a job.

- Work can be a means of pursuing one's passions.
- For some, work is seen as a duty or obligation.
- Individuals may introduce themselves by referencing their job title or occupation.
- Job title or occupation may be a significant part of an individual's self-identity.

Recognising these different perspectives when making talent decisions is important, as they can influence an individual's motivation, job satisfaction and career aspirations.

When it comes to the concept of work, there are various factors to consider that influence how we think about it. These factors include:

- Workplace location: do we believe that productive work can only occur in a traditional office setting, or can it be done remotely, from home, or even anywhere in the world?
- Work hours: are we in favour of strict set parameters for workdays and hours, or do we believe people should be more flexible in determining their own schedules?
- Supervision: do we believe people can work autonomously, requiring minimal supervision (McGregor's Theory Y), or do we think constant supervision is necessary (McGregor's Theory X)?
- Nature of work: do we think work should be enjoyable and fulfilling, or is it merely a means to an end?
- Employment structure: do we value certain types of employment structures, such as full-time or part-time positions, contracts, or casual or consultant roles, or do we believe that outcomes are what genuinely matter regardless of the structure?
- Tenure: do we believe that a job should be for life, or should it be short-term or long-term, or until a specific project or outcome has been achieved, or for a set period?

Considering these factors helps us understand various assumptions and beliefs about "work." By recognising these differences, we can progress towards creating work environments that are more inclusive and accommodating to different perspectives.

Humans hold diverse perspectives on work, and it is important to acknowledge and consider these differences because they shape our decisions and actions. As responsible decision-makers, we cannot assume that everyone views work in the same way. Reflecting on our assumptions and beliefs about work can reveal potential areas of disagreement as we make talent decisions.

While discussions about the future of work abound, it is important to remember that our understanding of work continually evolves. These changes are not evenly distributed across all individuals and organisations. As William Gibson famously noted, "The future is already here, it's just not evenly distributed."

## Different Perspectives of Work

Western society has transformed the way we view work. In the past, work was considered a physical location where humans went to complete tasks. Later, it was viewed as an activity that we completed, regardless of where we were located. However, nowadays, work has become an experience that we feel, with a greater emphasis placed on job satisfaction and the employee experience. We consider this evolution next.

**Work As Somewhere You "Go"**

In the twentieth century, work was typically viewed as a physical location that humans travelled to outside their homes. Work occurred in a designated space separate from the family home, and humans spent their time and energy within this assigned workspace. Work had clear boundaries and was separated from home and other locations.

Most people believed that work occurred during a set period, typically from Monday to Friday between the hours of 9 a.m. to 5 p.m., and working hours were captured as humans entered and left the workplace, often using technologies such as swipe cards and Bundy Clocks. Financial gain in the form of wages was the reward for attending the workplace, with wages generally calculated on minutes and hours between the arrival and departure times.

Despite technological advances and the transition towards digital ways of working, many people still regard work as a physical place where they complete tasks in exchange for financial compensation. This exchange of labour over time for financial gain is the foundation of many global industrial relations and workplace systems.[12]

The COVID-19 pandemic highlighted that a physical workplace is still required for some occupations, jobs and tasks. Nurses, medical doctors and front-line workers are examples of individuals who need to travel to a specific workplace to perform their jobs. For these individuals, work is still a place to which they must travel.

Work, therefore, can be viewed as somewhere we "go" with work a noun.

---

[12] Australia, my home country, established the foundations for our industrial relations system in 1904. The industrial relations system, whereby there is an iterative negotiation between employers and employees, sets up minimum standards associated with working hours, sick leave, annual leave, equal pay for equal work, maternity leave and a minimum wage. Australia's first minimum wage – a basic living wage for a (male) worker to support a family of five (himself, a wife and three children) – was established in 1908. Minimum wage remains a core aspect of work in Australia today with many individuals considering work as a place where they go.

### Work As A Set of Activities That You "Do"

There has been a rise in the perspective of work as an action or set of activities individuals perform. From this perspective, work is something humans "do," a verb that describes a set of activities.

These activities can occur and be completed in various locations, as there is no longer just one designated workplace. With the proliferation of digital technologies, work can happen anywhere with an internet connection. Home offices have become popular for this type of work, but cafes and other public spaces can also serve as workspaces. Some people work from beaches, as depicted in popular social media feeds like Instagram and TikTok.

Distinguishing between framing work as a place versus what individuals do can be challenging. For example, my children sometimes struggle to understand what work is and what their parents do for work. When I talk about work, I sometimes refer to it as "going to the office," as this concept is familiar to many people. However, this can confuse my children, as they witness most work-based activities occurring in the home-based office where I am currently typing these words. Distinguishing between work activities that happen at home and those that occur outside the house becomes the focus of many everyday conversations. As a result, conversations between family members often seek clarification about each other's movements, such as "Are you going anywhere today?" or "Where are you going today?" When I say "Remember, I am going to work today," it is code for "I am leaving the house today" – I am going somewhere as per the first notion of work.

Work, therefore, can be viewed as a set of activities that we "do," with work as a verb.

### Work As An Experience

Another perspective on work is to frame it as a set of experiences. From this point of view, work is a collection of experiences where individuals "feel" a range of emotions.

These emotions can take many different forms, including:
- Positive or negative feelings about their job
- Positive or negative feelings about the workplace
- Positive or negative feelings about co-workers
- Positive or negative feelings about work activities and tasks
- Feelings of being motivated versus unmotivated
- Feelings about being accepted versus an outsider
- Feelings of being listened to/heard versus ignored
- Feelings of being considered core to the team/organisation versus dispensable

- Feelings of being valued versus taken for granted
- Feelings of being overworked
- Feelings of being considered talent versus non-talent.

The perspective of work as an experience has given rise to a new industry and research area. Proponents of employee experience, also known as EX, encourage investments in everyday work processes, activities and physical spaces. Work as an experience includes considering not only the "what" of work but also the "where" and "how."

Work-as-an-experience involves examining the intersection between the individual, including their sense of belonging, purpose, achievement, happiness and energy; talent management, such as aligned practices, personalisation, new career pathways and job progression; and the broader organisation, including work design, trust, empowerment and voice.

Organisations can create a more positive employee experience. Maya Angelou's quote, "People may forget what you say, but they will never forget how you made them feel," should be a guiding principle. Making employees feel valued and appreciated can be an underappreciated source of competitive advantage.

# Chapter 7
# (Re)Thinking Technology and Digitalisation

We have established that technology is a central aspect of (re)thinking talent decisions. Digitalised talent management involves technology, and digitalisation and its associated technologies enable automated decision-making. Therefore, allocating time, energy and attention to how we talk about technology in our everyday experiences is crucial to enact responsible talent decisions.

Talking about technology is akin to the debate about pronouncing the word "potatoes." You say po-tah-toes, and I say po-tat-oes.[13] While correcting each other's pronunciation of potatoes may be playful banter, differences in how we talk about technology are a serious matter. Our thoughts influence our word choices, affecting whether we consider technology a source of fear and trepidation or a solution to our problems. Our ideas affect our conversations, interactions, decisions and actions. Therefore, it is essential to be deliberate and thoughtful in our discussions about technology and its role in talent management.

---

*Our thoughts influence our words. Beliefs also influence whether we think technology will impact (determinist) or influence (constructionist and socio-material) choices, decisions and outcomes.*

---

## What Does Technology Mean To You?

It is essential to reflect on the meaning of technology and what it represents to each individual when (re)thinking talent decisions. Being conscious of our thinking processes and questioning the underlying reasons behind our beliefs is crucial. Humans benefit from thinking about what they think (and why, why, why they think that way).

Agreeing on standard definitions and terms of reference is essential to avoid misunderstandings and miscommunications. It is vital to establish whether differences in thinking are merely semantic – po-tah-toes versus po-tat-oes. Or whether the differences are conceptual – I think of potato as a white carbohydrate versus a vegetable, or you eat potatoes because they are nutritious versus the idea that consuming potatoes is taboo.

---

**13** Searching "How to pronounce potato/es" generates videos illustrating different pronunciations.

https://doi.org/10.1515/9783110756326-009

How we conceptualise technology plays a significant role in talent decisions. Establishing a shared understanding of key concepts, such as technology, is essential to ensure that the (re)thinking journey is productive and leads to our desired outcomes.

Let's start to (re)think about technology.

How do you define technology?
What does the term technology mean to you?

If we ask the same question within the home context, it can elicit a different response.

What comes to mind when we think of technology at home? Do we think of specific technologies like Suri or Google or companies like Apple, Amazon, or Samsung (I tend to think of companies)?

Walk around your home and identify how technology is integrated into everyday life. In my house, we have a robot vacuum (which we affectionately call Maxy), an automated coffee machine (like the ones in Italy, not the percolated American kind) and a sit/stand desk where I am currently typing this sentence. I also recognise that technology has physical and material components, like my monitor, keyboard, mouse, printer (the hardware) and Microsoft Word (the software). I am using technology (Mozilla Firefox) to access YouTube where my speakers play music in the background. Even my Oura ring, a wearable technology, captures my resting heart rate and activity levels. This reflective exercise illustrates how technology has become ubiquitous and integrated into our daily lives.

I'll (re)pose the question and ask you to reflect on your technology in your "work" context?

How do you define technology within the context of your work? Do you think about the software used to complete task-based activities?

Consider the technologies you use daily, monthly, annually, or at certain times of the year. This may include Microsoft Word, email, communication and collaboration tools like Slack, Twitter, LinkedIn, Microsoft Teams and phones. It's important to recognise the various technologies that assist with getting work done, and understanding their roles can help with (re)thinking talent decisions.

The above differences illustrate that context influences how we think about technology. In a personal context, we may first share what comes to mind when thinking about technology in a general sense. However, when framing our talk about technology in the workplace, we may reflect on how technology helps us achieve specific tasks or how it helps automate processes. The focus shifts from a broad perspective to a more task-oriented view. Understanding these different perspectives is crucial in enacting responsible talent decisions.

> *We benefit from (re)thinking about what technology means to you and me. We should not assume that our thinking is synonymous.*

Human characters generally agree that there are various types of technology. However, context plays a significant role in how they talk about it. Complexity arises when we consider the various perceptions of technology within the context of work and the workplace, as The Workforce has different ideas and mental images of technology.

Now, let's complicate matters further. How would you define the term digitalisation?

The definition of digitalisation can vary based on context, which leads to differing perceptions of what it entails. Does digitalisation refer to:

- Anything involving transitioning a process from paper to computer?
- Making things (whatever the things are) electronic?
- The use of information technology to accomplish tasks?
- Anything to do with computers?
- An activity or process where the computer does the work?
- Making processes better (with "better" undefined)?
- Making processes better (with "better" pre-defined)?
- Where technology becomes the (process) driver?

It's useful to reflect on whether your meanings of technology and digitalisation differ. Do your thoughts infer that technology and digitalisation are synonymous?

Next question. What does automation mean to you?

Do you think of automation as:

- A method for optimising labour?
- A way to save on (human) labour costs?
- Using technology to eliminate the human glue between two or more process steps?
- A method to remove manual aspects of a particular task or process?
- A process requiring no human intervention?
- A way to remove the human element from decision-making?
- The computerisation of predictable and repeatable tasks?
- A way to ensure less "time" is wasted?

- A method or excuse for (human) Redundancies?
- A source of change, change and more change?

Answering these questions highlights the potential for similarities and differences in our ideas about technology. The term automation can evoke different mental images depending on one's experience and point of view. My talk about technology can be synonymous with your talk about digitalisation. Conversely, my talk about digitalisation may differ significantly from your automation perspective. Context plays a crucial role in shaping our understanding and definition of these terms, and it is important to establish a shared knowledge to avoid confusion and potential miscommunication.

> *Technology is the software; the codes; the algorithms; the systems supporting decision-making.*

Scientists intentionally reflect on different types of technology. The terminology for people-based information technologies has changed regularly as technological innovations have advanced.[14] Some elements of technology addressed by the scientific community include Enterprise Resource Planning Systems (ERPs), Human Resource Information Systems (HRISs), Human Capital Management (HCM), Electronic Human Resource Management (e-HRM), Electronic Talent Management (e-Talent), Digitalised Talent Management (DTM), Cloud-based technology, Software-as-a-Service (SaaS), Social Media, Artificial Intelligence, Machine Learning, Digital Humans, Quantum Computing, Blockchain, Internet of Things (IoT) and Virtual and Augmented Reality (VR/AR).

The above is far from an exhaustive list. And while the specific definitions and conceptualisations differ, we benefit from remembering that all technologies have physical, material and social elements.

When making talent decisions, it is important to understand and recognise the similarities and differences in using technology-related terms such as technology, digitalisation, or automation. Sometimes, our understanding of these terms may be merely semantic, like the difference between saying "po-tah-toes" and "po-tat-oes" – but we agree that potatoes are edible root vegetables. Or whether the differences are conceptual, where we think about potatoes differently. You may position potatoes as a source of nourishment, while I may avoid eating potatoes because I think they are of limited nutritional value. We potentially think about technology in distinct ways. For instance, one may view technology as a tool to enhance productivity, while another may see it as a potential threat to job security. Thus, it is essential to clearly understand how we define technology-related terms when making talent decisions.

---

[14] Please don't get too hung up on specific definitions and questions of whether my definition is better than your definition. Do, however, grasp the essence of various technology discussions.

Assuming that humans pronounce the word "potatoes" the same way does not necessarily mean their thoughts and beliefs about technology align. The differences in the conceptualisation of technology can be significant, and understanding both the points of convergence and divergence is crucial. The absence of shared meanings and beliefs can lead to misunderstandings and hamper the collaborative efforts of the workforce.

Defining concepts and establishing shared meanings of key terms is necessary to establish effective collaborations. Groups of humans should discuss their beliefs, ideas, mental impressions and thoughts to ensure they have a shared understanding of the key concepts that form the basis of their talent decisions.

By asking what people mean when they discuss technology, we can move towards establishing a shared path and a foundation for responsible talent decisions. But how often do humans take the time to pause, reflect and capture what key concepts mean to them? How often do groups of humans come together and discuss their beliefs – whether they have a feeling about something existing or being accurate and that they hold an opinion? How often do groups of humans come together and discuss their ideas – their mental impressions and their thoughts or suggestions about a possible course of action? How often do groups of humans take the time to establish shared meanings which form the basis of their (talent) decisions?

Understanding where, when and how thoughts differ is crucial for pursuing knowledge and strategy. We need to establish a shared path to journey along. We can foster effective collaborations and responsible talent decisions by comprehending differences and establishing shared meanings.

# Chapter 8
# (Re)Thinking Talent Management

Our (re)thinking journey continues by considering what we mean when talking about talent management. Our understanding of what talent management means may differ between individuals. Differences of opinion exist because talent management is used to organise our ideas and beliefs. There is no universally accepted definition to discover; instead, individual humans decide what talent means to them within their home and workplace context. Remember that talent management, like talent, does not exist outside of our thoughts. Talent management starts with our thoughts, which reside in the human mind.

This section ponders the nature and structure of talent management, including a conceptual conflict. On one side, some believe that talent management and human resource management are synonymous. Discussing talent management is the same as talking about HRM. The differences between them are merely semantic (you say po-tah-toes and I say po-tat-oes, but we agree that potatoes are edible root vegetables). Conversely, some argue that talent management is distinct from Human Resource Management. While talent management and human resources may be siblings, they are different.

However, another perspective on talent management goes beyond semantic and practice-based debates. It proposes that talent management is about making decisions based on subjective value judgments. This view acknowledges that talent management is not just about the efficient and effective use of human resources but also about how organisations identify, develop and retain employees with exceptional skills, knowledge and abilities. This approach recognises that people are not interchangeable resources and that each individual has "talent." Ultimately, the (re)thinking of talent decisions requires us to consider and reconcile these different perspectives and find a way to make talent management work for everyone involved.

---

*Talent management involves decisions and actions based on subjective judgments of value.*

---

## Differentiating Between Talent Management and Human Resource Management

There is an ongoing debate about whether talent management and human resource management are the same. Some argue that talent management is simply a new name for Strategic Human Resource Management or human capital management. Talking about talent management is akin to human capital management because all humans possess valuable expertise. The two terms are interchangeable. The only difference is the name (and maybe better branding?).

However, this belief overlooks the distinctive features of talent management. I often encounter this misconception, and my role is to challenge it by initiating conversations that differentiate between the two. It is not merely a question of semantics where two parties agree on the same meaning of a word but may use different terms to describe it. The differences between talent management and human resource management are conceptual. They go beyond word usage and entail different perspectives, goals and values. I frequently declare that talent management and human resource management are different. I believe, and yes, this is my perception, that talent management and human resource management are not synonymous. We are not discussing a semantic difference. A semantic difference where you say po-tah-toes and I can po-tat-oes but we are both imagining an edible root vegetable. We are experiencing conceptual differences. While you may think of potatoes as a vegetable, another human may imagine potatoes as a white carbohydrate. Another human may be thinking of vodka. Instigating conversations that differentiate between the two is something I like to do.

Ignoring conceptual differences can have significant consequences for talent decisions. Conceptual differences affect the "who" and "what" of talent decisions.

What are the differences, then, you may ask (please do ask).

A fundamental differentiating element between talent management and human resource management is the focus on the who. Human resource management concentrates on the workforce as a collective. In contrast, talent management concentrates on individuals or a select group of individuals.

Another crucial distinction is related to who is involved in what activities. Human resource policies and activities apply to the entire workforce, irrespective of their roles or talent levels. All members of "The Workforce" have access to human resource practices.

On the other hand, talent management activities only apply to specific individuals or categories of individuals, such as high performers, future leaders, etc. While human resource practices embrace inclusivity and apply to all, talent management practices tend to favour exclusivity and apply only to selected individuals. The beneficiaries of talent management activities are talent and talent alone, while human resource practices encompass the entire workforce.

---

*Human Resource Management is about doing the same thing to everyone. Talent management is about doing something (a practice, resource allocation) to someone (a specific individual).*

---

Fairness is a crucial aspect that distinguishes between human resources and talent management. Human resource management practices promote fairness by implementing procedural justice and distributing resources equally to everyone in the workforce. Resource allocation processes are the same for all employees, and the outputs of human resource decisions are also similar. This approach reduces the subjectivity of evaluation processes and resource allocations, making human resource management fairer.

In contrast, talent management assumes that some individuals are more valuable than others, making it less fair than human resource management. Talent management focuses on workforce differentiation, which is not about fairness. The decision-making process in talent management is subjective, and not everyone is judged as valuable according to pre-defined rules. As a result, resource distribution is unequal, and some individuals receive more benefits than others. Therefore, talent management does not emphasise fairness in the same way that human resource management does.

## Scientific Talent Management Perspectives

Talent management experts emphasise the connection between talent decisions, actions and outcomes. They agree that strategic objectives drive talent management activities. Strategy is the foundation of all talent decisions. Strategy, strategy, strategy; all talent decisions focus on strategy. Therefore, talent management is not just about managing individuals but also about aligning talent with the organisation's strategic goals and objectives.

In 2006, Robert E. Lewis and Robert J. Heckman (yes, we have talked about these two Roberts previously) published a critical review in *Human Resource Management Review*, which gained considerable attention in scientific talent management discussions. This paper was the first to comprehensively consider the parameters for differentiating between human resources and talent management. The authors proposed three ways to conceptualise talent management after analysing the talent management literature up to 2006:
- Talent management **as a collection of human resource activities** (whereby talent management and human resources are synonymous),
- Talent management **as a set of activities focusing on establishing talent pools and ensuring an adequate flow of individuals** into jobs within the organisation (whereby talent management shares similarities to human resources' focus on succession planning or human resource planning), and
- **Talent management as a set of activities focusing on the workforce and their talent more generically**. We can further consider talent management which involves managing performance whereby high performers are to be sought, hired and differentially rewarded regardless of their roles or the organisation's specific needs. Another way includes talent as critical because it is the role of a strong HR function to manage everyone to high performance or because external factors make talent more valuable. The Roberts argued that this third perspective also struggled to provide meaningful points to differentiate between talent management and human resource management.

Lewis and Heckman determined that there was a ". . . disturbing lack of clarity regarding the definition, scope, and overall goals of talent management." They arrived at this scathing determination because they believed practitioners and scientists had not yet established a core set of principles. At the time, the differences between human resource management and talent management were mainly semantic.

Scientists continue to categorise talent management similarly to this day, almost two decades later, with three dominant approaches:[15]

- **The management of designated individuals** with activities focusing on specific individuals regardless of their position. We are still thinking of high performers and high potential humans.
- **A set of activities** including talent acquisition (rather than recruitment and selection), talent identification (rather than performance management), talent development (rather than learning and development) and retention of valuable humans; or
- **The creation of talent pools** with a focus on allocating resources (time and financial) to creating talent pools. Succession planning is regularly associated with this approach because the talent supply chain is a focus.

## Talent Management as A Judgment-Orientated Activity

I propose an alternative way to approach talent management that acknowledges the subjective nature of value judgments in deciding who will be the focus of talent management activities. The dominant perspectives of talent management – which emphasise the management of designated individuals, a set of activities, or the creation of talent pools – fail to meaningfully differentiate talent management from human resource management. They also fail to provide decision-makers with guidance on what talent management requires on a day-to-day basis. In my view, talent management involves determining which individuals are of greater value than others, with decision-makers judging the value of The Workforce based on their perception of what talent looks and acts like. Therefore, subjective judgments of value lie at the heart of talent management.

My approach involves recognising that decision-makers use talent management practices – whether talent identification, talent development and talent retention – to identify individuals who will receive talent management interventions. Specific individuals become the recipients of talent management activities.

---

**15** Learn more about the different talent management perspectives in Chapter 2 "Talent management" (definitions, conceptualisations and frameworks) in *Talent Management: A Research Overview*, co-authored with Anthony McDonnell.

Three elements form the basis of my judgment-orientated perspective:
(1) judgments about value
(2) decisions
(3) resources

Human decision-makers assess and "judge" the "value" of individuals based on their perception of talent; subsequent "decisions" regarding talent management activities are made based on these value judgments; resource allocation is based on these prior judgments of value.

*Talent management is a judgment-orientated activity where humans judge the value of other humans. While mediated by various contextual factors and variables (such as technology), these judgments should be informed by and aligned to current and future strategic ambitions and goals.*

Talent management entails the identification of individuals, known as talent subjects, who are perceived to have greater value than their counterparts. These individuals are then afforded additional resources (e.g., development opportunities, secondments) than their (perceived) lower-value counterparts.

## Talent Management Involves Subjective Judgments of Value

Framing talent management as a judgment-oriented activity rather than a set of practices highlights the crucial role of human judgment in the process. Talent management is essentially about evaluating The Workforce and determining which individuals are most valuable. This evaluation involves subjective perceptions, as each human has their own ideas about what constitutes talent and what outcomes should be achieved through the identification process. Subjectivity is, therefore, a critical factor in talent management, as individual perceptions influence the judgment of which employees should be invested in. Talent management requires subjective judgment regarding what people say and do and identifying individuals who best exhibit their talent. Put another way; talent management involves subjectively judging what people say and do and investing in individuals who best act out their talent.

In our journey of (re)thinking talent management, we must confront an uncomfortable truth: subjectivity is an inherent part of our decision-making processes. This uncomfortable truth centres on the fact that talent decisions are ALWAYS subjective, as human judgment is the foundation for these decisions, and human judgment is inherently subjective.

## A Few Words Before We Continue on Our Journey

We should assume that humans think differently about work, technology and talent management (we'll do talent next). We benefit from knowing what pictures and images arise in the human mind before deciding upon what talent means. Start with reflective questions: what does [insert key term here] mean to me? What does [insert key term here] mean to others?

We benefit from (re)thinking about the meanings that underpin key concepts. Understanding the extent to which we hold shared pronunciations and ideas of potatoes is necessary. Collaborating to establish perspective alignment is core to ensuring a compelling journey down the yellow brick road in our tale of complexity, technology and subjectivity in the pursuit of strategy and knowledge.

Considering this, it is worth questioning whether talent decisions should solely be the responsibility of human actors or whether technology should play a more prominent role in executing talent decisions. As we rethink aspects of talent decisions, we must consider the potential benefits and drawbacks of incorporating technology into the decision-making process, whatever form that may take, because talent decisions are a tale of complexity, technology and subjectivity.

Part 4: **(Re)Thinking Talent**

# A Few Words, and A Visualisation Exercise, Before We Continue On Our Journey

Let us continue our (re)thinking journey with a visualisation exercise.

Imagine work and think of work as occurring in a specific physical space – a workplace.

What do you see? Are you standing at the front door of a building, in a conference room or desk?

Direct your eye gaze downwards. What do you see on the floor? Do you see marble, concrete, carpet, sand, or a different floor covering?

Let us involve our sense of smell.
Does the workplace smell a particular way? Is the smell of coffee permeating the airspace? Or does this question take you back to when your co-worker reheated X (insert smelly food here), and it stank out the lunchroom and your workspace?

How about the feelings which arise when you think about work (remember, some humans think of work as a feeling-based experience)?
Which emoji would you use?
Some options are happy, angry, sad, frustrated, sleepy, confused, impatient, excited, grumpy, proud and nervous.
What physiological responses does this question ignite?
Do you smile?
Does your heart rate increase?
Do your palms start to sweat?
Or do you not notice a physiological response?

Let us take a walk together. Imagine we are walking through work or the workplace. You encounter other individuals as you walk. Try and picture specific faces. Who do you see? Do you walk by characters you know well, say hello and extend your hand? Are there others you smile at as you walk past, even though they are unknown to you? Are there specific workplace characters who you avoid at all costs? Characters to whom you will put down your head, avoid eye contact, take a sigh of relief as you walk on and say "phew."

Let us do this same activity again. This time we turn our attention to questions about talent. Close your eyes and imagine retaking the same walk. Which individuals would you describe as talented?

Now expand your awareness to include your peripheral vision. Think more broadly about the characters in the workforce. Think about which individuals ignite a cheer. And consider whom you prefer to walk past. Think about being asked to work with specific individuals. To whom would you respond, "Oh dear!"

https://doi.org/10.1515/9783110756326-011

Next reflection task. Consider whether the day of the week influences you. Are your thoughts influenced by whether you see them on a Monday or a Friday? Your perceptions of someone's value can be malleable, whereby a particular behaviour annoyed you on Monday. Come Friday, however, you were willing to provide some additional leeway.

Starting with our eyes closed reminds us that talent meanings arise in our minds. Talent does not exist in and of itself from a positivist view. Instead, talent definitions are based on what we imagine and "see" because talent only exists in our minds. Talent is essential as it represents a concept through which we organise our ideas. Understanding talent meanings involves considering the images that arise and reside in our minds.

Applying an imaginary lens when thinking about talent allows me to highlight that we visualise talent differently depending on our perspectives. I can also illuminate that we think of talent as individuals who add value to us somehow.

This exercise communicates that our journey focuses on "work." We are (re)thinking talent decisions at work, regardless of whether you are working in a designated physical space or typing on a keyboard in a café or remote workspace.

The visualisation exercise also illustrates that we tend to define talent within the context of our everyday experiences. We can reflect on an individual's talent status before formal evaluation processes because we judge individuals based on our interactions with them. While some decisions use data, others are superficial. Some individuals garner positive attention, while others we avoid. Notably, talent evaluations materialise through our actions, such as whether we smile or put our heads down when walking past a specific individual or whether we say "G'day."

---

*We tend to think about talent within the context of our daily interactions.*

---

The exercise has a further benefit as it incites an awareness that our judgments of individuals are malleable. How we view the value of certain characters can change depending on whether we encounter them on a Monday, Friday, or a particularly stressful day.

# Chapter 9
# (Re)Thinking Talent Meanings

Given that our (re)thinking tale is about talent decisions, it makes sense to dedicate a separate chapter to illuminating the complexity of talent. This chapter begins by exploring what talent means to you personally. We will then consider what talent means to others and share examples of definitions from both the public and scientific domains. Discussions about talent definitions will precede various sub-sections offering different ways to think about talent. Together, these sections will show the kaleidoscope of talent colours in the human mind.

## What Does Talent Mean to You?

Defining what constitutes talent forms the foundation of effective talent management strategies. While all members of The Workforce are valuable (otherwise, why hire them?), talent management asserts that specific individuals provide greater value than others. We refer to these individuals as "talent."

(Re)Thinking talent decisions is a complex task due to talent itself. Talent is a concept or category that helps us organise ideas. "Talent" has no inherent meaning, and organisations do not have a set definition of talent. Rather, specific individuals within an organisation "create" or "establish" talent meanings within organisational boundaries.

Talent meanings start with Y.O.U. – Your Own Understanding. Begin by asking yourself, "What does talent mean to me?"

Understanding what meanings and images occupy our minds is the first step in thinking about talent. The human mind is a crucial character in talent decisions.

Take a moment to close your eyes and imagine talent.
What do you see?
Do you imagine a specific person, someone who elicits a smile during your imaginary walk? Or do you imagine a generic set of skills and capabilities?
Perhaps you consider anyone with Excel or Canva skills as talent.
Or are there particular roles and positions you value?
Maybe you treasure executive assistants, event organisers, or legal appointments.

Only when we are tasked with answering "What does talent mean to you?" do ideas about talent come to life. Our thoughts and opinions about talent are purely theoretical until we vocalise them. Language plays a pivotal role in establishing what talent is because language, words and conversations make the talent meanings that reside in our minds "come to life." Talent is a concept in our minds until we communicate our meanings and understandings through language and talk.

> *Remember: talent only exists in our minds – what's in your mind?*
> *Talent is a concept – a way to organise the world.*
> *Talent is social and highly contextual.*
> *Talent is dynamic – meanings can and do change.*

So, what is on my mind? What does talent mean to me – Dr. Sharna Lee?

Talent, for me, is a term used to refer to individuals who are judged to be of greater value. The context of greater value can differ: from greater value relative to their peers, having greater value compared to previous performance and greater value for strategic goals.

*Talent – a term used to refer to an individual who is judged to be of greater value.*

I am fascinated by individual talent meanings and their implications for talent decisions. As thoughts about talent reside in the human mind, exploring what talent means to different people is essential. I often say, "What talent is to you influences your perception of what you think I can be." This highlights the importance of understanding how individuals think about and communicate talent, as it can impact how they identify, manage and reward talent. Therefore, in our (re)thinking journey, examining what talent means to others, including in the public, scientific and executive domains, is crucial.

## Public Definitions of Talent

(Re)Thinking talent decisions requires a clear definition of key terms, and talent is arguably the most crucial of these terms. My *Compact Oxford Dictionary and Thesaurus* offers the following noun-based definitions:
1. Natural ability or skill
2. People possessing such ability or skill
3. People seen in terms of their sexual attractiveness or availability
4. An ancient weight or unit of currency

I have utilised technology as a tool to aid in our understanding of what talent means. In today's digital age, many of us turn to technology when we need to learn something new (I realise many of you use Google as an information tool).

Googling "talent" returned 1,110,000,000 results. The top results offered the following definitions:
- A natural aptitude or skill – Google word box at the top of the page
- A special natural ability or aptitude; a capacity for achievement or success; a talented person; a group of persons with special ability; professional actors collec-

tively, especially star performers; a power of mind or body considered as given to a person for use and improvement: so-called from the parable of Matthew 25:14–30 – the results of Dictionary.com
– A natural aptitude, an inner quality that emerges effortlessly – suggests Workable.com
– (Someone who has) a natural ability to be good at something, especially without being taught –the Cambridge Dictionary definition

ChatGPT answered "What is talent?" with:

> Talent refers to a natural aptitude or skill that a person possesses in a particular area. It can be seen as an innate ability that allows a person to excel in a specific field, whether it is in music, sports, art, or any other area of interest. Talent is often seen as a combination of abilities and traits, including intelligence, creativity, perseverance, and the ability to learn quickly. However, it is important to note that talent alone is not enough to achieve success, as hard work, dedication, and practice are also necessary to develop and maximise one's talents.

Posing the question "What is the definition of talent?" to ChatGPT yielded:

> Talent can be defined as a natural aptitude or ability in a particular area, which enables a person to perform at a high level in that field without extensive training. It is often characterised as an innate or inherent quality that allows individuals to excel in certain areas such as music, art, sports, or academic pursuits. However, it is important to note that while talent may give an individual an initial advantage, it must be nurtured and developed through practice, hard work, and dedication in order to be fully realised and utilised.[16]

## Scientific Talent Definitions

The knowledge-generating literature similarly returns mixed results. Sample talent definitions proposed by talent management scientists over the years include:[17]

---

[16] Note these are not the responses ChatGPT generated for me. ChatGPT, because it is trained to learn more about me and my writing, proposed very different responses to what the broad public would receive. My responses included "Talent is a term used to describe individuals who are judged to be of greater value or potential than others in a particular context. It can refer to a person's innate abilities, natural aptitudes, learned skills, or a combination of these factors. The context in which talent is evaluated can vary widely, from specific industries and professions to sports, the arts, or any other area where individuals are recognised for exceptional performance or potential. Defining what constitutes talent can be complex, as it often involves subjective judgments based on a range of factors, including past performance, potential, and cultural or organisational norms" and "The definition of talent can vary depending on context and perspective. In general, talent refers to a natural aptitude or skill, often in a specific area, that is recognised and valued by others. However, the exact definition may differ depending on who you ask and the context in which it is being used."
[17] The vast array of talent definitions is outlined in my book *Talent Management: A Research Overview* (co-authored with Anthony McDonnell). We highlight that researchers are unable to undertake a

- We define talent as the resource that includes the potential and realised capacities of individuals and groups and how they are organised, including those within the organisation and those who might join the organisation – John Boudreau and Peter Ramstad
- Talent has been used broadly to describe an individual's skill, aptitude and achievement ... The four elements of individual talent are potency (person's power, influence and capability to achieve results), truest interest (passion), skill intelligences (mental and physical learning and performance abilities to compete, conquer and survive) and virtue intelligence (moral excellence and integrity) – Hilligje Gerritdina Van Dijk
- From a human capital perspective, talent refers to the human capital in an organisation that is both valuable and unique, with an employee's contribution to the organisation the main criterion of interest – Nicky Dries
- Talent refers to systematically developed innate abilities of individuals that are deployed in activities they like, find important and in which they want to invest energy. It enables individuals to perform excellently in one or more domains of human functioning, operationalised as performing better than other individuals of the same age or experience or as performing consistently at their personal best – Sanne Nijs, Eva Gallardo-Gallardo, Nicky Dries and Luc Sels

## Executive Definitions of Talent

At the beginning of my presentations, I always ask the attendees, "What does the term 'talent' mean to you?" Sample responses include:
- "An attitude or skill to get something done."
- "Being able to excel in an area of focus."
- "A commodity."
- "A superior level of skill in a particular subject, field, or profession."
- "A developed skill or combination of skills that can be leveraged for both personal and/or group advantage."
- "A nurtured professionalism that encompasses many skills that is used to set an example and benefit others."
- "An individual's expertise or skills that may have been gained through experiences or have come naturally."
- "Individuals who perform well and are acknowledged for it."
- "Having an ability or skill that's valuable to a third party."

---

series of experiments to see what talent means, or prove which precise definitions exist, and if one is better than another. Instead, individuals and social groups decide – and socially construct – what talent means to them within the context of their social history.

- "Individual that an organisation wishes to attract as a new employee."
- "Individuals with fixed skills and attributes, in particular intelligence, expert communication and strong work ethic."
- "People who benefit financially."
- "Someone that is purely gifted and skilled."
- "An ability which an individual has which is inherent and is the trait which differentiates them from others."
- "An ability to do things better, faster, and more unique than others."
- "A trait of a person that captivates the attention of surroundings because of his/her uniqueness."
- "Scoring well in exams."
- "God's gifting."
- "A skill set that can be homed or developed with a combination of time, effort and consistency which is perceived or recognised by others."
- "Those that are naturally gifted."
- "Latent potential in a person that could be unlocked in whatever capacity needed, with only a little direction and guidance to foster and nurture that talent into something special."
- "An advanced ability or value a person can naturally produce without exerting as much effort as others do."
- "Something that comes naturally and that one shouldn't put too much effort into developing or worry about learning new skills because they are inherent qualities."
- "People that are good at sport."
- "High academic achievers."
- "A singular ability that one has that is above the ability of others in a certain field."
- "The set of skills or abilities that an individual can use to contribute to the success of theirs or a common goal."
- "Something I am born with, something that comes naturally and to be discovered during the course of my life."
- "When an individual attains the skills to achieve superior performance."
- "Natural ability in action."
- "An inner quality or ability in a person which emerges effortlessly but is not enough to guarantee success."
- "An individual who has a natural ability or aptitude to do something well."
- "A set of genealogical and acquired skills."
- "The workforce."
- "A God-given, natural born ability."
- "A skill set or quality people naturally possess within themselves that can be further refined so it holds a positive value in our everyday lives."
- "A natural ability or aptitude."

- "A gift or an inherent ability that enables someone to be more special than others in a particular area."
- "Someone possessing a strong sense of ability and knowledge to effectively achieve results."
- "A particular skill that someone holds. The term skill being referred to as being great at something."
- "A point of difference."
- "The natural competence to excel in a particular task or activity."
- "A person or group of people that have skills a business requires or desires to support the business strategy."
- "Having the natural ability to significantly excel at a task better than the average person."
- "To be able to demonstrate an aptitude for an activity and for at least one person to recognise that aptitude as valuable."
- "A speciality in a particular area."
- "A skill, aptitude, or affinity for a particular skill or activity that is a natural predisposition towards particular pursuits, something which is innate, untaught."
- "An innate quality that can be found across organisations."
- "Talent is an ability or attribute a person possesses that most if not all others do not possess."

The above list show that individuals think of talent in ways that resemble the generic definitions on Google. However, it is worth noting that many people mention a sports-centric image when visualising or imagining talent. We consider the influence of sport on talent meanings later in this chapter.

When John Boudreau and I asked a specific cohort of characters – senior HR executives – this question in April 2019 (pre-COVID), their responses focused specifically on the workplace context. Some of the definitions they provided included:
- "The high-potential employees who are identified for significant advancement."
- "The inherent capability that exists in each of our employees."
- "The competencies that we identify in our internal system."
- "The capacity that our employees have to do their jobs."

In February 2022, during the global pandemic and when workforce issues were at the forefront of organisational priorities, asking the same question resulted in the following responses:
- "The degree to which people are contributing and they're helping to achieve outcomes. But I am also looking at . . . growth potential. And if you've someone who is performing at the job today, but if you're understanding where you need to be tomorrow and actively developing towards those future needs, there is a strong talent there. And it's not something that we get across the board . . . they dive right in, they're coming with ideas and they're getting things done . . . talent is

the dual nature of people that are helping get outcomes today but they are also the ones that you feel like there's also the potential to develop into whatever they need to be or whatever they can be tomorrow."
- "The action or displayed abilities necessary to drive our strategic mission."
- Noting that their people strategy enables their business strategy – "An individual's knowledge, skills and abilities, or experiences that can help us accomplish team, business, enterprise goals. I think of like, can they currently do it? And when I think of potential then I think certain talent can be considered high potential."
- "Encompasses all people."
- "Demonstrated capacity to perform valuable work in a desired way."
- "The people resources that applies skills and capabilities to how they perform."

I make two critical points after receiving responses. First, I explain there is a wide range of definitions and perceptions of talent operating in society and workplaces. There is, I propose, "A kaleidoscope of talent colours." As responsible decision-makers, we aim not to bring everyone together and establish one definition of talent overall. Society benefits from a range of talent. We need a spectrum of talent to make the world go round. I encourage all humans to "look left, right, up, and down" when considering who makes them smile when they walk around. Who do they have no affiliation with and who makes them frown? Observing the people around us – as in our opening visualisation exercise – helps us learn who makes us feel positive and who makes us feel negative.

---

*A kaleidoscope of talent colours operates in people's minds.*

---

The second point emphasizes the importance of context and strategy. I remind my audiences that defining talent is about personal perceptions and how talent fits within an organisation's strategy. It is crucial to consider talent in the context of strategy, as responsible talent decisions should be aligned with the organisation's goals and objectives. Talent decisions should support the organisation's strategic goals.

---

*Talent definitions are informed by, and aligned, to strategy. Remember to start with the organisational, digitalisation and talent management strategies when establishing talent meanings.*

---

There are infinite possible definitions of talent due to the diverse ways individuals perceive and establish their meanings of talent. This variability is influenced by the individual's reality and their understanding of ontology and epistemology. It explores whether the truth can be discovered (positivist) or if knowledge and facts are complex due to multiple subjective realities (social constructionism and interpretivism).

Some believe that an individual's true talent can be uncovered, and that their natural abilities and skills can be identified. This positivist perspective is prevalent in popular media and scientific literature, often referring to talent as a natural, innate and internal element. However, it is essential to consider whether these ideas align with your own definition of talent. Are such terms the hallmark of your description? Others may hold a different perspective. Other humans believe that defining talent and understanding what talent looks like is, well . . . it's complicated.

# Chapter 10
# (Re)Thinking Talent Categories

The next step on our journey is to move from the various meanings of talent to talent categories (meaning groups) as we try to understand the different perspectives of talent within the human mind.

## Scientific Talent Categories

We have already established that asking humans what talent means to them as part of general or work-based conversation elicits diverse responses. Considering "scientific" answers generates a similar divergence. Each "scientist" thinks about talent in their own way. In their knowledge-creation pursuits, scientists aim to shape conversations and knowledge by offering their insights and perspectives. Scientists are not neutral characters. Scientists may also prescribe how we should talk about talent, particularly in cases where they lack empirical data or industry experience.

The challenge is to make sense of the vast complexity of talent definitions. We can identify themes and patterns and reconcile various perspectives into different talent categories. Several conceptual frameworks (see Figure 10.1) differentiate between talent meanings.

**Inherent versus acquired**. Questions surrounding whether humans are born with specific or unique talents or not fall within the inherent versus acquired framework, which is an extension of the nature versus nurture debate. The inherent perspective of talent holds that humans are born with their talent. Individuals are endowed with certain qualities that are biological and hereditary. According to this perspective, talent is part of the innermost nature of a person or thing, arising from nature itself. Terms such as built-in, constitutive, hardwired, ingrained, native and deep-rooted are often associated with the talent-is-inherent perspective.

On the other hand, the talent-can-be-acquired perspective holds that a person's skills can expand and develop over time. While humans may be born with specific skills and qualities, these are only part of the story, and humans can acquire new skills, capabilities, and experiences that influence their value. This perspective holds that talent can be obtained, developed and taught.

**Inclusive versus exclusive approach**. The inclusive versus exclusive framework pertains to the "who" of talent management, questioning whether talent management prioritises an all-of-workforce or some-of-workforce approach. Those who advocate for an inclusive approach assert that all employees are talent, meaning that everyone in the workforce has the talent that the organisation requires. The Workforce comprises individuals who have already been deemed valuable by decision-makers, which is why they were selected to join the organisation.

Conversely, the exclusive approach maintains that some individuals possess more talent than others, and processes should prioritise investments in this exclusive group of people.

**Subject versus object**. A subject perspective on talent implies a focus on identifying and developing talented individuals, whereas an object perspective focuses on identifying and developing the characteristics of talented individuals.

**Everyone is talent versus specific individuals versus specific skills and capabilities versus specific jobs, roles, or positions**. My framework categorises talent meanings into four perspectives. The first is the everyone-is-talent perspective, which aligns with the inclusive approach and considers The Workforce talent; therefore, all employees are talent.

The second is the specifically designated individual perspective. Talent as specifically designated individuals focuses on the individual and will assert that – Sharna Lee, Alec, Jenn, Mohammad, Jade, Charlie, Yijia and Ashita – are talent. Such individuals may be high performers, high potentials, future leaders and/or rising stars.

The third is the specifically designated skills and capabilities perspective, which identifies specific skills and capabilities critical to operational needs, strategic direction, or organisation performance as defining factors for talent. In this perspective, an individual gains talent status based on their skills and capabilities rather than their individuality. Sharna Lee is talent because she has (and effectively uses) her scientific knowledge, understanding of decision making and experience with structuring talent resources for strategy execution to advance responsible talent decisions. These skills, capabilities and experiences are the defining factors. Alec can sub-in for Sharna Lee and gain talent status if he can replicate and perform these skills.

Finally, the specifically designated jobs, roles and positions perspective, derived from John Boudreau and Peter Ramstad's Talentship framework, recognises particular roles crucial to strategic success. The "what" is identified first. Then the "who" – individuals with the required skills and capabilities to perform these roles effectively. This perspective acknowledges that while all roles contribute to operations, not all are essential for executing the organisation's strategy.[18]

---

[18] You can find a detailed explanation of these four categorisations in my book *Talent Management: A Research Overview* (co-authored with Anthony McDonnell).

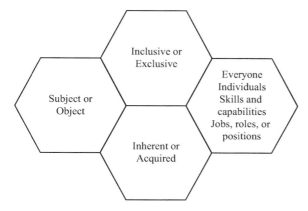

**Figure 10.1:** Overview of scientific talent categories.

## (Re)Thinking Talent Categories

Two additional questions help us understand the practical implications of talent meanings. The first question is: what does talent look like? I am fascinated by the mental images people associate with talent. In our workplace visualisation exercise, I asked you to imagine talent to reveal how our definitions and meanings of talent may differ from the mental images we have of talent.

The second question is: what does talent do? Focusing on specific behaviours and actions helps us identify the unique ways talented individuals approach their work. Through these positive divergent behaviours and actions, talent "stands out" or is what "sets them apart" from their non-talented peers.

---

*(Re)Thinking talent involves understanding what humans think talent means (talent meanings) and learning what humans think talent does (talent in action).*

---

Based on my experiences of asking thousands of executives what talent looks like in practice, I have realised the limitations of scientific perspectives. While talent categories, including mine, may provide some structure, they often miss the nuanced understanding of talent meanings, and the value humans bring to the workplace.

It is essential to move beyond talent meanings and focus on understanding the defining attributes of a talented individual versus a non-talented individual and the different actions that "set them apart." This understanding can serve as the epicentre of talent decisions and lead to better outcomes in the workplace.

Our goal is to (re)think talent decisions by considering the various ways humans think about talent and the resulting categories that emerge from these different perspectives. We reflect on whether talent is viewed as something individuals possess – in terms of skills and capabilities – or something that people do – in terms of effectively performing their talent. We also consider the extent to which people judge talent based on performance against expectations or their peers and whether they are interested in current talent or potential future value. Talent encompasses more than the categories in the scientific literature; it includes value, embedded attributes, strategy, expectations and many other factors. Figure 10.2 illustrates the talent categories that feature in thoughts and lived experiences.

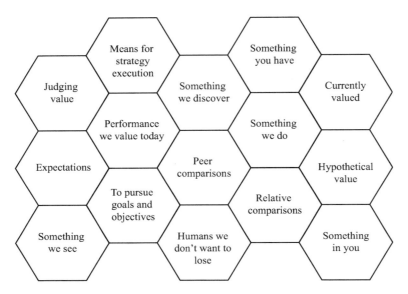

**Figure 10.2:** Talent categories.

## Talent as Judging Value

I believe that the central concept of talent management is value. Talent management involves making judgments about the value of individuals, and it asserts that some individuals are more valuable than others. Therefore, talent is a term that is applied to individuals who are of value or valuable.

*Talent = individuals judged as valuable.*

Talent as judging value refers to humans who possess a quality that makes them unique and valuable or those considered useful or important. Value judgments are highly subjective and are often based on individual preferences and experiences.

These judgments are reflected in statements such as "I value the way that [specific human] performs X [an action]," "I appreciate when [specific human] is there when I need them" and "I highly regard [specific human's] ability to anticipate my needs."

Our story of complexity continues because talent decisions are, in essence, based on subjective perceptions of value. Different talent definitions will prevail because humans value other behaviours and actions based on their unique value frameworks. Everyone's value framework influences how they judge, evaluate and interpret behaviours and actions, which is the basis for talent identification. It is important to inquire about what talent "does" to understand the defining attributes of talented individuals and the actions that set them apart from their non-talented peers. Understanding what key individuals believe about the behaviours and actions of talent is crucial to our journey of (re)thinking talent decisions.

## Talent as Something in You

Most people believe that talent is an inherent quality that exists within individuals. This perspective sees talent as something within us – talent is within our bodies and/or minds. It asserts that every individual has some talent and is predisposed to excel in a particular activity, whether music, sports, maths, spelling, problem-solving, singing, flexibility, endurance, creative arts, or another endeavour.

When asked about what talent means to them, many people express this perspective, indicating that talent is something embedded within the individual, and the ownership of talent resides with the individual. Figure 10.3 shows some ways that the talent as something in you perspective features in everyday conversations.

*Talent = something inside us.*

Talent as something inside us is commonly attributed to genetics and genetic predisposition. "They get it from me" is a common parental expression representing this view (I certainly claim aspects of my children's capabilities and outcomes result from having me as a parent. Do you, or have you done the same? Did your parents make such statements about you during your childhood?).

Although believed to reside within an individual, talent may also be seen as a mysterious and unpredictable quality, not easily accounted for, or explained. This "random" idea of talent still features in our daily interactions and conversations through various terms and statements such as "I don't know where they get it from" or "I don't know where I get it from."

Humans are socialised to believe that talent is an inherent trait of an individual. This belief starts early in life, as we judge and perceive others as gifted, special, or geniuses. This perception is not limited to adults, as we often believe we can identify

**Figure 10.3:** Talk about Talent as – Something in You.
Source: Copyright © Sharna Wiblen. All rights reserved.

and recognise talent in children. This is evident in the distinctions between talented and non-talented children across various domains, including gifted and talented programs in schools, specialised sports, music and performing arts schools. These are the material outcomes of the belief that all humans possess some form of talent, with some being more talented than their peers. The perception of talent as an inherent trait is easier to distinguish during a human's formative years. It is common to hear the phrase "destined for greatness" used to describe exceptionally talented individuals, regardless of age.

Notions of "Being born with it" or "Having IT" are common in popular culture. Maybelline's "Maybe She's Born with It" campaign is a well-known example. Maybelline positioned its advertisements in the realm of talent being something innate within a person. The catchy tagline "Maybe She's Born with It" was ubiquitous in the 1990s, and the jingle is still memorable today.

An example of advertising copywriting in 1991 was:

Some faces look fine.
Others look (pause) flawless.
Porcelain-smooth.
Even without powder.
Is it in their genes?
Yeah right.
Finish Matte Makeup (the product name)

> Maybe she's born with it.
> Maybe it's Maybelline.

Maybelline played with the notion that some women are born beautiful; some women are genetically blessed. Born-beautiful women can look flawless without makeup, while others may need to use makeup to enhance their looks. Maybelline's makeup products were so good that they could help women achieve a flawless look like those born with "natural" beauty. The advertisement campaign implied that the difference between the two types of women was almost indistinguishable.

Maybelline replaced the "Maybe She's Born with It. Maybe it's Maybelline" in 2016 with a "Make it happen" tagline. The assertion that some humans are born beautiful remained despite the change. Print advertising text read:

> Some of the lucky ones were born with it.
> The rest of us . . . We make it happen.

Notably, the talent as something in you implies that we can control our talent. The ability to control our talent infers that humans can turn on and off their talent. Do you think you can turn on and off what you have inside you? Do you think you can turn on and off your talent? Maybe these embedded assumptions falter when we consider and acknowledge the complexity of "talent."

## Talent as Something We Discover

The belief that all humans possess talent is common among many people. It is thought that each of us has something special within us, waiting to be "discovered." Some individuals may uncover their talents at a young age. Others, however, don't always know what makes them special or unique. The challenge, therefore, is to find, uncover, hunt out, figure out and discover our respective talents over a period of time.

---

*Talent = something we discover over time*

---

### Discovering Talent: The Case of *My Little Pony*

Talent as being something that we can discover features in various social contexts and encounters, some of which may be unexpected. One story time undertaken with my daughter featured the book *My Little Pony: The Cutie Mark Crusaders*. The My Little Ponies – Apple Bloom, Sweetie Belle and Scootaloo – sought to acquire a "cutie mark." The task to acquire the cutie mark was gained "upon realising their unique talent." The journey of discovering their talent was taking too long. The ponies set a plan: to try other ponies' talents for themselves and see if they could find their talent. The planned journey navigated to the sweet shop, boutique, library and farm, whereby they each learn about their inability to bake muffins, become a fashion designer, help a friend with magic, picking apples (and yes, there are some gender issues embedded here, but we'll leave this topic for another day).

An inability to adopt others' talents was met with the following response: "Earning your cutie mark ain't about trying to be someone else. It's about finding who you are. It's about being yourself. By focusing on what you are good at, you'll have your cutie marks in no time!" Applejack continued, "In time, you'll discover your talents. I promise."

The story instils in young children, specifically girls, the idea that everyone has a talent that resides within them and that they can discover their unique abilities with time.

---

The notions of talent as something in you and talent as something we can discover are grounded in positivist perspectives of talent (remember the section highlighting how humans establish knowledge and truth). Positivist perspectives assume that individuals have inherent talents and encourage them to search for and discover their talents. According to this view, everyone has a talent, and it is only a matter of time before we find it. Discovering one's talent may take experimentation and time, but it is possible for everyone. Time is the primary variable affecting one's talent status. These perspectives promote the idea that we are each unique and possess something special within us that we need to uncover. In *My Little Pony*'s words, we should go out and find talent – "seek and you shall find" your talent.

### Talent as Something We Discover Over Time and Finding One's Mission and Purpose

The notion of talent as something we discover asserts humans are unique. Humans possess specific skills and capabilities that set us apart from one another. This uniqueness makes each of us special and gives us our mission and purpose. We can and should "follow our passion." While some individuals may discover their "calling" early on or from a young age, others may take more time to find their unique path. However, the message is clear: by discovering our passion, we can find our purpose in life and pursue it with determination and fulfilment.

Many self-development and career books focus on discovering one's mission and passion. This is also the case in Stephen R. Covey and Cynthia Covey Haller's *Live Life in Crescendo: Your Most Important Work is Always Ahead of You*. The book encourages readers to reflect on their passions and values and the importance of finding their mission and purpose, emphasising that lifelong pursuit evolves. Sample excerpts connecting mission, talent and time are:

> As we work to uncover and utilize our skills, beliefs, talents, passion, abilities, time, resources – all we are – we will ultimately discover our own unique mission. When we listen closely and follow our conscience more regularly, the ability to discern whom to help and what to do grows stronger. The answer will come.

> It's important to discover your purpose and mission in regard to your family, your occupation, your community and in whatever other roles you may play. Then you must live by that purpose.

> It is essential to discover our gifts and talents, develop and expand them, and then apply them so they can benefit others.
>
> I have always believed that we don't invent our missions, we detect them . . . we can also detect or discover what our own unique mission in life is meant to be.

It is understandable why humans talk about talent as something to be discovered, especially since we are often encouraged to find our unique mission and purpose. Discovering our mission and purpose is closely linked to discovering our talents. By discovering our talents, mission and purpose, we understand who we are and what we can contribute to the world.

## Talent as Something That You Have

Talent is often perceived as an individual's specific attribute or skill. This perspective sees talent as something that people either have or do not have and is associated with judgments and perceptions of individuals based on their possession of it. Humans judge humans according to their perceptions of whether that individual has "something." Humans are not necessarily born with the relevant "something." Humans can acquire certain types of talents. The talent as something you have perspective positions talent as acquirable attributes. While some talents may be innate, others are gained through practice and hard work. Cultivating talent is a process that takes time and effort. People can develop their talents by investing in certain behaviours and activities that help to enhance their skills, capabilities, experiences and qualifications. In some cases, individuals may even receive recognition for their talents, which can further motivate them to continue developing and improving their abilities.

*Talent = individuals that have something*

The good news is that humans can acquire different types of talent, regardless of whether they possess innate characteristics (talent as something in you) or successfully discover their abilities through exploration (talent as something you can discover).

### Talent as Something That You Have and Talent Acquisition

Talent as something you have dominates talent acquisition. The talent acquisition process assesses whether specific individuals have particular "somethings." When hiring employees, HR executives often evaluate whether candidates A, B, C, etc., possess the specific attributes identified during the job analysis process and stated in the position description. Job advertisements list the necessary qualifications and experience that successful candidates should have.

*Talent acquisition prioritises talent as something individuals do or do not have.*

A Lecturer/Professor, for example, requires (aka needs to have):
- A PhD in a relevant field
- Teaching experience
- Experience in curriculum development
- Experience in devising and executing research-based projects
- A record of research outputs
- Interpersonal and communication skills
- Digital literacy and technology systems skills
- A collegiate and collaborative spirit

Human Resource positions can require:
- Thorough knowledge and understanding of industrial relations and employee relations
- Ability to influence senior executives
- Exceptional written and verbal communication skills
- Understanding Profit and Loss and associated financial statements
- Bachelor's degree with a major in Human Resources
- Professional qualification
- Working with Children Check
- Experience in using HRIS, HR technology systems
- Experience in different practices – organisational development, talent acquisition, employee engagement, performance management, compensation and benefits, HR compliance

Some of these "somethings" are easier to evaluate than others. For instance, it is relatively straightforward to determine whether a human has specific degrees and qualifications. However, assessing communication and collaborative skills is more subjective. What criteria should we use to gauge whether a human possesses exceptional or thorough skills in these areas? How can we evaluate a human's talent for collegiality and collaboration?

Assessing humans according to this perspective often results in a binary outcome. Despite the complexity and subjectivity involved, hiring managers must often make a yes or no determination as to whether a candidate possesses the specific talent they seek. Hiring humans will usually decree: yes, Human A has the [insert relevant something] we want and/or need; no, Human A does not have the [insert relevant something] talent we want/need. A favourable determination increases the likelihood of a job offer.

## Talent as Something That You Have and Performance Management

Performance management also prioritises talent as something you have. Many leadership and capability frameworks serve as the foundation for performance management. These frameworks provide decision-makers with multiple evaluation points, including leadership, capability and competency. When evaluating an employee, decision-makers must subjectively determine if they possess the specific skill-based talent required for a particular task or role. Does Human A "have" the specific (skill-based) talent? The "haves" of performance management are usually pre-defined.

*Performance management encompasses judging whether an individual does or does not have something.*

## Talent as Something That You Have and Stereotypes

Stereotypes, generalisations and cliches often stem from the belief that talent is an attribute that individuals "have."

*Humans associate certain "haves" with different cultures, genders, ages, personalities and social groups.*

**Cultural associations.** Our minds often predict a person's value based on our ideas about what certain cultures or groups of humans can or cannot do. These perceptions of culturally based talents are reflected in some discussions. For instance, the idea of "talent" as an inherent trait one has or does not have can perpetuate stereotypes and generalisations, such as if all members of a particular culture possess specific talents or abilities.

The following statements reflect commonly held stereotypes about certain groups of people and their abilities:
- Africans are often perceived as having exceptional long-distance/marathon running skills.
- Asians are often thought to be proficient in mathematics-based skills.
- Indians are often believed to possess extensive information technology-based skills.
- Germans are often viewed as having a solid appreciation for rules and systems.
- Americans are often stereotyped as having a solid work ethic and a willingness to work long hours.

The following statements reflect negative stereotypes about certain groups of people:
- Germans are often perceived as lacking a sense of humour.

- Americans are sometimes stereotyped as overly obsessed with pursuing financial goals or outcomes.
- Australians are sometimes portrayed as lacking a strong work ethic.

People often associate certain groups of humans with specific categories of talent, consciously or unconsciously. Broader societal beliefs shape these associations and can influence decisions related to talent, as we tend to associate human qualities with geographic regions.

**Gender associations.** Gender is often associated with specific skills and capabilities, perpetuating stereotypes and cliches that permeate society and workplaces. Examples include:
- Men are often assumed to be born with innate leadership skills and capabilities.
- Women, on the other hand, may be perceived as lacking leadership skills and capabilities.
- Women are often thought to possess caring-based skills and capabilities, while men are assumed to have interests in science, technology, engineering and mathematics (STEM).
- Men are sometimes stereotyped as having rational decision-making skills and capabilities, while women are believed to have emotions-based decision-making skills and capabilities.
- Women may be labelled "bossy," while men are considered "assertive."

Gender-based stereotypes are inaccurate and limiting, with some individuals excluded from talent pools because of gender-based factors.

**Age associations.** Age-based stereotypes can also shape perceptions and attitudes towards individuals. Examples include:
- The saying "You can't teach an old dog new tricks" suggests that older individuals are resistant to change and unable to learn new skills.
- Older workers may be stereotyped as less proficient in technology than younger workers.

These stereotypes can be harmful and limit opportunities for older individuals who may be skilled, experienced and willing to learn. It's important to recognise that age is just a number, and individuals of any age can bring value and expertise to the workplace. Age-based stereotypes can perpetuate ageism, a form of discrimination that can prevent older workers from accessing employment opportunities, being treated fairly in the workplace, or being identified as "talent."

**Personality associations.** Stereotypes based on personality and social traits are prevalent in everyday conversations and can perpetuate bias and discrimination. Examples include:

- Introverts are often stereotyped as risk-averse and less likely to take chances, limiting opportunities to showcase their strengths.
- Extraverts may be assumed to be the best at socialising and interacting with others, but this overlooks the fact that individuals have unique social styles and preferences.
- Individuals who are labelled as "nerds" or "brainiacs" may be stereotyped as socially inept and wearing glasses, which can lead to unfair treatment and a lack of recognition for their talents and skills.
- People who are seen as "boring" may be thought to lack interpersonal warmth or have lower social skills, but this stereotype is often based on limited or biased perceptions.

---

In a 2022 scientific paper on perceptions of "Boring People," Wijnand van Tilburg, Eric Igou, and Mehr Panjwani examined the stereotypes and associations people hold about boring individuals in the United States and United Kingdom. The study found that boring people are generally considered dull, uninteresting and bad conversationalists. They are also associated with certain occupations, such as data analysts, accountants and taxation, and are believed to enjoy activities such as sleeping, participating in religious activities, watching TV, observing animals and engaging in mathematics and statistics.

The study also found that perceptions of boringness can impact interpersonal warmth and competence judgments, with boring people being perceived as less warm and competent. This has implications for talent decisions, as individuals who are perceived as boring may be less liked and we tend to avoid people we like less. Being perceived as boring is likely to have social implications. Being perceived as not having something – not having conversationalist skills or specific interests – can have consequences for talent decisions.

---

It's important to recognise that these stereotypes are often unfair and inaccurate. Individuals within these groups are diverse and may not conform to these narrow and limiting assumptions. Although these beliefs may be reinforced by cultural and societal factors (such as media representation), making talent decisions based on stereotypes are always irresponsible.

## Talent as Something That We Do

Remember our workplace walk where we imagined walking past specific individuals and reflecting on how these individuals made us feel?

Who elicited a cheer?
Who did we smile at superficially?
Who did we try to avoid?
Did you consider whether your reactions were based on what that individual has – their skills, capabilities, and attributes, or were they influenced by how that individual helped you?

Did you value them because of their Excel, PowerPoint, or Canva skills, or were you grateful because they were always "There when you needed them" and "Anticipated your needs?"

Ask yourself if you thought of an individual as talent because you admired how they performed certain tasks, or if you disliked how others went about their daily activities. Is talent a question of whether you like or dislike how an individual performs tasks, activities and/or jobs?

The reflective question above highlights that we often perceive talent as something an individual "does." We value how individuals act and behave.

---
*Talent = how individuals act and behave*

---

The perspective of talent that I have developed from my research, teaching and experiences in managing talent frames talent in a performative way. (Re)thinking talent decisions involves reflecting on what talent looks like in practice. From my perspective, "talent" is best framed as a verb rather than a noun. We judge individuals based on what they "say" and "do." Therefore, we are interested in talent-in-action.

---
*Talent is a verb; talent is a performative construct. We are interested in how individuals act and behave. We are interested in talent-in-action.*

---

(Re)Thinking talent decisions recognises that, rather than framing talent as a noun, where it is assumed to be embedded within all of us, it is more accurate to view talent as a verb, a doing word.

---

**Asking, "What do you value?"**

An exercise that asks executives to reflect on what they value and do not value in their colleagues elicits responses that frame talent as a verb. Responses concede that their perceptions note how an individual adds value to their lives. How an individual or group of individuals "do" "something" which is valuable.

These reflections include valuing individuals who can "anticipate their needs," "provide output of high quality," "follow instructions," "take feedback," "show up to meetings on time" and "show up to meetings prepared."

By connecting what they value to their thoughts about talent, executives understand how talent meanings influence their everyday interactions.

---

Talent as a verb and talent as something an individual does perspectives are useful because, within workplace contexts, talent is more about how individuals perform their tasks and activities in alignment with decision-makers' expectations.

Talent determinations are based on how well individuals can complete their jobs, which are aligned with the preferences and goals of the judgers. Talent, within workplace contexts, is more about what decision-makers think about how individuals "perform" their talent. Talent determinations ask individuals to conduct themselves and complete their tasks, activities and jobs in alignment with the judgers' desires. Talent, therefore, is a performative construct.

(Re)conceptualising talent as a verb is pivotal to our (re)thinking journey as we continue to unpack talent's complexity within our lived realities.

## Talent as Something That We See

Talented individuals exhibit certain actions and behaviours that distinguish them from their non-talented counterparts. However, talent decisions are based on a series of observations, which are particularly significant when we view talent as a verb – something we do. In this sense, we observe an individual's talent in action. Observations are salient when we think of talent as something that we do because we are watching – aka observing – an individual's talent-in-action. We may feel that we "See something in you" and "See you as a future X." Conversely, others may have their career prospects diminished if decision-makers don't perceive their potential or talent. If decision-makers "Don't see 'it' in them."

Observations are crucial when we think of talent as a verb because we watch individuals perform their talent. We may observe individuals who excel in their tasks, anticipate and meet the needs of others, or consistently produce high-quality work. Conversely, we may observe individuals who struggle to complete tasks, fail to meet expectations, or display negative attitudes. These observations inform judgments and influence decisions about who to promote, who to hire and who to invest in. As such, talent decisions can be based on observable actions and behaviours that indicate talent-in-action.

*Talent = a series of observations of talent-in-action*

My awareness of talent as something that we see arose from my empirical research (which includes non-participant observations) that found that many senior decision-makers assert they "know talent when they see it." A research paper titled *Do you see what I see? The role of technology in talent identification*, co-authored with Kristine Dery and David Grant, details these findings. We were interested in understanding how HR, line managers and senior executives (all key characters in our tale) framed technologies (primarily HRIS modules) value and use in talent identification. We found that some parts of our Professional Services Firm relied on technology as the key decision-maker (more on this later). We also found a completely different approach to talent identification based on subjective observations and "seeing" talent. Some decision-makers relied solely on observations as the sole basis for talent evaluations. Some individuals were deemed "talent" based on what the specific decision-maker saw. Conversely, some individuals were not "talent" because of what they did not "see." Kristine, David and I noted,

> Many interviewees commented that they were able to "see" talent. That is, business unit managers, in combination with their HR managers, could accurately evaluate whether someone was deemed as talent by observing their activities and behaviours.

Illustrations of this perspective are represented by,
- "Partners should be able to evaluate talent through observation."
- "People within the business should be open to seeing talented people."
- " . . . and by the end of today you will be able to see the top 10% stella talent."

Our scientific paper illustrated that a key character – the CEO – advocated for talent as something that we see, with a HR character declaring, "[The CEO] has a view that any partner should be able to identify talent like that [and they clicked their fingers]. As in they can just see it. They just know it]." Many others believed that "seeing" talent was fundamental to talent evaluations.

Others used their own experiences as the basis of talent determinations. A HR executive commented that line managers

> that have risen to the top have tended to have an intrinsic insight into what it takes to get there so they are able to see these traits or behaviours or abilities in others. So, they tend to overlay their own experience when they are actually identifying who we think are in the upper echelons of potential.

Framing talent as something we can see reinforces the subjective nature of talent decisions. Talent evaluations are based on subjective interpretations of observable actions, making judgers both observers and evaluators. Judgers form differing perspectives on an individual's value and impact by observing talent-in-action.

---

*Talent evaluations are based on subjective perceptions of an individual's talent-in-action.*

---

Talent is inherently dynamic, and our subjective understandings of what talent is and is not change over time. Our subjective interpretations of what talent "looks like" also change. An individual can attain talent status, but they can also lose it. Talent, seen as something that we see, gives rise to ever-changing talent status because, in reality, observation-based views can become a case of "Now you see it, now you don't."

---

**Is "I see me in you" a compliment?**
How often do you and your peers discuss talent in terms of being able to see it? Phrases like "I see myself in you" and "You remind me of me" are often used in conversations around talent. I have received such comments, including one from a senior colleague to whom I directly reported, who once said, "I see a younger version of me in you." While initially surprised by the comment, my background as a social scientist led me to immediately question what they saw in me and what I was doing that reminded them of themselves.

However, I was unsure whether to take this comment as a compliment or not. I had no idea if they saw positive qualities in me or not. To this day, I still have no informed basis for understanding what they saw in me and whether they still see talent in me.

## Talent as Something That We See and Sports

Responses to "What does talent mean to you?" frequently elicit sport-based references. Sport is a common factor that drives talent meanings and explains why they have that view.

I understand why. It is common for society to classify individuals into performance categories based on their talents or abilities in various domains. The tradition of segmenting individuals into performance categories in both school and sports remains prevalent today, and references to "talent" are often made during childhood concerning these areas. I was exposed to gifted and talented programs in my early years, and these memories and experiences have shaped how I view and approach talent (sports and academics are part of my "why" of talent. Are they part of yours?).

Another "why" is that humans of all ages enjoy participating in or watching organised sports. Many spend hours or even entire days engaging in or watching sports activities. For example, parents often watch their children participate in various individual and team sports. Similarly, many spend leisure time watching professional athletes perform on the court, field, stadium, track, pool, rink, or course. Watching sports events can be an engaging and exciting way to pass the time, unite people and establish social connections. It can also be a source of emotional connection, as fans become invested in their favourite teams or athletes.

Sports also allow learning about the game, its rules, and its strategies. They are an example of strategy in action with the desired outcome known to all parties – to win. While watching, spectators regularly evaluate the "talent" and judge how a specific individual or team performed their "talents" in a particular instance or throughout the game. Spectators may share their talent judgments directly by cheering or yelling, or commenting on the decisions of sporting humans, officials, and coaches. In doing so, humans use their observation skills and (perceived) expertise to judge others' talent and whether what they saw aligned with their (internal) perceptions. This evaluation of talent adds another layer of enjoyment and engagement to the sporting experience, as fans can feel a sense of satisfaction or disappointment based on how they judge the performance of their favourite teams or athletes.

The structure of sports reinforces the importance of seeing talent-in-action. An entire industry is about "seeing" sporting talent. As Wikipedia describes, Sports scouts are "experienced talent evaluators who travel extensively to watch athletes play their chosen sports and determine whether their set of skills and talent represent what is needed by the scout's organisation." These scouts are a crucial part of the sports ecosystem, as they help teams identify and acquire the best talent available to improve their chances of winning.

*Moneyball* is perhaps one of the most well-known and accessible examples of how talent is framed as something that can be observed and evaluated. The book and subsequent film adaptation focused on using statistical analysis to identify undervalued players in baseball, challenging traditional scouting methods that relied on subjective judgments and perceptions of talent. Next, we will examine *Moneyball* as a case study to further explore the concept of talent and how it relates to seeing talent-in-action.

**Moneyball: an Example Questioning Humans' Ability to See Talent-In-Action**

Many of you may be familiar with sports scouting in American baseball through the story of *Moneyball* by Michael Lewis, which has become a cultural reference for talent identification through observation. The book and subsequent 2011 movie featuring Brad Pitt and Jonah Hill tell the story of Billy Beane and the Oakland Athletics' success in creating a winning baseball team comprised of undervalued players. Beane questioned traditional talent-based assumptions and baseball traditions and adopted a statistics-driven approach to identify undervalued players ignored by other teams.

Michael Lewis begins his book with the following preface, which captures the essence of talent identification through observation:

> I wrote this book because I fell in love with a story. The story concerned a small group of undervalued professional baseball players and executives, many of whom had been rejected as unfit for the big leagues, who had turned themselves into one of the most successful franchises in Major League Baseball.

I enjoy discussing and teaching about *Moneyball* because it offers insight into how humans perceive and identify talent. Specifically, the film highlights how human talent scouts rely on their ability to see, watch and observe talent-in-action to judge an individual's potential to make it to the Major League. This emphasis on observing and judging talent based on physical abilities such as running, throwing, fielding, hitting and hitting with power is exemplified by talent scouts who travel to watch players train and play baseball and put them "through their paces." Talent scouts serve as a compelling example of the importance of defining talent based on what we can see rather than what we cannot see.

According to *Moneyball*, talent scouts often believe if they "see" talent in a player then that player is talented. They adhere to the notion that "If you see it once, it's there" and that only they know the true meaning of what they see. The "discovery" of a talented player is considered a transformative moment for the scout who found them. However, talent status can also be influenced by the perceptions of others. The book shares a story of a player who was asked to change positions from catcher to first baseman because a coach felt that "you could see he shouldn't be out there." This illustrates the extent to which individual scouts and broader social and cultural factors influence talent perception.

*Moneyball* is, from my perspective, a story about talent identification. It is a story that pits humans – who are talent scouts – against Bill James' mathematical approach. *Moneyball* addresses a pertinent question – who is better at identifying talent? Is it the human talent scout or is it mathematics and statistics?

**Evaluating talent-in-action and *Moneyball*'s talent scouts**. *Moneyball* includes many examples of the connection between observing talent-in-action and talent scouts' careers. I highlight some here:
- The power of imaginations: talent scouts (generally older men) like to identify players they can "dream on" and imagine what kind of pro ballplayer a young man might become.
- Focused on potential: scouts are interested in identifying players with untapped potential that can be later "brought out of them."
- Talent scouts are talent bouncers. Although invisible to ordinary fans, talent scouts are the heart of the game. They decide who gets to play and how baseball is played.
- Role of appearances. Some scouts believe they can tell a young man's future in professional baseball by the structure of his face, and they look for players with a "good face." They may also judge whether someone "looked" like a big-league player and make career predictions based on appearances.
- Past player experiences. If talent scouts are also former players, they may bring their playing experiences, feelings, hunches and instincts to their scouting work.
- Entrenched perceptions. Talent scouts may hold on to their beliefs even when evidence contradicts them. For example, a scout may ask for a re-do of a foot speed test if he doesn't believe the result.

Reflecting on *Moneyball* can help us recognise that our perceptions of gender, race, age and other factors influence whether we believe we "see" talent in action. Our judgments are often influenced by what we think we "should see."

**Evaluating Talent-in-action via a mathematic system**. *Moneyball* presents an alternative approach to talent evaluation that minimises the emphasis on talent scouts. Instead, the book focuses on Billy Beane and Paul DePodesta's pursuit of sabermetrics, systems and math-based talent evaluation approaches.

The system-based approach was inspired by the work of Sandy Alderson and Bill James, who challenged the traditional evaluative approach and the entrenched belief that a player's performance could be judged simply by watching it. James believed that the naked eye was an inadequate tool for learning what you need to know about baseball players and games. He argued that one could not tell the difference between hitters just by watching and that the differences are not visible to the naked eye:

> Think about it. One absolutely cannot tell, by watching, the difference between a .300 hitter and a .275 hitter . . . It might be that a reporter, seeing every game that the team plays, could sense a difference over the course of a year if no records were kept, but I doubt it . . . The difference between a good hitter and an average hitter is simply not visible – it is a matter of record . . . we can't tell accurately from watching . . .

Instead, James proposed that counting things like on base and slugging percentages could provide a more accurate assessment of a player's value. A system-based approach considered wins a process-based outcome. In this approach, "the system was the star" and on-base percentage became the new talent metric. This approach was adopted by all but one Major League team – the Oakland Athletics. Billy Beane was introduced to the ideas of Bill James via Eric Walker, who advocated for an "objective view" of baseball and offered an alternative to the entrenched approach founded almost exclusively on "subjective opinions." They sought to expose the illusions of the insiders.

Billy Beane says, "We're blending what we see, but we aren't allowing ourselves to be victimized by what we see." This quote illustrates the importance of stepping back from preconceptions and biases to objectively see the data.

*Moneyball* illustrates how we approach observing talent-in-action:

- Talent, numbers and sports are interlinked: highlights the interconnectedness of talent, numbers and sports. Numbers are critical in how we watch sporting events and evaluate performance. Sports analytics involve tracking data such as balls, strikes and runs, which can offer valuable insights that would otherwise remain hidden.
- Identify the desired outcomes: highlights the importance of identifying desired outcomes because observing and measuring talent-in-action is associated with "outcomes." For example, the main factor influencing game outcomes in baseball was "getting people out."
- Identify which factors/variables influence outcomes: Paul DePodesta studied why teams win and found that two statistics disproportionately influenced success: on-base and slugging percentages. The on-base percentage was three times as important as the slugging percentage, making it a leading indicator of success.
- Performance and outcomes matter: emphasis should be on an individual's performance and outcomes rather than their appearance or subjective opinions.
- All statistics value past performance: no matter how accurate the calculations and the correlations are, the statistical outcomes rely on past performance. Statistics are an "uncertain guide to future performance." Despite this limitation, the book believed that the number-based approach, while imperfect, was better than rendering decisions through gut feel.
- Time of evaluations (may) influence talent determinations: The timing of talent evaluations can also affect determinations. Billy Beane did not watch games live, stating, "All they provide me with is subjective emotions . . . and that can be counterproductive." Instead, he framed baseball as a social science, with the game following odds, laws of probability and predictable patterns. While all players are unique, baseball players follow patterns etched in historical records. Therefore,

"watching" games was not always necessary. Despite this objective approach, Billy Beane attempted to influence player behaviour, with subtle direction from viewing game footage.[19]

Whether using talent scouts or numbers, the perception of talent in sports relies on observing talent-in-action, which involves identifying and assessing how humans "perform." The ability to perform one's talent, during competition and training, influences sporting careers.

## Talent as Something That We See and Stereotypes

Talent decisions are never perception-free. When we observe talent-in-action, we tend to evaluate it based on what we expect to see, which differs between you and me. In terms of what we see, our perceptions of talent are often influenced by stereotypes and biases, which can limit our ability to recognise one's value. Our (re)thinking tale acknowledges the relationship between talent as something we see and stereotypes.

> *Talent decisions are influenced by what we expect to see.*

The influence of stereotypes on perceptions of talent is a key takeaway from *Moneyball*. The book tells how Billy Beane and Paul DePodesta challenged long-held perceptions about what makes a talented baseball player, many of which relied on stereotypes and biases.

Paul DePodesta was particularly aware of the limitations of relying on traditional metrics and stereotypes when evaluating talent. He recognised that players who didn't fit the traditional ideals of what a talented baseball player should look like could still have valuable skills and abilities that were being overlooked.

Rather than using the common language of calling such players "defective," DePodesta referred to them as having "warts." He saw these "warts" as non-outcome-based factors and variables that were often overlooked by talent scouts, such as a person's age, physical appearance, or previous position on the field.

Their ability to perform despite their "warts" set these players apart for DePodesta. He stated, "What gets me really excited about a guy is when he has warts, and everyone knows he has warts, and the warts just don't matter."

By placing less emphasis on traditional metrics and more on the ability of players to perform despite their perceived limitations, Beane and DePodesta were able to

---

19 Note the perceived differences between watching the game live and viewing the game after the outcome and the belief that post-game observations were less emotive with evidence that Billy Beane was/could be very emotional when watching live games.

identify undervalued players who had the potential to be top performers. The "system" placed less emphasis on non-outcome-based factors and variables, including those embedded in the decision frameworks of talent scouts.

The movie portrayed this point in one scene where Paul DePodesta (played by Jonah Hill) speaks about how numbers and metrics help overcome appearance perceptions and embedded stereotypes:

> It's about getting things down to one number using stats the way we read them, we'll find value in players that nobody else can see. People are overlooked for a variety of biased reasons and perceived flaws. Age. Appearance. Personality. Bill James (?) and mathematics cuts straight through that . . . I believe that there is a championship team of 25 people that we can afford because everyone else in baseball undervalues them. Like, an island of misfit toys . . . Chad Bradford . . . he is one the most undervalued players in baseball. His defect is that he throws funny. Nobody in the big leagues cares about him because he looks funny. He could not only be one of the most effective pitchers in our team, but one of the most effective relief pitchers in all of baseball.

*Moneyball* also sheds light on how age, body associations and perceptions of gender also played a role in talent evaluations. Scouts assess whether players were "in their prime" or too old, whether they had "juice" in their body or the potential to hurt others with their throws or pitches and whether they "swung like a man."

Ideal throwing and pitching techniques are regularly associated with gender-based stereotypes. How often have you heard an individual's sporting talent devalued or shamed because they "throw like a girl?"

Let's shift our focus from baseball to basketball. You might automatically think of a tall person if you describe a basketball player. Height is a key characteristic of a basketball player, and many assume that talented basketball players are tall.

The connection between basketball and perceptions of the need to be tall exemplifies how we establish and reinforce talent-based stereotypes in sports. It's common for people to see a tall person and automatically assume that "they'd be great at basketball." However, this stereotype can be limiting, as it overlooks individuals who might not fit the traditional mould of what a talented basketball player should look like.

The complex relationship between talent status and stereotypes in sports is an important topic that deserves further discussion. It's important to acknowledge that our perceptions about what we expect to see in talent can influence talent determinations and individual careers. It is essential to realise that stereotype-based expectations are outside an individual's control.

## Talent as a Means For Strategy Execution

(Re)thinking talent decisions involves appreciating that all talent decisions are associated with strategy execution. Strategies come to life via the actions and inactions of The Workforce. I frequently say – "Talent management starts with strategy, strategy,

strategy." We pursue and realise organisational, talent management and digitalisation strategies via talent decisions.

It should come as no surprise that talent, when considered in the context of The Workforce, is a means for strategy execution.

---

*Talent = (specific humans) involved in, and required for, strategy execution.*

---

Others have also recognised the interrelationship between strategy and talent. For example, Lucien Alziari notes that talent categorisations and strategy are closely linked. Alziari argues that "Strategies define capabilities and capabilities define talent . . . Business strategy defines the capabilities needed to win. Those capabilities drive the definition of talent and the decisions about how it is deployed organisationally." In other words, talent decisions need to be aligned with an organisation's strategy and the capabilities required to achieve strategic objectives.

It is essential to align our understanding of talent with the strategic ambitions and goals of the organisation. Business strategies define the capabilities required to achieve success, and those capabilities drive the definition of talent and its deployment within the organisation. To (re)think talent decisions, we need to consider how talent aligns with our current and future strategic plans. Which talent categories are required to execute our current strategy and which ones do we need for future strategies? Where are our talent gaps, strengths and weaknesses?

Talent management is a means to execute strategy through The Workforce, and understanding the different talent categories associated with work is crucial. By acknowledging the interdependence of talent, talent management and strategy, we can begin to ask more focused questions about talent within the context of different strategies. Our fundamental question should be: talent for what?

The following sections present three other talent categories: talent as a time-based concept, talent as a relational concept and talent as humans you do not want to lose.

## Talent as a Time-Based Concept

Talent as a time-based concept explicitly recognises the dynamic nature of talent, where the value of an individual's talent can change over time. This concept differentiates talent for performance that is valued today versus talent that is valuable for future days. In other words, the value of an individual's talent is not static and can vary based on the time horizon. We enquire about talent for what? What day? Today? Tomorrow?

## Talent as Something We Currently Value

Effective strategy execution today requires specific talent-based somethings essential for organisations to achieve their desired outcomes. These talent-based somethings are valued for their ability to contribute to results in the present moment. Certain "somethings" attain talent status because they are valuable today – at this moment, right here, right now.

(Re)thinking talent decisions involves recognizing that talent and "performance" are twins. Discussions about performance should focus on talent for the now – the current day. We value certain talent-based somethings, whether they are individuals, jobs, tasks, or activities, because they assist with performance. Talent as performance means that talent is being executed effectively via actions. Individuals know their talents and perform them professionally, effectively and positively.

Talent as something we currently value can be synonymous with talent as performance we value today.

---

*Talent = performance we value in the current jobs, tasks, activities and strategic activities.*

---

Talent as current performance features in most, if not all, work-based contexts. Evidence shows that the talent as performance we currently value is the foundation of many talent management strategies. Most conversations assume that talent and performance go together.

Let me illustrate the pervasive nature of the automatic connections between talk about talent and references to performance. Asking an individual, "What does talent mean to you?" regularly elicits references to "performance."

Reflect on your Y.O.U. (Your Own Understanding). Did you reference performance or (high) performers in your talent meaning?

The strong connection between talent and performance is understandable. After all, talent management is fundamentally concerned with The Workforce's performance. It deals with the where, when and how of individual and team performance. Talent management involves scientifically analysing where, when, how and why specific pre-defined performance measures are achieved. It also examines where, when, how and why specific performance measures remained unrealised. Moreover, talent management involves judging how individuals perform in relation to various criteria. It is, therefore, not surprising that talent and performance are considered inseparable.

Talent as performance we currently value dominates scientific conversations. Many academic publications refer to "performance" when defining talent and/or talent management. Examples include (underlined emphasis added):

- [Talent management] Activities and processes that involve the systematic identification of key positions which differentially contribute to the organisation's sustainable competitive advantage, the development of a talent pool of high potential and high performing incumbents to fill these roles, and the development of a differentiated human resource architecture to facilitate the filling of these positions with competent incumbents and to ensure their continued commitment to the organisation – David Collings and Kamel Mellahi
- Talent management typically focuses on a specified pool of employees who rank at the top in terms of capability and performance – Kristiina Mäkelä, Ingmar Björkman and Mats Ehrnrooth
- Talent management typically involves the identification, development, appraisal, deployment and retention of high performing employees. It is a distinct business activity because it calls for greater focus on employees and positions that have the greatest differential impact on business strategy – Anthony McDonnell
- TM [talent management] is aimed at the systematic attraction, identification, development, engagement/retention and deployment of high potential and high performing employees, to fill in key positions which have significant influence on organisation's sustainable competitive advantage – Eva Gallardo-Gallardo and Marian Thunnissen
- Talent refers to systematically developed innate abilities of individuals that are deployed in activities they like, find important and in which they want to invest energy. It enables individuals to perform excellently in one or more domains of human functioning, operationalised as performing better than other individuals of the same age of experience, or as performing consistently at their personal best – Sanne Nijs, Eva Gallardo-Gallardo, Nicky Dries and Luc Sels
- [Talent] refers to a select group of employees, those that rank at the top in terms of capability and performance – rather than the entire workforce – Günter Stahl, Ingmar Björkman, Elaine Farndale, Shad Morris, Jaap Paauwe, Philip Stiles, Jonathan Trevor and Patrick Wright

The above definitions also highlight the connection between talent categories and management activities. Many academics suggest that identifying and developing (high) performers should be a priority in talent management. They argue that (high) performers are the key focus of talent management policies and practices.

Pausing and reflecting on the connections between talent categories and decisions allows us to consider how language can influence talent decisions. We need to focus on outcomes since talent and performance are so closely connected. Talent as performance raises further questions about what we aim for with that performance. What outcome are we trying to achieve? What aspect of strategy execution are we targeting with this performance?

When (re)thinking talent decisions, we must consider the measure of performance that we value. Do we value individuals who perform their talent

– Adequately?
– Consistently?
– Above expectations?
– At a higher level than their peers?
– At a higher level than their predecessors?
– At a higher level than the evaluator when they were at that level/position?
– At a higher level than set goals/targets/outputs?

Despite unanimously agreeing that talent and performance are connected, we must move beyond abstract or vague discussions about performance. Predefining essential performance parameters underpins many aspects of talent management, including performance management and talent identification. Conversations about talent as performance must include questions about performance for what purpose or goal.

## Talent as (Hypothetical) Value for a Future Day

Many talent conversations focus on categorising talent as a time-based concept when discussing strategies for the future. There is also the idea that we value talent for a future day. Framing talent in terms of "potential" focuses on perceptions of value at a later date. Talking about talent in terms of potential implies that we are concerned with talent for a future day.

Talent with potential means that someone believes that a specific individual has talent inside them that they have not yet realised or applied. Evaluating questions focus on whether the individual has the potential to become valuable in the future. A key evaluating question is – Does Human A have talent inside them that they are yet to realise and/or apply? Discussions about what might happen in the future are the foundation for this talent category. Notably, this talent category refers almost always to an individual – someone who is talented because their value will increase over time.

*Talent = someone who will increase in value.*

Reflecting on the concept of potential sparks our imagination because it is inherently future-oriented. We imagine that high-potential individuals can become something more valuable in the future, with our creativity being the only limit to our perceptions of what that could be. The sky's the limit.

References to "rising stars" and "future leaders" fits within this talent category. As are statements about an individual's potential to "climb to the top" or perceptions about whether a specific individual has a "bright future." Regardless of the language used, framing talent in terms of potential is always based on subjective perceptions.

Defining the characteristics required may be challenging. It can be difficult to pinpoint the "X factor" or consistently measure potential to determine whether an individual "Has what it takes." Conversations about potential often involve phrases such as "They have it in them" or "I can see something in them." In contrast, others may fail to achieve potential status because the evaluator "doesn't see them doing X in the future" or "They don't have it in them."

The talent as – (hypothetical) value for a future day – is fraught from the start. I intentionally frame talent as potential in terms of "hypothetical" value because talking about an individual's potential brings us into the realm of possibility and purely hypothetical outcomes.

Potential is considered hypothetical because it is impossible to predict with certainty whether particular talent decisions will ultimately prove successful in the future. Evaluating the value of talent is theoretical and speculative, as it is based on assumptions and projections. Talent decisions based on potential exist in the realm of speculation and are often subject to uncertainty. Some evaluators may use their assumptions as the starting point for a series of talent decisions and actions, which can also introduce additional hypothetical elements into the decision-making process.

*Talent as a hypothetical value in the future involves imagining what is possible. Talent decisions focusing on potential are always speculative.*

I purposely chose "hypothetical" instead of "guessing" because the latter can often carry a negative connotation. People may be more likely to defend their perceptions and decisions if they are described as mere "guesses." I have tested the influence of different terms on individuals' reactions and found that "guessing" can elicit stronger negative perceptions than "hypothetical." However, it is worth noting that "potential" and "guessing" could be synonymous. The distinction is that "guessing" may be perceived as more opinion-based and less scientific than "hypothesising."[20]

Let us acknowledge the uncomfortable truth about potential: the realm of possibility is inherently uncertain. Outcomes are never guaranteed when investing in po-

---

20 I've also connected potential and gambling. Proposing a relationship between talent decisions based on potential and gambling makes executives even more uncomfortable.

tential. While we may make cause-and-effect inferences, confirming or refuting them scientifically can be difficult. Establishing causal relationships between talent investments and outcomes is complex, as various factors influence talent decisions. This complexity arises from the interplay between technology, subjectivity and other factors. Recognising this complexity is critical to making responsible talent decisions that are deliberate, intentional and informed. Doing so can mitigate the inherent uncertainty associated with investing in potential and increase the likelihood of positive outcomes. Recognising the complexity is core to responsible talent decisions, whereby our decisions are deliberate, intentional and informed.

## Talent as a Relative Concept

The concept of talent as a relative notion recognises that comparisons, which serve as the basis for talent decisions, involve relationship comparison points. This means that talent is relative and involves comparisons between individuals or groups. Decision-makers prioritise certain behaviours and actions when making talent decisions. For instance, they may ask questions like: Is there a positive relationship between behaviour A and outcome X? Are outcomes X and Y connected, and if so, how strong is the connection?

*Talent = a series of relations between comparison points.*
*(Interrelations, correlations, equivalency, connections, sameness, linkages, bonds, conformity, and comparability)*

The significance of relationships lies at the core of talent management, evident from the numerous discussions on talent as a relative concept. The following sections present some examples of this.[21]

### Talent as a Relative Concept and Talent Management

Let's revisit the fundamental differences between human resource management and talent management. Human resource management, I propose, is about doing the same thing to everyone. Talent management, however, is about doing something to someone. Emphasising judgments, specifically judgments of value, helps us differentiate between human resource management and talent management. Talent management involves comparing the value of individuals against specific criteria and other individuals. Talent management, therefore, encompasses relative judgments.

*Talent management relies on relative judgments.*

### Talent as A Relative Concept and Workforce Differentiation

Scientists agree that workforce differentiation is at the heart of talent management. Workforce differentiation emphasises talent as a relative concept. While all humans in The Workforce are valuable (otherwise, why hire them?), workforce differentiation asks, "Who is of greater value?" Specific individuals who are differentially valuable

---

[21] Some of the discussions in this section are repetitive because of the inability to draw hard boundaries between the various ways that we frame talent as a relative concept.

are allocated talent status. In the form of particular humans, "talent" becomes the beneficiary of talent management policies, activities and investments.

## Talent as A Relative Concept and Talent Identification

Decision-makers establish differences within The Workforce via talent identification because talent identification focuses on establishing "who" becomes the recipient of "talent management." The connection between talent management, talent and relative notions of value features in my talent identification definition. Talent identification is:

> The process of workforce differentiation is a judgment-orientated activity whereby we make judgments to determine which individuals are of value, or greater value.

Talent identification involves a process whereby relevant decision-makers, consciously or unconsciously, make comparative judgments. Talent identification also establishes a relationship between different humans relative to "something" (we reflect on the other "somethings" in the next section). The outcomes of this comparative process are illustrated in talent rankings (usually highest to lowest performers) and talent lists (e.g., top 5%, or top twenty individuals according to X or overall). Both talent rankings and talent lists communicate an individual's importance – aka value – relative to someone or something.

---

*Talent as a relative concept comes to life via talent rankings and lists.*

---

Brené Brown highlights the inherent tension in comparison discussions, as they ask individuals to fit in and stand out simultaneously. On the one hand, there is pressure to conform and be like everyone else, while on the other hand, there is an expectation to perform above their peers. This tension resonates with talent decisions that rely on relative judgments, which evaluate how individuals compare against pre-defined criteria (fitting in) and whether they outperform their peers (standing out). Comparison says, "Be like everyone else, but better." For individuals seeking talent status, this tension creates inherent challenges. They must decide whether to stand out from the crowd, excel at the fringes and edges, or shrink from the limelight. While talent management can offer many benefits, it can also create pressure to outperform one's peers constantly. Everyday challenges include whether to "stand out from the crowd," "excel at the fringes and edges," or "shrink from the limelight."[22]

---

[22] Standing out from the crowd is considered a social taboo in Australia. Gaining talent status by standing out is associated with the Tall Poppy syndrome – the critique of an individual's successes and achievements.

**Talent as A Relative Concept and Talent Pools**

Talent as a relative concept is closely tied to the creation and development of talent pools. By emphasising workforce differentiation, talent management assumes that grouping specific individuals into talent pools benefits the execution of organisational strategies. This culminates in a particular group of individuals achieving talent status and gaining admission to a talent pool. Talent pools may be broad or focused on high performers, high potentials, future leaders, rising stars, etc. Establishing talent pools also encourages transparent conversations about talent decisions and strategic outcomes, which can shed light on the strengths and limitations of the current talent supply chain.

**Talent as A Relative Concept and Talent Development**

Individuals included in the talent pool/s are considered worthy of talent development. Talent development is a strategic practice that focuses on investing in activities that significantly impact the execution of organisational strategies. Organisations can undertake workforce differentiation by investing in talent development, with specific individuals gaining more development opportunities and resources than their non-talented peers due to their talent status.

**Talent as A Relative Concept and Talent Retention**

Bringing up talent retention again emphasises the link between talent as a relative concept and talent decisions. Many decision-makers have a list of individuals they consider crucial to retain – individuals they want to "keep." Discussing talent retention from this perspective suggests that some individuals are more valuable to the organisation than others. Maintaining their employment, therefore, becomes a priority.

Our attention now turns to questions about the relationship between relative judgments and outcomes. The key question becomes: talent relative to what?

# Talent as Relative to Performance

A focus on relations stems from the desire to establish (and prove) relationships between humans and performance outcomes. Talent management advocates are, as stated above, interested in an individual's performance. That is, decision-makers are interested in understanding human-to-human relationships. Human-to-human relationships include how individuals perform according to pre-defined outcomes, perform according to explicit and implicit expectations, or perform according to their peers (more on performing relative to peers later).

## Talent as Relative to Goals and Objectives

Decision-makers regularly evaluate how individuals perform regarding set goals and objectives. Talent determinations occurring within the context of talent as relative to goals and objectives enquire whether individuals are below, meeting and or exceeding pre-defined goals and objectives. We can frame talent as relative to goals and objectives.

*Talent = performance of talent compared to set goals and objectives.*

Certain occupations, such as sales-based roles, significantly emphasise talent in relation to achieving specific goals and objectives. In sales-based positions, individuals are evaluated based on their ability to meet predefined targets, including total or unit sales, sales revenue, profit margin and commissions. The fluid nature of sales-based roles means that individuals are frequently evaluated, with some being assessed daily, weekly, or monthly. Therefore, talent decisions in sales-based occupations are heavily influenced by performance, with individuals' talent status being subject to change based on their recent performance. The axiom "You are only as good as your last sale" exemplifies the influence of recency bias on talent decisions in sales-based roles.

Have you considered how talent is evaluated in your organisation, occupation, or industry? Are relative judgments used to determine who is deemed more valuable? Are individuals assessed based on their performance according to specific goals, objectives, or targets?

## Talent as Relative to Peers

Defining who has talent is also influenced by how specific individuals perform compared to their peers. In this way, talent involves comparative judgments, with talent status influenced by the individuals we are compared to. Therefore, talent is a relative concept because talent decisions involve judging two specific individuals against each other. Peers are the comparison points.

*Talent = performance of talent compared to another someone or other someone's.*

Sanne Nijs, Eva Gallardo-Gallardo, Nicky Dries and Luc Sels' talent definition effectively captures the notion that talent decisions focus on relative performance:

> Talent refers to systematically developed innate abilities of individuals that are deployed in activities they like, find important, and in which they want to invest energy. It enables individuals to perform excellently in one or more domains of human functioning, operationalised as <u>performing better than other individuals of the same age or experience</u> or as performing consistently at their personal best.

The above talent definition declares that talent decisions can focus on an individual relative to other individuals of the same age and the same experience levels (known as an experienced proxy).

Previous and current peers also influence an individual's talent status:
- Previous peers – because you judge my value according to how you think I perform my talent relative to individuals who have held the same or similar position.
- Current peers – because you judge my value according to how you think I perform my talent relative to others in my team, function, or location.

Comparing humans within the context of other humans becomes the focus of this talent category regardless of whether the relative judgments relate to age-based, experience-based, previous, or current peers.

An outcome of viewing talent as relative to peers is decision-makers expressing that Human A is of greater value when compared to Human B.

**Talent as Relative to Peers and the Need for a Proxy**

When (re)thinking talent decisions, it is essential to consider the concept of a proxy. This is because comparing an individual's talent relative to their peers requires a minimum of two individuals: the individual to be judged and the individual to be judged against, who is the proxy. The proxy is a benchmark against which evaluation occurs.

Researchers Jerry Suls, René Martin and Ladd Wheeler flag the role of proxy performers in comparative judgments. While their work relates to social comparisons, their insights help us reflect on how we undertake comparisons:

> Social comparison consists of comparing oneself with others in order to evaluate or to enhance some aspects of the self. Evaluation of ability is concerned with the question "can I do X?" and relies on the <u>existence of a proxy performer [an experienced other].</u> A proxy's relative standing on attributes vis-à-vis the comparer and whether the proxy exerted maximum effort [rather than ambiguous or unknown effort] on a preliminary task are variables influencing [their] informational utility . . . Important variables that affect an individual's use of social comparison to evaluate [their] opinions are the other person's expertise, similarity with the individual, and previous agreement with the individual.

The challenge, however, is ensuring that comparisons occur between similar attributes. Undertaking comparisons between dissimilar others is potentially troublesome.

We must acknowledge another limitation of thinking about talent regarding how individuals perform relative to their peers. Their behaviours and actions do not solely determine an individual's talent, performance and potential. Instead, the behaviours and actions of those around them influence their talent status. Thus, talent as relative to peers acknowledges that an individual's peers influence talent decisions. The degree to which an individual's peers effectively perform their talent can affect whether decision-makers consider my talent or identify me as talent.

---

*Caution, caution: my talent status may be influenced by those around me.*

---

**The Influence of a High-Performing Proxy: The Case of Shane Warne and Stuart McGill**
An example of the potential impact of peers on talent status relates to the experiences of two cricket players: Shane Warne and Stuart McGill. While those unfamiliar with cricket may have heard of Shane Warne, it is less likely that you will have heard of or know of Stuart McGill (stay with me even if you do not know or like cricket because the example makes an essential point about talent decisions).

Let's start with Shane Warne. Shane Warne was an Australian right-arm leg spin bowler who reached the pinnacle of cricket.[23] Shane enjoyed a fruitful career involving 145 Test matches (played over five days) and 194 One Day Internationals (one hundred overs in one day) for Australia, and a stint in the Indian Premier League. Shane took over one thousand wickets over both forms of the game. Shane was one of the "best" bowlers relative to other spin bowlers and other bowlers compared to country-specific and global counterparts.

Stuart McGill is also a talented leg spin bowler. Stuart's career, however, transpired very differently. Stuart played for Australia in (only) forty-four test matches and three One Day Internationals.

The lower representative numbers are because of two factors. The first factor is associated with the traditional composition of a cricket team. While there are eleven players in total, only one of these places is (generally) for a "spin bowler," resulting in all Australian spin bowlers competing for one position.

The second factor relates to the quality of one's peers. Stuart McGill is considered a talented spin bowler. However, Stuart was considered less talented than his peer – Shane Warne. Stuart usually only played when there was room for two spin bowlers (e.g., when playing matches at the Sydney Cricket Ground) and when Shane was injured or unavailable to play. No matter the quality of his bowling talent, Stuart could not achieve the same career heights as Shane because Shane was considered "The King of Spin."

There is frequent conjecture about how Stuart's career would have unfolded if Shane was not his peer. Would we know more about Stuart McGill if Shane Warne wasn't his proxy?

---

Reflecting on the story of Shane Warne and Stuart McGill highlights the potential influence of a particular proxy on one's talent status and career. This story emphasises the importance of ensuring that talent comparisons are appropriate, given the potential for peers to distort or shape talent decisions.

---

23 While Shane is best known for his cricketing prowess, "flipper" (a particular ball delivery) and talent, others may know of him because of his romantic endeavours with the movie star Liz Hurley.

## Talent Relative to A Decision-Maker's (Subjective) Expectations

All members of #Teamhuman operate under the guise of expectations. Humans generate various thoughts about how they expect "things to unfold," how "things will turn out," how individuals will respond in pressure situations or what type of partner or parent an individual may be.

Think about your daily interactions. How often do you say, "That was unexpected!" Expectations guide our thoughts. Expectations, whether met or not, form the basis of many judgments.

Brené Brown writes about expectations in *Atlas of the Heart*. Sharing some of her prose provides some valuable reflection points as we (re)think talent decisions. Brené recognises the pivotal role of expectations in our daily lives: "Every day, sometimes every hour, we are consciously and unconsciously setting expectations of ourselves and the people in our lives."

Another aspect that considers talent as a relative concept is the idea that talent is judged relative to the decision-makers' subjective expectations. Talent as a relative concept emphasises "expectations." This talent category involves decision-makers basing judgments on their subjective expectations. Subjective expectations inform talent decisions and careers. I connect a decision-maker's expectations and talent determinations by saying, "What talent is to you influences your perception of what you think I can be."

Talent decisions ultimately reside within the mind of the decision-maker. Decision-makers mentally evaluate an individual's talent by calculating and comparing their performance to their internal (and mostly theoretical) expectations.

---

*Talent = judgments based on a decision-maker's theoretical and abstract notions of how an individual will perform.*

---

### Talent as Relative to A Decision-Maker's Y.O.U.

From this perspective, talent recognises the critical role of Y.O.U. – Your Own Understanding – in talent decisions. The decision-maker's expectations are shaped by abstract and theoretical ideals of how an individual should or will perform, which reside in their mind. Thus, the connection between subjectivity and talent decisions highlights the importance of understanding "thinking." In this way, the human mind is a crucial character in our tale (the connection between subjectivity and talent decisions again reinforces the importance of thinking about how decision-makers think. Hence, I positioned the human mind as a key character in our tale).

Brené Brown also recognises the connection between expectations and the human mind. Brené writes,

When we develop expectations, we paint a picture in our heads of how things are going to be and how they are going to look. Sometimes we go so far as to imagine how they're going to feel, taste, and smell. That picture we paint in our minds holds great value for us. We set expectations based not only on how we fit into that picture, but also on what those around us are doing in that picture. This means that our expectations are often set on outcomes totally beyond our control, like what other people think, what they feel, or how they're going to react. The movie in our mind is wonderful, but no one else knows their parts, their lines, or what it means to us.

The mindset of the decision-makers themselves influences talent decisions. Some decision-makers may have a negative attitude and go into workplace interactions "expecting the worst." Others may choose to lower their expectations to avoid disappointment. It can be challenging to discern which mindset a decision-maker has. Do you expect the worst from some of your colleagues? Do you know if others expect the worst from you? Understanding expectations begins with your own self-awareness. Understanding expectations starts with Y.O.U. – Your Own Understanding.

## Talent as Relative to A Decision-Maker's Expectations and Performance Management

The notion of talent being relative to a decision-maker's expectations is a prevalent feature of performance management frameworks. Such frameworks often require decision-makers to evaluate how an individual's performance matches their expectations, which can determine their talent status. Individuals who perform "above expectations" or "exceed expectations" may be granted talent status.

However, talent decisions are less sound if decision-makers are limited in the quantity of "above expectations" scores they can attribute.

Expectations can manifest as questions reflecting the internalised and theoretical expectations of talent. For instance:

- Did X perform as expected?
- Did X exceed or fall short of expectations?
- Is X demonstrating the abilities we hired them for?
- Are they performing at their full potential?
- Do I think they perform a specific task or act in a certain role?

---

**Performance management memes**
The complex reality of thinking about talent decisions this way features in various performance management memes. My presentations regularly include memes highlighting the influence of internalised perceptions of a judger on an individual's performance evaluation. I particularly enjoy one where the decision-maker (aka judger) notes, "I know that you exceeded expectations, but at your level, I expect you to exceed expectations. Since I expected you to exceed expectations, you met my expectations. And since you met

my expectations which I expected you to exceed them, I have no choice but to give you a grade of failed to meet expectations."

The reality of positioning talent decisions within the context of a decision-maker's subjective expectations is the potential for theoretical expectations to be outside the realm of probability and possibility. Consider how often decision-makers set realistic expectations. How often are expectations unreasonable? How often are expectations founded on hypothetical ideals of how things should be and how individuals should effectively perform their talent?

Further complexity arises when we evaluate whether decision-makers effectively articulate their expectations. How often have you said or heard, "You should have said so" or "You should have told me X"? The assertion is that individuals will revise their behaviour to abide by the decision-maker's expectations. Effectively performing one's talent is influenced by whether the rules of the (talent) game are known and available to be seen.

But how often are expectations unknown?

We consider the dangers associated with undefined expectations next.

## Talent as Relative to A Decision-Maker's Undefined Expectations

Decision-makers who state, "I know talent when I see it," essentially base their judgments on undefined expectations. Decision-makers that "see" talent may not know their expectations before seeing the desired talent-in-action. Operating with vague expectations requires individuals to perform their talent within undefined parameters. A significant challenge with talent – as relative to a decision-maker's expectations – is the assumption that decision-makers know their expectations before judging.

Although some characters in our (re)thinking talent decisions tale advocate for pre-defined evaluation criteria, the uncomfortable reality is that many talent decisions are founded upon in-the-moment judgments. In-the-moment judgments prevail because expectations are not clearly understood. Therefore, many talent decisions are based on hazy or vague ideals of what talent "looks like" and "acts like."

*Talent decisions can occur "in the moment" on undefined expectations.*

Brené Brown's discussion of stealth expectations applies to this discussion. Brené helps us (re)think undefined expectations by shining a spotlight on the connection between stealth expectations and disappointment. Brené shares that stealth expectations are those expectations that are unexamined and unexpressed. Unexamined and unexpressed expectations can give rise to disappointment – disappointment because the picture or movie in one's mind didn't come to fruition. Reflecting on stealth expectations allows us to notice situations whereby specific individuals are excluded from talent pools because their behaviours and actions "disappoint" the relevant decision-makers.

## Talent as Humans Who We Don't Want to Lose

All talent categories, thus far, imply that talent decisions focus on keeping the identified "somethings" and "someones." There are individuals and skills and capabilities that decision-makers want to retain. There are individuals, skills and capabilities that decision-makers want to keep in their possession, to own and control.

Thinking about talent this way paints an incredibly positive picture of talent management. A picture whereby decision-makers think about strategic imperatives when judging value. A positive image whereby decision-makers are initiative-taking, discerning and insightful. However, we should hold our applause because the reality is less flattering.

Some decision-makers may not consider the value of an individual until that person declares their intention to leave or submits their resignation. The decision-maker may not have considered this person's talent before that moment. The reality is that some individuals may gain talent status because decision-makers want to retain them. Talent is humans that decision-makers "do not want to lose." Some decision-makers think of talent as individuals they do not want to lose, individuals whose absence would be felt. The decision-maker may miss having that person around or miss the support they provide. Loss aversion plays a role here because humans tend to feel loss more acutely than we feel gain. Thoughts about losing someone may matter more than retaining someone.

---

*Talent = an individual whose absence would be detrimental.*

---

The nuances between talent perspectives matter, as it is not merely a matter of different terms used to describe the same idea. There is a critical distinction between focusing on the talent you want to keep versus those you don't want to lose. Value and retention-based talent decisions are proactive, focusing on the outcome-critical talent. On the other hand, loss-based talent decisions are reactive and only made when an organisation risks losing a valuable employee. Value and retention-based decisions are about an individual's worth – the individual is the focus. On the other hand, loss-based decisions are about deficiency and shortage – the focus is on the decision-maker (and their expectations).

---

*Loss-based talent decisions are reactive.*

---

I use NKOTB's song *Please Don't Go Girl* as a tool to illustrate this point. As a child, I enjoyed singing along to NKOTB. As an adult, I use the song to initiate a (re)thinking about the differences between talent in the hypothetical realm versus our everyday experiences. Imagining me singing to executives may seem humorous, but the message is serious: the decision-makers' perspective on talent can significantly impact their decision-making process.

Ok, back to NKTOB's song (you may like to search for the song on YouTube to understand the song I am referring to). A boy band of five openly declares they do not want the talent to leave them. Talent, in this instance, refers to a "girl."

Here is a sample of the lyrics I love to sing:

Please don't go girl
(I just can't live without you)
Please don't go girl
You would ruin my whole world
Tell me you will stay
Never go away
I'm gonna love you girl until the end of time
Tell me girl, (Tell me girl) you're gonna always be mine

Followed by copious lines of "Please don't go girl."

The song encapsulates how declarations around talent can centre on loss aversion. Getting the girl to stay is an inward focus. As NKOTB say, if you – the talent or the girl – leave, it would "ruin their world." While you may not be valuable within the context of the organisational strategy, the present day or a hypothetical day, this human's departure would make that character's life harder.

I am fascinated with talent meanings at the individual level. I hope after reading this chapter, you are too. Understanding what talent means to you and what talent means to me influences talent decisions. Different talent Y.O.U.'s influence talent decisions inform the who of talent management – the "someones."

# Chapter 11
# External Character's Talent Categories

Talent is, as the previous chapter shows, contested terrain. Contested terrain because a kaleidoscope of talent colours operates in the human mind. Contested terrain because humans hold different beliefs about what talent "looks like" and expectations about how an individual should perform their talent. It is a contested terrain because a plurality of interests exists and interact.

Rather than focusing solely on how humans as individuals perceive talent, this chapter takes a different approach. It explores the meanings and categories of talent from the perspectives of character groups. More specifically, we examine how external characters view talent because they influence talent decisions.

It is crucial to ask, "What does talent mean to character X?" because acknowledging different perspectives helps establish a foundation for talent decisions.

However, the answers to this question show that each character group advocates for particular talent meanings which align with their interests.

---
*Talent = domain where external groups wrestle for their interests.*

---

As the following prose will show (see Figure 11.1), each group of characters holds different ideas about the defining characteristics of "talent."

**Figure 11.1:** External characters interested in talent decisions.

## Scientists

The previous chapter on (re)thinking talent highlighted that scientists have differing opinions on how to define talent (talent definitions) and categorise talent types (talent categories). Scientists continually debate whether talent is:
- Inherent (born with) versus acquired (learnable)
- Inclusive (The Workforce) versus exclusive (specific someones and somethings)
- Subject (specific someones) versus object (specific somethings-in-individuals)

I propose framing talent in a novel way that differs from previous scientific peer-reviewed contexts. My talent categories include:
- specifically designated individuals
- specifically designated skills and capabilities
- specifically designated (e.g., pivotal) jobs, roles, or positions.

While scientists excel at prescribing what talent could or should be within a hypothetical or specific organisational context, they are limited in their ability to shape talent meanings or decisions within industry.[24]

## Consultants

Consultants shape the defining characteristics of talent. Consultants benefit from proposing talent meanings and developing talent frameworks. However, consultants may be less interested in advocating for specific talent meanings with opportunities for consultants to engage with organisational strategic imperatives.

Consultants can serve in a variety of roles, including:
- Assisting with establishing talent meanings and frameworks that are context and strategy specific.
- Helping to update existing talent meanings and frameworks to align with changing business needs.
- Aiding with updating talent frameworks even if decision-makers are using a vendor-designed system.
- Generating talent management insights through white papers, discussion papers and other means.
- Commenting on the validity of specific talent policies and practices based on the broad spectrum of data collected through industry surveys and interviews.

---

[24] See Chapter 3: A kaleidoscope of 'talent' definitions and conceptualisations in *Talent Management: A Research Overview* which I co-wrote with Anthony McDonnell to learn more about how scientists define and conceptualise talent.

It is crucial to approach consultancy perspectives with caution. The consultancy industry operates on a competitive business model offering clients financial gain solutions. Consultants may focus on promoting talent-based problems they can address or fix through their consulting services, potentially creating a conflict of interest. It is worth noting that the infamous "War for Talent" was initially spawned by McKinsey, highlighting the potential for consultants to benefit financially from identifying talent challenges and providing solutions to address them.

## Customers

Customers represent another group of external stakeholders with a vested interest in talent decisions. While an individual's hypothetical value for future development may not concern customers, they tend to advocate for talent categories that emphasise performance, skills, capabilities and expectations.

My research has found that customers can play a pivotal role in shaping an organisation's definition of talent and identification process. Individuals may sometimes gain talent status because customers perceive them as having valuable skills or capabilities. Alternatively, individuals may be identified as talented because they have a strong relationship with a specific high-revenue or sales customer.

This customer-driven approach is particularly relevant in professional services and sales-based industries where customers seek specific talents to address their identified problems or needs. Customers are "buying" particular talents to help them achieve their business objectives.

## Unions

Unions can significantly impact shaping talent meanings within contexts underpinned by industrial relations systems, as is the case in Australia. This character group often plays a key role in negotiating wages, salaries, conditions and entitlements on behalf of The Workforce. Doing so can influence talent definitions, decisions, policies and practices.

Through their advocacy, unions can shape how talent is defined. This may include advocating for specific skill sets or capabilities to be recognised and rewarded or negotiating for more inclusive talent development and management practices. Overall, unions can be powerful in shaping how talent within The Workforce is identified, developed and rewarded.

## Experts, Admired CEOs or Business Gurus

To (re)think talent, it is important to recognise that the words and thoughts of others can have a significant impact on how we perceive and value talent. Experts, admired CEOs and business gurus are a specific category of external stakeholders that can influence talent decisions. An expert is someone I think knows more than me. An admired CEO has or is excelling in a particular organisation. A business guru is someone with influential ideas or theories about business.

Humans want to learn and expand their knowledge base, particularly regarding high performance, technology, social science and lifestyle design. As such, we often consume content related to these areas from various sources, including podcasts, books, online programs, YouTube, TikTok and more.

It is important to note that these individuals and their content may significantly influence our thinking and decision-making processes. Engaging with content "does something."

Listening to the thoughts of others also shapes our thinking. We may think differently about a topic based on the conversations and insights shared.

The process of shaping our thinking occurs both consciously and unconsciously. A conscious review involves taking notes and subsequent actions – after learning a new idea, we may consciously change certain aspects of our behaviour or activities.

Have you ever witnessed an executive returning to work after a conference or seminar and announcing, "We are now doing X (insert activity here)?" Or have you heard someone say, "We need to be more like X (a company or individual)" due to the content they have consumed from an expert, admired CEO, or business guru?

On the other hand, unconscious shaping occurs because we can't disengage or "unlearn" the content we consume. Memories and reflections may arise later, often without our conscious awareness. Our mind plays a significant role in this process, as it filters and interprets the information we encounter. We allow certain voices to penetrate our minds more than others. Our brains do not process and hold consumed information equally.

It's important to remember that experts, admired CEOs and business gurus often have commercial interests associated with their thinking. Their ideas and recommendations may benefit their businesses or generate revenue if we engage with or implement their suggestions. Thus, this group of external stakeholders is not neutral and is vested in advocating for a particular way of thinking or doing. We must approach their advice with a critical eye and carefully evaluate how their recommendations align with our strategic goals and values.

## Vendors

The increasing digitalisation of talent management has given vendors a significant role in shaping talent decisions, as they provide many of the technologies used within organisations. However, it is essential to recognise that vendors are not a unified group of external characters; they are competitors who seek to persuade decision-makers to adopt and implement their thinking and tools.

Vendors tend to advocate for particular talent categories presented in the previous section.

- **Talent as relative to peers**. Several popular leadership and competency frameworks push the talent as relative to peers approach. The *Lominger Leadership Architect*, for example, encourages number-based evaluations. Using a score scale allows for a relative comparison of performance against peers.

    The vendor designed and provided *9-box* framework also advocates for talent relative to peers' thinking. The ability to classify individuals according to their performance and/or potential is a core element of the *9-box* framework. At the touch of a "generate report" button, decision-makers can access a report which visually plots individuals against each other – individuals evaluated as high performers and high potentials take pride of place in the top right-hand corner. Individuals with lower performance and potential will reside in the bottom left-hand corner. Therefore, decision-makers can see how individuals perform according to set criteria and how they compare to their peers.
- **Talent as something that you have**. Vendor-designed competency models/frameworks strongly emphasise talent as something individuals have. We are reflecting on vendors here because vendors are key characters in our (re)thinking talent tale and play a significant role in shaping our understanding of talent. Each vendor offers various characteristics to judge an individual's value against: value, if often measured according to performance and/or potential. Vendor-designed frameworks require internal decision-makers to subjectively assess whether a human has a specific "something." Scales, typically ranging from 0–5 or 0–1, are used to evaluate this individual's talent concerning the predetermined criteria. The predetermined criteria are the "something." We reflect further on vendor views and motivations later in our journey.
- **Talent as (hypothetical) value for a future day**. Various vendors play a role in talent decisions by offering pre-designed frameworks to evaluate potential. One of the most well-known examples is the *9-box* framework, which judges individuals based on their current performance and potential. Vendors can, for a fee, offer different ways to (subjectively) judge whether an individual "has" potential.

Vendors' talent beliefs are part of their talent frameworks. Implementing and using a vendor's framework sees that organisation adopting the vendor's view of talent. The extent of a vendor's influence is primarily determined by whether internal decision-makers amend criteria and processes to adhere to the technology or customise.

The above discussion illuminates the role that external characters play in talent decisions. External characters, however, are not a homogeneous group. External characters are also not neutral. External characters are vested in advocating for particular ways of thinking or doing. We benefit from recognising that – not all voices are equal within and between organisations. Our (re)thinking journey involves recognising that external characters influence talent decisions, with the potential for talent meanings to arise outside an organisation.

## A Few Words Before We Continue Our Journey

Let's pause and reflect on where we are on our (re)thinking journey.

So far, we have established that (re)thinking talent decisions is a tale of complexity, technology and subjectivity in the pursuit of strategy and knowledge:

- **Complexity**. Talent decisions are and always will be complex because talent management is complex. Our tale is one of complexity because talent and talent management are socially constructed concepts – categories and ideas which only exist in the human mind – which can, and do, change over time.
- **Technology**. Talent decisions and technology enjoy a reciprocal relationship whereby talent availability influences technology processes and projects, and technology selection and use affects the talent required to realise the benefits of digitalisation. We have explicitly acknowledged technology's leading role in talent decisions.
- **Subjectivity**. We have accepted an uncomfortable truth about the subjective nature of talent decisions. Conceding that talent decisions are always subjective helps us recognise that all decisions include an element of bias because perceptions of talent are within the eye of the beholder – the judger.
- **Strategy**. Talent decisions and actions are means to pursue and realise strategic plans. I contend that the "somewhere" of talent decisions is realising strategic ambitions and goals.
- **Knowledge**. I also contend that you, my reader, engage with these words to advance your understanding of what you know and garner an awareness of unrecognised or overlooked areas. We have learnt, however, that humans think about knowledge differently. Some humans believe knowledge and truth are objective and discoverable (Positivism). Others think knowledge and reality are co-created and associated with subjective experience (Social Constructionism). Knowledge-centric perspectives influence how certain characters think about talent and technology.

We have also established the importance of asking questions about key concepts. Questions about what work, technology and talent management mean to you and me are pivotal. Pivotal because there are a multiplicity of perspectives. We must, therefore, establish, rather than assume, that everyone knows what they mean when talking about work, technology and talent management. We have also learnt that defining key concepts is essential. Establishing shared meanings is foundational to effective collaborations because we want to know which differences are semantic or conceptual. Unidentified conceptual differences may jeopardise both talent decisions and outcomes.

We have developed an informed perspective on talent, which is one of the three core elements of responsible decision-making. This chapter featured many talent categories and showed that human characters define talent differently. In addition to the

dominant ideas which frame talent as specific individuals, specific skills and capabilities and pivotal roles as positions, this chapter has expanded our knowledge by framing talent as:
- Judging value
- Something in you
- Something we discover
- Something that you have
- Something that we do
- Something that we see
- A means for strategy execution
- A time-based concept
- A relative concept
- Humans, we don't want to lose.

Overall, there is a kaleidoscope of talent colours!

Gathering diverse perspectives increases the complexity of talent decisions. The alternative, however, whereby we assume that all stakeholders know what they mean when talking about talent or thinking that everyone agrees, is worse. Acting on implied rather than explicit assumptions and meanings can lead to disastrous outcomes. My research shows that even when stakeholders use the same language to talk about talent, they may have different meanings and perceptions of what a talented individual looks like, the defining characteristics of talent and what individuals do or don't do.

Acknowledging and embracing these different perspectives is crucial for building a common foundation for effective talent decisions. Rather than striving for convergence, we should aim for foundational alignment that provides a solid basis for decision-making.

Different perspectives on talent are semantic and conceptual, with some believing that individuals are born with their talent, while others think they can develop their value over time.

However, most of the prevailing ideas of talent miss the performative aspect. By framing talent as a performative verb, we acknowledge that decision-makers judge an individual's value and allocate talent status based on observing talent-in-action. Explicitly recognising the performative aspects more accurately represents the realities of talent decisions.

Part 5: **Negotiating Talent Decisions**

# From Theory to Negotiations in Work-based Contexts

The next step in our journey is understanding how individual perspectives (a sample size of one, i.e., Y.O.U.) becomes the collective perspective (a sample size of many, i.e., The Workforce). We are transitioning from developing an informed perspective (which involves understanding the science and theory) to the reality of making talent decisions. Moving from theory to reality (even if hypothetical) helps us understand the crucial link between talk and action. Different ways of thinking can result in different actions, and various forms of thinking influence decisions.

In this section, we reflect on how different voices and interests come into play in the workplace. You will learn how particular ways of thinking are emphasised during negotiation processes. Recognising the various character voices is crucial because talent decisions do not exist alone. Instead, all aspects of talent decisions arise from negotiation processes where characters negotiate to determine which meanings, frameworks and systems become the accepted path.

## Using a Stage Play to Think About Negotiation Processes

The negotiation processes are presented as a stage play to establish "sticky" associations between thinking, behaviour and actions that transcend reading this book.

The stage play consists of three scenes revolving around a central collaboration or conflict. We first consider talent meanings, followed by talent identification and decision systems. The order of the scenes is crucial as establishing a shared understanding of what talent is and looks like is essential before designing the identification processes. We need to know and agree on the defining characteristics of talent and identification processes before selecting specific decision support systems (e.g., technology).

Each scene details the setting, location, props and character interactions. Each scene also features a new character – a narrator – allowing me to speak directly to you and provide information or commentary.

I suggest reading and reflecting on each section individually. Start by reading the prose about negotiating talent meanings. Then, pause, close your eyes and imagine the scene. Try to create a mental picture of the characters performing their respective roles. Do this for each section before moving on to the next. Creating individual mental images can help you remember and recall the essence of these discussions later.

# Chapter 12
# Scene 1: Negotiating Talent Meanings

*Collaboration/ Conflict: we are negotiating what talent means within a specific organisational context.*

We now understand that talent is a concept, representing a way to organise ideas. As a concept, talent only exists in our minds. We bring talent meanings to life through words and conversations. To learn what talent means, we ask questions such as "What does talent mean to you?" and "What does talent mean to me?" We also consider what talent meanings operate within broader society.

Asking questions about Y.O.U. – Your Own Understanding – is pivotal for effective decision-making because talent decisions start with a specific human – a sample size of one. We establish what talent means within Organization X by understanding what talent means to specific humans and character groups.

The question becomes: what does talent mean in our organisation?

*Key question = what does talent mean in our organisation?*

Answering this question is essential because organisations do not have a predetermined definition of talent. Instead, they create or establish talent meanings through negotiation processes. In other words, certain characters within an organisation must decide and socially construct what talent means for their own operational needs and strategic imperatives. Establishing a shared meaning, or multiple meanings, is vital for effective talent decisions.

This scene takes place in a room with a large table, where our characters gather for a negotiation. The scene builds on our previous understanding that internal and external characters hold diverse ideas about talent, and each character thinks about talent from their individual, team and functional context.

In this scene, we also recognise that many external characters come to the table with various commercial interests, leading to conflicts and disagreements as they seek to convince others that their talent ideas are the best. Some disputes may be overt and played out for all parties to see, while others may be more covert, with characters arguing for their talent meanings in corners of the room or whispering in their ears.

## Scene Setting – Table Seating Positions

The scene opens with characters assuming positions at the negotiation table. The Chief Executive Officer (CEO) sits at the head of the table, symbolising their high status and indicating to others that they possess a lot of power.

The CEO is flanked on either side by other senior leadership team members, including the Chief Finance Officer (CFO), Chief Operating Officer (COO) and Chief Strategy Officer (CSO). These internal characters support the CEO and ensure that conversations cover issues related to the strategic, financial, and operational implications of specific talent meanings.

Opposite the senior executive team are members of Finance and Procurement. The Finance characters control the money and hold the purse strings. The Finance department and the CFO help decide where, when and how (and if) money is allocated. The Procurement team is also interested in the monetary aspects, particularly cost-efficiencies.

HR team members may or may not be seated at the table. HR's seating arrangements depend on whether they assume a business partner, facilitator, or spectator role.

- **Business Partner role**: HR counsels the senior leadership team and provides insights about current policies and workforce capabilities. Hopefully, the CEO will look to this character, value their talents and view the HR function as a strategic business partner.
- **Facilitator role:** HR starts and directs the conversation as characters present their respective talent meanings. HR can ask or encourage questions as they speak to identify areas of agreement and those areas that are the source of conflict.
- **Spectator role:** Rather than provide counsel or facilitate the conversation, the spectator role sees the HR characters standing off the side. HR does not come to the discussion with status and power. Some characters may even consider HR "a pain in the backside."

An Information Technology (IT) team representative is also at the table. The IT team supports the organisation's technological infrastructure, including HR and enterprise decision systems. This character will share their thoughts on the feasibility of adopting particular talent meanings within the existing IT framework and how it may impact the organisation's operations.

Representatives from different parts of the organisation may also be present in the room, including individuals from specific business units, geographical regions, or plant locations. However, it is unlikely that they will play a pivotal role in shaping the conversation. In some cases, these characters may be present to represent diverse voices, but their participation may be purely tokenistic. They may assume a non-speaking role or cannot insert their perspective and thoughts, playing a spectator role only.

Line managers rarely have a chance to voice their opinions in this scene. They might be standing in the corner or absent altogether, even though line managers are the ones who carry out most talent decisions. This limited role for line managers is problematic because they are the ones who understand the day-to-day realities of their teams and have first-hand knowledge of the skills and abilities required for success in their specific roles.

Now to external characters' placement.

Scientists are not involved in this scene, as internal characters have already dismissed their definitions as prescriptive and limited in practicality.

Unions and customers are also not present.

On the other hand, vendors are eager to be part of the negotiation process and campaign for a seat at the table. They have a commercial interest in defining talent and can generate sales and revenue if they convince internal characters that their talent meanings are best. Vendor characters play a more prominent role in subsequent scenes.

Leadership capability, competency and talent framework characters are seated at opposite ends of the table. The CEO sits at the head of the table, facing the technology vendor directly. However, there is an empty seat between the vendor and the leadership capability and competency models. This positioning suggests that while their interests are similar, they are not fully aligned. Tension exists at this end of the table.

## "And Action . . ."

The scene unfolds as follows:

### External Characters Share Their Ideas

These three external characters present their talent meanings, articulating their ideas directly to senior executives. They understand that gaining the commitment of senior executives from the start will significantly impact their overall role in the process.

External characters may use pre-prepared presentations that address cost efficiencies, best practice processes, standardisation and consistency, and desired outcomes. They may also demonstrate examples of their user interfaces, offering a list of possible reporting criteria and an array of complementary dashboards.

Vendors often claim that their framework is easy to change when asked about possible customisations and that they are there to help. However, they exchange knowing smiles as they understand the high costs of customising frameworks. Vendors may also emphasise their existing customer base, citing Fortune 500 companies such as S, L and W as examples of organisations adopting their platform. Their message is clear: adopting their framework will ensure that the organisation does not suffer from the fear of missing out (FOMO).

**Internal Characters Deliberate**

The discussions between the internal characters unfold as follows:

HR needs more details about each framework and the embedded judging criteria. They want to ensure that the talent definitions align with the organisation's goals and values.

Finance contributes their perceptions of the platforms' value and may want more information about the costs. They want to ensure that the investment is justified, and that the organisation gets the best value for its money.

Procurement declares that they see little need for changes. They are interested in cost efficiencies and know that "no changes" are the cheapest regarding capital outlays.

The IT representative comments on the practicalities of integrating the new/revised talent meaning into the existing infrastructure. They focus on how they will make any changes "work" and express the need to consider implementation and integration requirements.

At some point in the conversation, the technology character advises the senior executive team that the external vendor frameworks will not integrate with existing software platforms. It's unclear whether these insights are appreciated or dismissed, with the technology character saying, "We will worry about that later."

Internal characters then engage in a conversation about what companies S, L and W are doing. There are discussions about whether they want to copy what these companies are doing or whether it doesn't matter. However, they agree that other companies' approaches are outside the scope of their conversations because all talent management strategies are contextually specific. They need to decide which methods are best for their organisation.

**Another Character (maybe) Enters the Discussions**

An admired CEO or business guru might appear in the scene if the previous conversation noted an interest in the activities of others. The admired CEO or business guru enters from stage left and walks towards the table. They walk towards a specific internal character confidently or cautiously to access that character's ear. The conversation can be loud enough for everyone to hear; in that instance, a character will ask everyone to pay attention. The conversation may also take the form of whispering. Hands are near each other's ears, and the characters may slouch in their chairs. They do not want others to know that they are listening to outsiders, or they do not want others to hear.

**External Vendors Campaign for Their Ideas**

Despite wanting to exclude external characters from selection discussions, the vendors are out of their seats and make a beeline for the other end of the room. They position themselves separately to listen to the conversation, eager to learn more about the basis of the decisions and whether any pain points or barriers have emerged. With additional information, they hope to reengage with internal characters and answer any questions. Vendors are aware that some aspects of their frameworks can represent sticky points, so in these circumstances they may avoid eye contact to decrease the likelihood of offering an answer.

**Narrator Commentary**

I have a few words to add as the characters think about the talent meanings and frameworks they will select and apply. This part includes a voice-over montage. The narrator (that is me) has insights to share:
- It's easy to get distracted by the external frameworks' shine when evaluating different frameworks and the ideas of talent embedded.
- Defining talent for strategy execution is a challenging task. The difficulty of designing talent meanings that facilitate strategy execution may explain why many decision-makers seek guidance or solutions from external parties. Vendors can be helpful in this regard as they provide predefined evaluation criteria.
- While potentially strategic upon implementation, external models are static and emphasise consistency in talent meanings. It's possible to update or iterate leadership capability, competency, or technology vendor software model in response to internal and external changes. However, it's unlikely that organisations will amend them as often as necessary. Furthermore, if talent is the most crucial asset, why outsource talent models to an external vendor whose primary interest is to sell a framework to as many organisations as possible?
- External characters create and offer organisations talent meanings and frameworks based on their selling ability. Vendor talent meanings are fit-for-sale, not fit-for-purpose. While talent is complex, externally designed frameworks are rarely strategic. They aim to cater to the needs of as many characters as possible, and vendor-created talent meanings are all-purpose.

Acknowledging the different characters and their interests generates a more informed perspective on talent management. This consideration process can lead to various thoughts, ranging from "I agree with your ideas on talent management and see that we have aligned interests here" to "That misses the point" to "I appreciate what you're saying, but you're an external character, and we'd rather you didn't interfere."

The (re)thinking process can only progress when we clearly understand what talent means and what it looks like within our organisational boundaries. It is crucial to recognise the different perspectives because assuming everyone thinks about talent the same way is a significant weakness.

Regardless of the thoughts and specific dialogues, a decision is required. However, the theme of complexity persists as we pose another pivotal question: whose perspectives serve the intended purpose?

At the end of the day, there must be a final determination. Is there a need for compromise? Should the CEO make a captain's call? It's important to remember that not all voices are equal, so who decides? And who decides who decides?

## The Ending: All-purpose or Specific Purpose Talent Meanings?

In this scene, the characters gather to create and establish a definition of talent specific to their organisation. As the conversation unfolds, two likely outcomes emerge: an all-purpose meaning or a specific-purpose definition. As the characters debate and discuss the pros and cons of each option, tensions may rise, and compromises may be needed. Ultimately, the characters must decide and ascertain their organisation's "best" approach.

### All-Purpose Talent Meanings – One-Way Applied to Everyone

The previous scene concluded with discussions about talent meanings. As the characters leave the stage, they share a common understanding of what talent means. Key characters may have realised that they similarly think about talent, and areas of agreement are listed as essential judging criteria. This hopefully indicates a shared understanding of what talent "looks like."

Applying an exact talent definition throughout the workplace is known as talent-by-design. This approach is associated with strategy-by-design and is known for its ability to follow a linear process. A one-way talent meaning allows for a step-by-step identification process, with the judging process starting in a predefined manner. Steps 2, 3 and 4 (and however many more) are also pre-designed. Talent-by-design means everyone must "jump through the same hoops" to be considered "talent."

*All-purpose talent meanings = talent-by-design*

Several aspects contribute to the allure of "one-way."
- **Consistency.** One-way values consistency whereby humans behave and act similarly. Talent identification processes are mandated, with characters required to follow the set processes. One-way increases the likelihood that various business units/divisions/functions similarly look at talent. One way creates a degree of agreement rather than a situation whereby everyone does their own (talent) thing.
- **Strategy.** All-purpose meanings can place strategy at the forefront of negotiation processes (remember strategy, strategy, strategy. All talent decisions are informed by and aligned to strategy). A predetermined talent meaning, therefore, increases the probability that strategy and talent decisions are aligned.
- **Justice and fairness.** The answer may lie in the (perceived) ability of processes based on one-way to promote procedural and distributive justice and (perceived) fairness in evaluating an individual's performance and/or potential because all individuals are subjected to the same, consistent and controlled criteria and processes. In theory, one-way approaches increase procedural justice because standardised definitions and structured methods decrease the likelihood of human error. In theory, all-purpose meanings reduce internal politicking. While these ideals are noble, the restrictive nature of one-way required a (re)thinking of the value of pursuing only one-way in talent decisions.

My teaching and research have brought to light the practical limitations of an all-purpose approach to talent. Applying one talent meaning to everyone restricts the ability to acknowledge unique characteristics outside of predetermined criteria. This approach could potentially result in a narrow, rather than a holistic, talent perspective, especially if talent status is based on looking, acting and performing the same as other talent subjects. The homogeneous, rather than heterogeneous, ideas of talent that underpin all-purpose meanings could lead to creating "talent clones" instead of embracing individualistic and human-centric talent concepts.

Furthermore, evaluating individuals based on specific criteria could result in some talented individuals being excluded from talent pools because they do not "fit the box" of the predefined criteria.

Despite the potential pitfalls, the one-way all-purpose approach remains widely accepted and heralded as the best way. Most scientific, technology, leadership capability and competency characters are card-carrying members of this approach. Vendors are also staunch advocates of all-purpose talent meanings, as they are codifiable and scalable. Codifiable and scalable talent concepts form the foundation of most vendor-designed decision systems.

**Specific Purpose Talent Meanings – Multiple Meanings**

The next potential ending is framing talent as talent for a specific purpose, although it is less likely than the all-purpose approach. Talent for a specific purpose emphasises diversity and recognises the complexity of talent decisions by accepting multiple talent meanings. This approach does not mandate or impose talent meanings, allowing for the appreciation of differences and diversity by judging individuals through multiple lenses. Applying one perspective is helpful, especially as differences between workforces can contribute to sustainable competitive advantages.

---
*Specific purpose talent meanings = talent-as-variety*

---

Notably, embracing multiple talent definitions can shift talent decisions towards a talent-as-variety approach. Instead of a single, all-encompassing talent definition, there may be Talent Definition 1 and Talent Definition 2, and the goal is to evaluate "talent for a purpose."

Evaluators are not restricted to answering in a binary yes or no manner. Instead, they recognise that there is always an asterisk (*) and terms and conditions to consider. Questions about whether an individual is talented elicit the response, "It depends" – on the context. An individual can be valuable for a particular task, outcome, skill, connection, product, team, or other reasons.

Adopting multiple ways enables dexterity. Characters can apply more than one talent definition, recognising that talent is more than a single set of criteria. Judges use both hands when reflecting, evaluating a person's worthiness for talent status by considering the all-purpose way and their specific skills and actions that are not captured by the all-purpose lens. Ambidextrous judges are like jugglers, capable of simultaneously keeping many balls (talent meanings) up in the air.

Using multiple ways allows key characters to view the workforce as a puzzle. They can adopt various lenses to zoom in and out, considering the bigger picture and examining the sizes and shapes of the different puzzle pieces. Are there missing pieces in the talent puzzle?

**Scene 1 Concluding Note**

The question transitions from "What talent meaning is best for strategy execution?" to "Are one-way or multiple ways of thinking about talent going to help us get to our predefined 'somewhere'?"

(Re)thinking talent decisions requires questioning the prevailing notion that one way is superior. While a single talent definition aids in maintaining consistency and control, the truth is that individuals will always apply their perspectives when judging The Workforce against the criteria. Acknowledging the intricacies of talent decisions and the desire for diversity in The Workforce motivates some individuals to define talent in multiple ways. This approach allows for recognising value outside of the confines of a singular definition. However, it is more challenging to incorporate fluid and adaptable methods into software and algorithms. As our story moves forward, I will expand on these ideas and explore how talent identification processes can bring these varied talent meanings to life.

# Chapter 13
# Scene 2: Negotiating Talent Identification

Scene 1 focused on establishing the meaning of talent within a specific organisational context. The scene highlighted the negotiation processes between different characters. I presented two alternative endings: one advocating for an all-purpose talent meaning and the other advocating for multiple frames of reference. The talent-for-a-specific-purpose approach contends that individuals can be valuable for various reasons.

---

*Collaboration/ Conflict: we are negotiating talent identification processes within a specific organisational context.*

---

Let us now focus on scene 2, which deals with the negotiation processes involved in talent identification. In this scene, we are focused on establishing the talent identification processes within the context of Organisation X by revealing our different characters' preferred talent identification processes. Talent identification is closely related to the definition of talent, and, therefore, organisations must negotiate, via certain characters, what talent identification process/es are best for their organisation.

The critical question becomes: "What talent identification process is best for our organisation?"

---

*The key question = what talent identification process is best for our organisation?*

---

Answering this question is essential because talent identification is where talent meanings transfer from theory to action. Talent identification is where the talent meanings discussed in our *(Re)Thinking Talent* and *Negotiating Talent Meanings* sections "come to life."

Evaluators judge an individual's talent according to a talent meaning – the talent meaning residing in their mind (Y.O.U.). Y.O.U.-based meanings shape and influence the criteria for judging and evaluating The Workforce. Regardless of an evaluator's (internalised) beliefs, talent identification focuses on identifying value. The goal is to differentiate between The Workforce to determine which individuals are of value or greater value. Talent identification centres around three aspects: (1) judgements about value; (2) decisions based on value judgments; and (3) resource allocations.

The desired outcome of talent identification is understanding the "who" and "what" of talent because this categorisation influences resource allocations and informs talent development and retention activities. The identification of valuable individuals is also crucial in executing strategy.

Scene 2 involves a set change to a workplace setting. You can imagine the workplace you envisioned before. The focus is on talent-in-action as we act out talent identification. The different talent meanings play out in the workplace, making it the context for our talent decisions.

The scene begins with a narrator's overview, informing the audience that we have progressed from discussing talent theoretically to taking action. The characters are now negotiating talent identification in the workplace, taking their positions on stage as the dialogue begins.

## "And Action"

The scene unfolds as follows:

### Agreement About The Importance of Workforce Differentiation

The scene begins with a sense of consensus as the negotiation starts. All characters agree that talent identification is crucial, and the organisation, through specific characters, must distinguish between different aspects of The Workforce. "Although we value all our employees, we acknowledge that some individuals and contributions hold more value than others."

### A Debate About What Talent Identification Process is Best

Agreement levels change when characters discuss identifying these valuable "someones" and "somethings." What talent identification processes enable the organisation to pursue and realise its strategic ambitions and goals?

### Scientists and Vendors Advocate for A Systemic Approach

The scene begins with the scientists positioning themselves at the front of the stage, advocating for a systemic approach to talent identification. They argue that having one way is correlated with a systematic approach, which requires applying the same criteria and process to the workforce. This approach brings all-purpose and talent-by-design ideas to life, with pre-designed processes dictating the whom, how and where of talent identification. The scientists assert that having a systematic talent identification method is essential for talent management, as it provides a set of procedures that allocate authority and offer mandates to act.

Vendor characters also move to the front of the stage. Technology vendors are on the left, and leadership capability and competency frameworks are on the right. This positioning indicates that while vendors encourage internal characters to outsource and buy talent thinking, they are on opposing teams. The vendors present their polished marketing spiel, highlighting how their respective frameworks provide a systematic evaluation mechanism. They proclaim that their one way is the "best way" and facilitates consistency and control. By comparing individuals against set criteria, goals and peers, their systematic approach enables key characters to understand who is "talent."

The audience watches as characters change their stage positions.

Technology vendors move to the middle of the stage, pushing scientists out of the way. The audience is encouraged to listen to them because they – technology characters – can provide a systemic approach. The technology character's voice booms loudly within the theatre. A systematic way affords consistency and control. Enacting talent management via technology is known as Digitalised Talent Management (DTM). DTM include well-defined criteria – the what – of evaluation. Standardising evaluative criteria and processes is the goal. DTM involves embedding structured terminology and standard definitions of the skills and capabilities to be evaluated against and thus explicitly encodes the talent classification criterion.

Second, the digitalisation of criteria (automatically) applies that single definition of talent to the workforce during the talent identification process.

Third, technology vendors define talent using data on required competencies, personal attributes, technical and professional knowledge and experience and attach labels like "high performer," "high potential" and success to the outcomes of the automated process.

DTM technology is part of the process as it collects, encodes, sorts and classifies the workforce against the single talent definition and according to the standardised procedure. Systematic methods are also a means to generate, capture and store data that inform talent decisions.

Technology characters provide algorithms embedded with consistent talent meanings. They offer access to step-by-step electronically encoded instructions that execute specific data management tasks in a particular order, with a priority or weighting. This approach allows for standardisation and consistent reproduction of talent identification by encoding processes for coding, sorting, filtering and ranking individuals. Algorithms enable organisations to implement new control mechanisms, and some characters want to control the process of talent identification in scalable ways.

Now to the battle between internal characters. Characters again change their stage positions. Two HR characters move to the front of the stage. One stands beside the technology character, while the other pushes the scientist character aside, causing them to move to the back of the stage. The HR character standing beside the technology character assumes an Amy Cuddy power pose and stands at the centre of the stage.

### The Narrator Re-Sets the Scene

Including two different HR characters is deliberate because my research shows that HR characters are not (always) a united team. Some HR characters stand with technology, leadership capability and competency model. In contrast, others argue against a systematic approach. These HR characters see the benefit of having flexibility in talent decisions.

### HR Present (Opposing) Views

The HR dialogue emerges as follows.

The HR character discusses the need to ensure alignment between the different business units. A systematic approach, this HR character believes, enables the identification of top talent through a robust and consistent methodology. Characters can do their own thing if they do not follow a systematic process.

There are even worse consequences, HR characters say. The HR character looks for the senior executive team because the next few lines apply to them. They comment that the inability to ensure talent decisions are informed by and aligned to current and future strategic imperatives should be of utmost concern. Talent decisions are the mechanism for strategy execution. HR argue that a systematic approach is the only way to ensure that there is a strategic approach.

Furthermore, a systematic talent identification process is a way to evaluate an individual's value consistently. Conducting the evaluation process through software also provides a way to quantify (aka measure) value. Systematic evaluation leads to metrics generation because measures and scores are allocated. Measures and scores are regularly allocated according to scales of 1–5, 1–7 or 1–10. Scores reflect an individual's (perceived) value. Garnering data and metrics about the workforce creates opportunities to identify various talent categories, including talent as performance we value today, as a set of expectations and as something that you have. Key characters adopted a targeted approach, regardless of the specific talent category.

Notably, digitalised talent identification plays a pivotal role in understanding talent as relative to peers. Algorithms encoded in the software can force rank employees – according to various criteria – by computing evaluation scores. They perceived an inability to communicate talent decisions if required. A well-defined process made this possible even though there was no desire to inform individuals of their talent status expressed. Characters could call upon the scores and measures to justify an individual's exclusion from talent development opportunities.

These HR characters describe a number-based systematic approach as "objective" and "fair."

## HR Campaign To Play A Role in Talent Identification

The following dialogue focuses on HR's interests.

The HR character pauses and reflects on their role in talent identification. They then communicate the belief that having one way to identify talent increases the probability that HR plays a role. HR could access information via technology. HR would also know the who, what and how of talent identification. HR knows the "who" because delegated authority is outlined as pre-determined roles and responsibilities.

HR know the "what" because they know the judging criteria. A systematic approach makes this possible because the all-purpose talent meaning is predefined, increasing transparency about the defining characteristics. HR understands "how" talent identification happens because processes are pre-designed and linear.

My research also suggests that some HR characters are open to a more flexible approach. One HR character stands at the centre of the stage, bathed in a bright spotlight, ready to deliver their monologue. While recognising that line managers are best suited for evaluation processes, HR characters also value a team-based approach to talent identification. They advocate for a collegiate method, where line managers can discuss and debate their judgments with them. HR characters acknowledge the subjective nature of talent decisions and openly discuss the role of subjective judgments. They understand that striving for objectivity is flawed and instead focus on ensuring that multiple perspectives inform talent determinations. Decisions tend to be made based on whether the group agrees on an individual's talent for a specific purpose.

## Introducing a Line Manager's Perspective

Line managers straddle both sides of the talent identification debate. Some line managers advocate for a systematic approach that prioritises consistency in criteria. However, other line managers value differences and prioritise creating a talent jigsaw puzzle where all the pieces differ in shape and size.

Line managers have different ideas about how to identify talent. Some believe an individual's talent is quantifiable, making it measurable. Others judge talent based on performance, relying on observations to identify talent.

Line managers also have different opinions about HR's role in talent identification. Some value HR's expertise and want to collaborate to balance talent determinations. Others prefer minimal collaboration and want HR to stay out of talent decisions altogether. These less favourable opinions explain why HR characters may use their voice to advocate for their expertise and involvement in talent identification.

### The Senior Executive Team Share Their Views

Senior executives speak next.

The CEO responds to the previous dialogue and the senior executive team positions themselves at centre stage. Interestingly, the response from the CEO was not as expected, despite the systematic HR character looking to the senior executive team before discussing the relationship between systems and strategy. The audience initially assumes that this stage position seeks to illustrate their power, but they quickly learn that the stage location serves two purposes. In this tale of (re)thinking talent decisions, the key human character of the CEO is not a fan of a systematic approach. There is unanimous agreement that talent decisions start with strategy (strategy, strategy, strategy). However, there is no need to predefine all talent aspects in advance. The CEO sees little value in adopting an "over-engineered" process. A systematic approach could result in a "cookie-cutter approach." A talent identification process that can recognise many forms of talent is preferred.

### Discussion Between Senior Executives and HR

At this point, the other HR character intervened and raised the issue of the potentially adverse effects of systematic approaches. The concept of "talent clones" was brought up again, and the Chief Strategy Officer (CSO) agreed that such an approach could lead to problems.

The CEO, on the other hand, expressed confidence in the ability of line managers to identify talent. The CEO says line managers "know talent when they see it." As a result, they should have the delegated authority to determine the what (criteria) and how (process) of talent identification.

This conversation surprised many, particularly the HR character advocating for a systematic approach. The HR character realises it won't be easy to get their way if the CEO and broader senior executive team do not share their views.

### Vendors Become Confused by Their "Outsider" Position

The expressions on the faces of the technology, leadership capability and competency characters change to reflect their confusion and surprise. They had assumed that the internal characters would value the frameworks they presented, leading to a conflict between the frameworks. However, this assumption was wrong, and this unexpected turn of events now shell-shocked the characters. The characters believed one vendor-designed framework would ultimately prevail, but the situation was far more complex than anticipated.

A battle then erupts on stage.

**Narrator Commentary**

As the characters debate and fight for their perspectives, the narrator interjects with a voice-over to remind the audience of the complexity inherent in talent decisions. The dialogue between the characters highlights the many factors at play:

– **(Cost) Efficiencies**. Systems often prioritise efficiency. Talent systems are no exception, with many organisations justifying their system selection based on the business need to increase efficiency through process standardisation. Vendor software focuses on standardising practices, with each vendor refining the processes embedded within their respective software to foster "efficiencies" and a shared outcome. Systematic approaches help facilitate cost efficiencies by adopting an all-purpose talent meaning. Codifying and scaling all-purpose talent meanings is cheaper.

– **Fairness and justice**. In theory, systematic approaches increase procedural justice because standardised definitions and structured methods apply to everyone. These systematic approaches share similarities with HRM ideals focused on "treating everyone the same way."

However, it is a misconception that standardisation leads to fairness simply because everyone is subjected to the same process. Standardisation and fairness are not synonymous. Standardisation does not necessarily result in fairness.

Cathy O'Neill makes this point in *Weapons of Math Destruction* when noting that scalable algorithms (which she focuses on WMD) tend to favour efficiencies: "By their very nature, they feed on data that can be measured and counted. But fairness is squishy and hard to quantify. It is a concept . . . And the concept of fairness utterly escapes them. Programmers don't know how to code for it . . . "

Instead, we may scale the production of unfairness.

O'Neill proposed the key question: who does this framework not work for?

Moreover, it is essential to recognise that talent management is inherently unequal and cannot be fair. The very essence of talent management is differentiation. In contrast to HRM, which treats all employees equally, talent management focuses on identifying and developing the top performers. This process inevitably results in unequal resource allocation, and distributive justice issues arise. The conflict between talent management and distributive justice is ongoing and unresolvable.

---

*Talent identification is never fair because we identify specific valuable "someones."*

---

– **Evidence-based decisions**. Day-to-day, vendor-designed software assists with people-based decision-making and helps organisations transition to or enact evidence-based decision-making. In many organisations, vendor software systems capture data, manage information and generate reports upon which many decisions, including promotions, rewards and resource allocations, are based. Systematic approaches and evidence-based decision-making are intertwined. We need data to make data-based decisions, and data is captured, stored and calculated through software. Executives can now compare employees through dashboards. With a click or two, an executive can identify the best and worst performers across a broad range of pre-determined criteria. The desire to enhance the quality of decisions is noble.

However, all talent measurements and scores come from somewhere, and humans are the "somewhere." Talent decisions, because of their close relationship with value, are subjective. Whether judged as a "3," "4," "5/5," or according to a scale out of 10, the number allocated is always a human's idea of what "3," "4," or "5" looks, behaves and acts like. Notably, what a "5" "looks like" to Sharna Lee can differ significantly from Darrell Lee.

Including data in decision-making can lead to better outcomes. However, humans are responsible for determining which data is included. Humans also choose which information is excluded and ignored. Conversations about pursuing evidence-based decision-making should consist of questions about whose evidence the decision is based on.

– **Measure and score talent**. Systematic talent frameworks assume that we can and should measure talent. Most talent frameworks require judgers to allocate scores. Scores indicate the judger's perception of an individual's actions relative to the pre-determined criteria. The score is indicative of the truth and viewed as an objective reality of the individual's value. Scores are proxies of that individual. We assume that higher scores are better than lower scores. Many frameworks focus on quantifiable attributes, representing what is easy and efficient (remember the emphasis placed on achieving cost efficiencies).

Executive characters may assume that standardised scoring practices generate data about individual value in ways that are good enough/close enough. Approximate scoring, therefore, is viewed as a proxy for the extent to which the specific individual is or is not talent.

The emphasis on measuring and scoring talent leads to some more significant questions. Can we measure what individuals have? Can we quantify an individual's value?

– **Scores are not proxies**. Talent scores are not accurate proxies for value. Research shows that evaluation scores are flawed. Prevailing performance management practices are essentially inaccurate. Research shows that judging performance is influenced by the opinions of the judgers.

There is also the potential for little to no questioning of whether the evaluative score is accurate and the reliability and validity of the initial and resulting measures. Seeing talent-in-action can be unique. Think of watching your favourite sports star performing on the field. You see that individual dodge the opponents. That same individual later sidesteps. They sidestep with ease. You enjoy watching this individual perform their talent. You think the individual is a 10/10. When asked what makes this individual a 10/10, you ponder . . . hmm . . . when asked to justify your score. You list a few things, but at the end, you declare, "It's hard to put my finger on it."

Systematic approaches, however, seek to predefine all talent elements, including the parts which are "hard to put your finger on." But talent is a concept. Some talent components are impossible to articulate. Some aspects of talent are unquantifiable. The desire to quantify a human's value is fraught.

I have a guiding principle to communicate my thoughts:

---

*Guiding principle:*
*Talent is so complex and includes all the subtleties of life that it cannot be reduced to a single score, digit, or numerical value. Talent is a rainbow rather than black and white.*

---

The (re)thinking tale can only progress when we understand how to undertake workforce differentiation and identify talent. Before we consider how this scene ends, it is important to reiterate some key points. First, organisations, through certain characters, must establish how specific individuals gain talent status. Second, there must be a final determination at the end of the scene. Negotiation processes, by nature, involve compromise, and we should be clear about the characters' interests throughout the process while ensuring that the strategy remains the guiding light. Third, we must consider who makes the final determination. Not all voices are equal, so we need to decide who decides and who decides who decides.

## The Ending: A Systematic or an Integrated Approach?

This scene occurs in the workplace, with characters shifting their positions on stage as negotiations around talent identification unfold. The question of "What talent identification process/es are best for our organisation?" has two potential answers: systemic or integrated. It is crucial to differentiate between integrated processes, where different components are interconnected and coordinated, and systematic approaches, where talent identification follows a pre-determined, fixed and static plan.

### A Systematic Approach – Static and Bounded Processes

A systematic approach (not to be confused with a systems approach), pursued under a so-called "best-practice" approach, could inadvertently result in a narrow perspective of talent rather than a holistic one. There is already recognition that systematic practices, facilitated through technology, can sometimes lead to conflicts or even paradoxes. While digitalisation permits consistent criteria and processes for talent pool determinations, a systems-based approach arbitrarily establishes boundaries around what talent is or is not. Systematic approaches can limit the ability to recognise distinctive and nuanced attributes and appreciate a kaleidoscope of talent colours.

### An Integrated Approach – Fluid and Dynamic Processes

An integrated approach whereby organisations are deliberate, intentional and cross-divisional in identifying talent may be of greater value. Multiple talent meanings can feature in an integrated approach. For example, Talent Definition B can be more nuanced than Talent Definition A because it has contextually specific criteria.

Multiple ways enable fluidity. Talent meanings are flexible and emergent rather than static. Talent meanings and frameworks can cater to external context changes or ensure alignment between operational and strategic requirements. Talent Definition C, for example, may also feature. Talent Definition C also informs talent identification with the workforce judged according to flexible criteria. An ability to amend, revise, reiterate and debate talent encourages the ongoing negotiation of talent meanings. Fluidity, by default, requires ongoing conversations. Characters question whether the current talent perspectives are "still right."

While of value today, these humans may not be considered talent when we re-evaluate them in a future day. We do not assume that the criteria and process for talent status are completely predefined, regardless of whether the workforce is judged according to Talent Definition A, B, or C.

## Scene 2 Concluding Note

The central question remains: what is the best approach for executing strategy – a systematic or an integrated way?

To rethink talent decisions, we must question the compelling rhetoric about the value of systematic approaches to talent identification. While systematic approaches are excellent for establishing codifiable and scalable processes, they rely on a one-size-fits-all talent meaning and method. This approach may lead to a fit-for-coverage rather than a fit-for-purpose approach.

An integrated approach offers a different perspective by emphasising "perspective alignment" rather than "meaning convergence." This approach advocates for multiple talent meanings and the potential for numerous talent identification processes within a single organisation. One of the main challenges in this scene is how to allow for flexibility while maintaining control afforded by systematic processes.

An alternative ending may be an "AND ending," where characters adopt systematic and integrated approaches. The question then becomes where systematic approaches are best, and where are integrated approaches best?

The future of talent management lies in appreciating the fluidity of talent meaning, talent identification and decision systems. Fluid and AND-based decisions can help organisations strategically align talent meanings and identification processes.

# Chapter 14
# Scene 3: Negotiating Talent Decision Systems

Scene 1 focused on establishing the meaning of talent within a specific organisational context and proposed that organisations adopt either an all-purpose or specific talent meaning.

Scene 2 took us to talent identification, where we reflected on how characters negotiate workforce differentiation processes to identify valuable individuals. Considering that talent identification is critical, as it is where talent meanings "come to life," Scene 2 offered two possible endings, with characters debating whether systematic or integrated approaches are "best."

Scene 2 noted that most characters advocate for systematic processes to facilitate fairness and evidence-based decision-making because "value" is quantified through talent scoring. Other characters believe in an alternative perspective – an integrated talent identification process that links and coordinates various parts. An integrated process is a better way to make talent decisions because it allows for fluid and dynamic talent meanings and methods. Another option is to adopt an AND approach, which involves adopting systematic and integrated processes within one organisation.

*Collaboration/Conflict: we are negotiating talent decision systems selection and use within a specific organisational context.*

Scene 3 focuses on the talent decision system and how characters negotiate the "best" system. Talent decision systems are not automatic but must be established through negotiation to determine which system becomes the foundation for talent decisions.

In Scene 3, technology takes centre stage as the "system" is synonymous with technology. Most organisations use a talent management system, which is a form of technology software that captures, stores and analyses talent data.

We seek to understand how specific technologies become the foundation for talent management. By examining systems within a technology context, we can better understand talent decisions as our tale of (re)thinking is one of complexity, technology and subjectivity.

The critical question becomes: "Which talent management technology system is best for our organisation?"

*The key question = Which talent management technology system is best for our organisation?*

Answering this question is crucial because talent meanings come to life through talent identification, and a talent management system represents a significant aspect of the "how." Information Technology developments, both hardware and software, offer various options for structuring workflow processes for "doing" talent management. I often write and talk about Digitalised Talent Management because I want to acknowledge the direct interrelationship between talent decisions and technology. While technologically embedded frameworks have undeniable value in guiding and organising talent decisions, delegating decision-making authority to technology is ill-advised. We must exercise caution when automating talent decisions, as the potential to "cause harm" is significant.

Scene 3 takes a different approach. The narrator (me) is the only character on stage.

## "And Action"

Scene 3 unfolds as follows:

### We Think About Talent Systems Broadly

One of my key learnings from engaging with the rhetoric, research and reality of technology systems is the need to define key terms broadly. Our (re)thinking tale includes a specific section on technology – a section that illustrates that technology is not a homogenous group.

Yes, we must acknowledge that there are different technology types (e.g., Enterprise Resource Planning Systems, Human Resource Information Systems, social media, Artificial Intelligence, Digitalised Talent Management etc). But do not get too caught up in establishing hard boundaries. Recognise that some differences are semantic (you say po-tah-toes, I say po-tat-oes), while others are conceptual (we are discussing different things).

We benefit from thinking about "technology" broadly. Let us include, rather than exclude, technological aspects. Microsoft Excel, as well as pen and paper, can be indicative of a talent "system" if they help humans make decisions. A broad rather than a narrow frame of reference enables us to include various perspectives and recognise that technology is ever-evolving.

---

*Technology includes the software; the codes; the algorithms; the systems supporting decision-making.*

---

## The Ever-Evolving Nature of Talent Systems – From Proprietary to Vendor Design Systems

The number of options for acquiring externally designed systems has grown dramatically over the past two decades. When I started examining and observing how specific organisations selected and used technology decision systems in 2008, there was a smaller selection of HR and talent management platforms.

At that time, the HR and TM technology market featured two teams: proprietary and vendor-designed systems. Proprietary systems were designed in-house by characters with specialised organisational knowledge, and system maintenance and updates resided with internal characters such as HR, Finance, or IT professionals. Organisations owned the systems, and internal characters accessed and acted on the data.

Vendor-designed systems were the other team. SAP and Oracle dominated the vendor HR technology market, with smaller best-in-breed platforms presenting as potential "better" options.

## Vendor-Designed Systems Represented a Different Way

The vendor-designed approach represented a different way. Vendor-designed systems had a different ownership model, whereby organisations could transition from owners to renters of their HR and TM systems. Internal characters such as HR, Finance, or IT professionals were no longer responsible for maintaining and updating the systems, as technology vendors provided those services for an ongoing fee. The licensing prices were significantly lower than those of a proprietary system. Gaining and proving direct cost savings was almost immediate as associated costs transitioned from a labour/human capital expense to an IT infrastructure expense.

Vendors claimed that their systems were more cost-efficient, as cost efficiencies were possible because their systems focused on standardising talent criteria and processes. Therefore, a vendor could sell the same software to numerous organisations. It's important to note that standardised technology encodes all-purpose talent meanings and systematic identification processes.

## HR Characters Become Fans of Vendor-Designed Systems

HR executives tended to be huge advocates of vendor-designed systems. Vendor-designed systems enabled HR to become "strategic business partners." Transitioning to a business partner role was possible because vendor-designed systems provided HR professionals with "time." Investing in Manager Self-Services (MSS) functionality allowed HR managers to "push" specific reports to managers. Managers could also access the MSS module to access information without HR. The decreased need to liaise with managers would "free up time." HR professionals would then "have time" to work on business-critical and strategic tasks.

Vendor-designed systems were also data warehouses that HR professionals could use to access people-based data. Some vendors intentionally glorified the data warehousing aspects of their products and connected data warehousing capabilities with creating a "single source of truth." A single source of truth was possible because the vendor-designed system encouraged all data to be captured and stored in one place.

Due to data warehousing, vendor-designed systems increased the likelihood that HR could generate real-time data and metrics on HR-related issues to support strategic decision-making. The ability to provide senior executives with data-informed diagnoses and solutions could help HR executives play a more strategic role because they could offer "evidence." The ability to provide "evidence" would facilitate a "seat at the table."

Whether to maintain a proprietary in-house or vendor-designed system is largely irrelevant today. Most organisations are members of the "vendor" team. More on this soon.

### Vendor-designed Systems Decrease Talent Risks (?)

Some considered relying solely on internal staff's knowledge and expertise to use and maintain in-house systems to be a "risky" approach. This is because the success or failure of in-house systems often relied heavily on specific individuals possessing the necessary knowledge and skills. Changes to the composition of these individuals' talents could have a significant impact on system operations. By turning to vendors for assistance and paying for access to their expertise, key decision-makers could decrease the likelihood of skills gaps and reduce their dependence on specific individuals.

Sharing with you the experiences of ManuOrg (an assumed name) illustrates this point.

**A Case Study: ManuOrg**

My colleagues, David Grant, Kristine Dery, Nick Wailes and Richard Hall, and I studied the implementation of a vendor designed HRIS module in ManuOrg as part of a larger longitudinal research project examining the impact of HR technologies on the HR function.

ManuOrg represented my first foray into exploring the relationship between talent management and digitalisation. ManuOrg was particularly interesting because the organisation – via its senior executive team – used the technology project to decrease HR's internal power. Yes, that's right. Senior Executives wanted to reduce the reliance on HR and decrease the importance of one particular HR professional. Over 20 years, ManuOrg built a proprietary system that addressed different business needs. The HR system was managed in-house. Maintaining the system relied on the knowledge of a particular group of humans. The HRIS team included the humans who built and developed the technology.

Seeking to break with the past, ManuOrg's senior executive team sought to select and implement a vendor-designed HR system. Two factors drove this decision: the pending retirement of an essential HRIS character who had been with the organisation for over four decades and the desire to restructure the business. This first reason was directly associated with de-risking talent management.

A newly appointed HR Manager quickly advocated for a vanilla implementation. Senior executives and the new HR manager believed a vanilla implementation would minimise the risks associated with having a proprietary system that relied on the knowledge of specific individuals (including the retiring individual). Certain key characters believed that relying on particular individuals had become untenable. Recruiting generic technology skills was less risky.

The selection and implementation of HRIS modules of SAP had talent management implications. Previously ManuOrg's talent conceptualisation emphasised history and loyalty, where longitudinal commitment to the technology and the organisation was valued. However, the value of organisational-based careers and context-specific knowledge began to wane. The selection of SAP increased the need for SAP skills, knowledge and experience. This change meant individuals with specific proprietary IT knowledge were no longer considered talent.

Transitioning to the new vendor-designed HRIS technology changed the HRIS team and the HR and IT functions. Centralising IT skills and talents saw the repositioning of the previous HRIS team from HR to Business Information Systems (BIS). Individuals with knowledge of the replaced proprietary HRIS would go from being considered HR professionals to IT professionals. The change, however, was short-term because the HRIS team was disbanded permanently shortly after the implementation. The shift from a proprietary to a vendor-designed system prioritised SAP-based skills over organisational knowledge.

---

The findings of the ManuOrg study illustrates the importance of characters in constructing and reconstructing the skills, capabilities, roles and positions valuable within the context of technology-based projects. As technology changes, so do talent definitions.

However, redefining talent in the context of changing technology and decision systems is not a one-time event. It is an iterative process as decision-makers grapple with the tension between existing skills and knowledge valued under the current strategic paradigm and the new projected requirements to meet future challenges. This tension is particularly evident during the implementation of new technologies. Predicting what might constitute talent is challenging due to a broad spectrum of unknowns, making it difficult for relevant characters to anticipate the implications for processes, behaviours and actions.

**Degree of Customisation**

One of the perennial issues key characters face when transitioning from an in-house to a vendor-designed system is how they will customise the technology. Internal characters must decide whether to tailor their existing processes to fit the new system's functionality or customise the system to match their current operations.

## Cost-Efficiencies Through A Vanilla Implementation

Many organisations pursued vendor-designed systems because they were more cost-efficient. Embarking on a vanilla implementation was the cheapest option. A vanilla implementation involved selecting and implementing the vendor-designed framework "as is" with little to no changes to the criteria or process. Customising the software was costly, so avoiding changes to the so-called "tried-and-true" methods was desirable.

## Software-As-Service Represents Another Evolution

Technology vendors have benefited from the ever-evolving technology space, driven by the growth and availability of cloud-based infrastructure. Cloud computing has further reduced software and hardware costs because organisations can move away from on-premise systems to a shared resource model. Vendors can now share their platform via "The Cloud," allowing for greater flexibility and scalability.

Cloud-based technology has led to the development of software-as-a-service (SaaS). SaaS has changed the technology landscape even further because organisations can now "rent" vendor software instead of investing significantly via a license fee. Instead of purchasing and installing software on-premise, organisations can access similar vendor services via "The Cloud" for a subscription fee.

## Benefits of a Technology-Enabled System

The reasons key decision-makers turn to vendors for technology-enabled talent management are compelling. Some of these reasons include:
- The ability to document and define profiles for "high performers," "high potentials," and success
- The capability to encode a universal talent meaning
- A systematic talent identification process
- Capturing and storing talent evaluations and scores
- Establishing a unified and accessible talent database
- Automating talent rankings with technology
- Generating talent metrics and analytics using algorithms
- Creating and sharing talent reports
- Sharing information with internal stakeholders through talent dashboards
- Setting automatic reminders for talent-related tasks
- Fostering transparency of talent definitions because predefined criteria are knowable.

## Vendor-Designed Systems Now Dominate

Many organisations have shifted to relying on technology vendors for their talent management needs, with evidence supporting vendors' pivotal role in talent decisions. This is evident in technology vendor annual reports and external marketing, which proudly declare the ongoing expansion of the technology systems industry. Among others, SAP, Oracle and Workday are driven by revenues and profits, effectively selling for-profit standardised software at the core of their business models.

## From "Which" Talent Decision System to "How May" Systems

My research on the transition from proprietary HR systems to vendor-designed decision systems began in 2009 when vendor-designed Human Resource Information Systems (HRIS) were heralded the "next best thing" for HR. However, times have changed. Today, most organisations use vendor-designed systems for talent decisions, and debates are now focused on which system to choose rather than whether to use a vendor-designed system. HR, IT and senior executive characters may still discuss the merits of different systems, but rarely debate the trade-offs between designing and maintaining an in-house system versus a vendor-designed one. The competition now lies between different vendors, with key questions being which vendor to choose – SAP, Oracle, WorkDay, or another system?

---

*Today's landscape involves choosing between different vendor-designed talent decision systems.*

---

It is no longer a question (if it ever was) about which system. Now it is a question of "how many" HR and talent systems will support talent decisions.

Our story of complexity continues as we acknowledge that many organisations use multiple vendor-designed systems to support talent management. My research revealed that an Australian professional services firm utilised 80 different HR technologies to capture, store and analyse HR data. Eighty systems is a staggering number!

When I ask HR and senior executives how many systems they use to support talent decisions, I find that organisations have moved beyond the decision between proprietary and vendor-designed systems. Instead, they have entered a complex situation where they maintain multiple vendor systems. Organisations, through key decision-makers, have selected multiple vendor-designed technologies. It begs the question: how many decision systems are too many?

**Misaligned Success Criteria**

Choosing a vendor-designed framework comes with many benefits, but selecting and using multiple vendor-designed systems also gives rise to notable points of conjecture around the notion of success. Reflecting on success is helpful because what success means to an organisation may differ from what it means to a vendor.

Furthermore, recognising that vendors' and internal success notions are misaligned is important. What success means to a vendor will always differ from an organisation's perspective. Vendors want to design fit-for-sale software and to sell their standardised software to as many organisations as possible.

A vendor's view of talent embedded in their saleable software may not fulfil your organisation's strategic needs. Key internal characters must keep their eye on the main strategy prize. Keeping an eye on the success criteria involves acknowledging where, when and how the vendor-designed talent framework covers the bases (compliance-based) and where, when and how it misses strategically relevant "someones" and "somethings." Recognising the limitations of vendor-designed talent systems is pivotal because such systems are rarely, if ever, fit-for-purpose.

Scene 3 concludes here.

# A Few Words Before We Continue on Our Journey

Part 5 covered the negotiation processes in defining talent, identifying talent and selecting a talent decision system. Reflecting on these three aspects is vital because talent meanings, identification processes and decision systems do not exist in isolation. Rather, all elements of talent decisions result from negotiation processes, where characters advocate for their ideas and methods to become the norm. Characters want their thoughts and methods "ruled in" and become accepted practice.

**Scene 1** focused on establishing what talent means within a specific organisational context and proposed that organisations adopt either an all-purpose or specific talent meaning. Considering the negotiation processes associated with talent meanings is core to effective talent decisions because organisations do not have a definition of talent. Instead, organisations, via relevant characters, create or establish talent meanings.

We must start at the individual level of Y.O.U. – Your Own Understanding. We learn about different talent meanings by asking, "What does talent mean to you?"

Scene 1 emphasised the differences in beliefs among characters regarding the definition of talent. Recognising that internal and external characters may not share similar views is important. Understanding the complexity of talent meanings is crucial because characters may frame talent differently based on their roles, power and agency within the organisation. It is beneficial to gain an understanding of the interests, power and agency of different characters because talent meanings are a contested territory, with some characters seeking to dominate the view with their perspectives. Negotiation processes can be overt, occurring at the forefront of the stage, or covert, happening offstage with hushed voices.

At some point, however, the relevant characters will come together to construct what talent means within the context of their specific organisation. Relevant characters must negotiate organisationally specific talent meanings.

The key question becomes, "What does talent mean in our organisation?"

Scene 1 presented two competing approaches to address this question. On the one hand, the negotiation scene could conclude with relevant characters agreeing that having a single definition of talent is optimal. A unified definition of talent promotes shared thinking, leading characters to converge toward a common concept, whereby The Workforce is assessed using the same criteria. An all-purpose talent definition becomes the accepted standard, with the defining characteristics applied to everyone.

Characters can, on the other hand, decide that having The Workforce converge to one talent meaning limits the ability to recognise that talent takes many different forms. Talent can look different, and what we value in one aspect of the organisation may not be valuable in another. A second Ending suggested that talent decisions benefit from recognising diversity whereby characters can judge individuals based on multiple lenses. Numerous talent meanings may operate. Characters want to identify talent concerning a specific goal or task.

Regardless of the ending, establishing what talent means – the defining characteristics required to be attributed talent status – has implications for talent decisions. How one thinks about talent influences judgment processes and determinations. And perspectives about talent and value materialise in behaviours, actions and specific talent management practices such as talent identification.

**Scene 2** recognised that how one thinks about talent has implications for identifying talent. We addressed the talent identification negotiation process and reflected on how characters negotiate workforce differentiation processes to determine valuable humans. Considering talent identification is critical as this is where talent meanings "come to life." Talent identification is where talent meanings transfer from theory to action because evaluators judge an individual's talent according to an all-purpose or specific-talent purpose.

Characters, again, must come together and negotiate how to "do" talent identification. We seek to answer the question, "What talent identification process is best for our organisation?" We want to establish the steps to determine which individuals are talent.

Scene 2 again showed that characters hold different views about the best way to identify talent. External characters, including academics and vendors, are fans of systematic approaches. Both these characters agree that evaluating The Workforce consistently according to one predefined talent framework is the best way. A systematic approach is best because they rely on predefined procedures (talent-by-design) that allocate authority and provide mandates for action. Because of the reliance on standardised criteria and processes, systematic approaches can be embedded in technology software and with talent decisions scalable through algorithms.

Internal characters such as HR and Senior Executives may disagree that one-way is the best way. My research suggests that these characters are more comfortable with ambiguity and advocate for fluid and flexible ways of identifying talent. Over-engineering and systematising talent identification processes may lead to the identification of talent clones. Judging individuals in multiple ways recognises a kaleidoscope of talent colours.

Scene 2 offered several "Endings," with characters debating whether systematic or integrated approaches are "best." Scene 2 noted that most characters advocate for systematic processes to facilitate fairness and evidence-based decision-making because "value" is quantified through talent scoring.[25]

Another potential Ending is an alternative perspective – an integrated talent identification where various parts are linked and coordinated. An integrated process is a

---

[25] I remind you here in the footnotes that the underlying premise of framing systematic processes as best because they facilitate objective decision making is flawed. All talent decisions are subjective. Hence all talent scores, including those generated via systematic talent identification process are subjective.

better way to make talent decisions because it permits fluid and dynamic talent meanings and methods. An integrated approach emphasises perspective alignment, not meaning convergence.

I offered a third Ending. An AND Ending suggested that organisations benefit from adopting systematic AND integrated talent identification processes. This ending recognises there are places where a systematic approach is best and others where an integrated system disproportionately contributes to strategy execution.

**Scene 3** put "technology" front and centre because we were interested in understanding how organisations decide which talent decision "system" to use. I suggested that we equate technology with systems because most organisations use some form of technology software to capture, store and analyse talent data. Most organisations use technology when making talent decisions.

Scene 3 started by reflecting on the history of HR technology. An account that sees organisations replacing proprietary HR technology with vendor-designed systems.

Questions about talent decision systems no longer ask whether a proprietary or vendor-designed system is best. Internal characters now ask which vendor system is best. My research suggests that characters debate how many vendor-designed systems are used because organisations rely on numerous vendors. The domain of talent decision systems has become increasingly complex, with internal characters needing to manage different technology platforms.

At the end of Scene 3, I make the point that vendors and internal characters do not approach talent decision systems the same way. Vendors and organisations have misaligned success criteria. Vendors want to create saleable systems – systems of decision-making that can be sold to as many organisations as possible. A vendor's view of talent or identification processes rarely fulfills strategic talent needs. Vendor-designed systems are seldom, if ever, fit-for-purpose.

**Part 5** makes another critical point; there must be a final determination at the end of the day. Someone, whether an internal or external character, as an individual or a team, must decide what talent means within the organisation, what processes guide identifying talented individuals and creating talent pools, and which and how many forms of technology systems support talent decisions.

Remember that not all voices are equal, so who decides? And who decides who decides? Because all aspects of talent decisions require delegative authority – a decision-maker. Talent decisions also lead to mandates for action – behaviours, activities and processes which guide the "doing" of talent management.

We reflect on the strategic and other implications next.

Part 6: **Implications**

# Recognising the Strategic and Knowledge Implications

I opened Part 2 by saying that– "Talent decisions help us get 'somewhere'." We make talent decisions because we want to journey towards an outcome. The "somewhere" is the "why." I want to remind you that we must reflect on the "why" of talent decisions. We benefit from knowing and predefining our desired outcomes – what do we seek to achieve? Knowing where we want to go helps ensure we stay the course. Our destination – the desired outcomes – acts as our map.

Our destination should also be our map as we navigate the negotiation processes. Negotiating what talent will mean how to identify talent and which talent decision systems best support our operational and strategic needs will always be complex. And while we cannot remove the complexity, we can negotiate the details with an awareness that the outcomes of these processes have consequences. Knowing and intentionally considering the implications of the negotiation outcomes helps us "keep our eye on the prize."

You are already familiar with these two "somewhere" because our journey is a tale of complexity, technology and subjectivity in the pursuit of strategy and knowledge. Strategy and knowledge have guided our talent decisions tale and acted as two different somewheres on our map. In Part 6, we consider our tale's implications for strategy and knowledge.

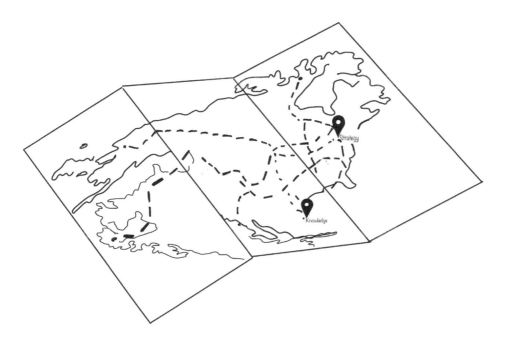

Source: Copyright © Sharna Wiblen. All rights reserved.

# Chapter 15
# Strategic Implications

A key "why" of talent decisions is "strategy." Strategy and talent decisions are interconnected. Strategies are realised or not realised because of talent decisions. (Remember that talent management involves assessing value judgements to pursue and realise strategic ambitions and goals, so talent decisions are all about strategy execution.) It is essential to explicitly consider strategic imperatives when discussing decisions and actions because realising strategies is the "somewhere" in our talent tale.

---

*Strategy is the "why" of talent management.*
*Strategy, Strategy, Strategy. Talent decisions start and end with strategy.*
*Talent decisions help us pursue (and realise) strategic ambitions and goals.*

---

As a proponent of human decision-making, I strongly believe that humans are highly skilled at making decisions, and I align myself with #Teamhuman. However, our comprehension of the crucial players executing strategies is constantly evolving. By examining how organisations handle human and technology interactions, I understand how humans contribute to strategic decision-making. I also delve into the human-technology interface to create knowledge and expand my knowledge of how individuals and groups of individuals perceive technology or technological tools.

Answering the question, "Which talent decision system is best for the organisation?" has resulted in vendors transitioning from a supporting to a leading role in our rethinking talent decisions tale. Vendors are increasingly responsible for designing and supplying the technology and decision frameworks. Vendors, therefore, are becoming both the designer – they decide the "what" – and driver – they decide the "how" – of talent decisions. Vendors take a position in the centre of our stage because they are the designers and drivers of talent decisions.

Selecting and using vendor-designed systems has implications for strategy. We must reflect on the strategic consequences because of the importance of strategy – "Strategy, strategy, strategy. All talent decisions start and end with strategy" – and our mutual desire to learn about the connection between talent decisions, technology and strategy.

---

*Choosing and using vendor-designed talent decision systems has strategic implications.*

---

## Implications for Digitalisation Strategies

There is ample evidence to suggest that the evolution of vendor-designed technology has driven a significant shift in the digitalisation strategies of most organisations. As a result, we are witnessing the emergence of a technology-driven approach to digitalisation.

This approach strongly emphasises vendor-designed software, codes and algorithms, which become the foundation for decision-making. Prioritising these systems influences resource allocation, the type and amount of technology investment and the scope of digital transformation initiatives.

In essence, deciding to prioritise technology-driven decision systems influences how an organisation structures, selects and implements various technologies to achieve its operational and strategic objectives. Many digitalisation strategies see vendors assuming a position at the front of the (strategic) stage.

## Implications for Talent Strategies

The rise and rise of vendor-designed talent systems has fundamentally changed how organisations "do" talent management. Technology-encoded criteria and processes have become the foundation of talent decisions, with vendors assuming leading roles in these processes. Vendors decide the who, what and how of talent decisions, making them the primary decision-makers in this field.

And while there is no denying the value that technology brings to talent decisions, we must exercise caution when permitting external parties to guide and, in some cases, dictate the who, what and how of talent management. Outsourcing decision design to vendors creates a situation where vendors can unknowingly or unintentionally influence strategic decisions. Key internal characters must keep a watchful eye on the organisation's strategic goals to ensure that vendor-designed systems support these goals rather than dictate them.

Key decision-makers must carefully consider the strategic implications of relying too heavily on vendor-designed systems. Adopting similar talent systems as other organisations may lead to an imitation strategy, where organisations are essentially "doing the same (talent) thing."

I understand that many decision-makers choose to purchase vendor-designed technologies and rely on the expertise of technology vendors to determine the defining characteristics of talent. However, regardless of this decision, key decision-makers must evaluate the outcomes of the predefined criteria to ensure that the embedded algorithms lead to better outcomes.

HR play a pivotal role because HR functions are responsible for assessing the effectiveness of the technological or algorithmic-based decision-making process. HR must also take responsibility for revising, reiterating, amending and/or updating the criteria and methodology used. Such revisions and updates are crucial to improving talent decisions and ensuring they align with the strategic goals.

## Implications for Digitalised Talent Management Strategies

Technology-driven strategies and an increased reliance on vendor-designed talent frameworks have implications for digitalised talent management strategies, including:

### An Increase in Vendor Power and Agency

If key decision-makers intentionally select and deploy vendor-designed frameworks as the critical mechanism for talent management, vendors, by default, become responsible for talent decisions. Adopting vendor-designed talent meanings and identification processes creates the potential for vendors to become the sole or primary decision-makers.

### Talent Decision Systems Encode A Particular View of Talent

Talent decision systems depict a particular view of the world. Outsourcing design elements of talent decision systems to vendors prioritises the *vendor*'s view of talent. The vendor's perspective becomes the foundation, the blueprint, the map for talent decisions.

Vendors encode a particular view of talent into their system because "the system" relies on programming. The programming of talent decision systems involves human decision-makers because humans programme algorithms. Algorithms do not programme themselves. Relevant vendor characters, therefore, are tasked with deciding the defining characteristics of talent (the what) and judgment processes (the how). Per the vendor's views, the defining characteristics and processes are programmed into the software.

Thorsten Grohsjean, Linus Dahlander, Ammon Salter and Paola Criscuolo, in an *MIT Sloan Management Review*, make a crucial point relevant to our talent discussion. The authors note that technology companies are not renowned for innovative and novel ideas. Vendors tend to focus on the technical aspects of an idea:

> Technology companies usually staff expert panels with scientists and engineers, who tend to focus on the technical aspects of an idea without sufficiently considering the business opportunities and challenges. Although some expertise is required, having only experts on a panel can be problematic. Panel members may have a bias for ideas originating from their own field of expertise, and experts are prone to systematic errors in assessing truly novel ideas.

The above quote encourages us to recognise that all forms of technology reflect and advocate for a particular view of "something" – the something which the technology company sells for profit. Technology companies champion a specific idea of talent. Therefore, the challenge is becoming aware of the perspective and judgment calls (trade-offs) made in the embedded code. Key characters benefit from asking questions about the assumptions embedded into the vendor-designed framework or the reasoning/ assumptions underpinning specific rules for action/inaction or degree of mathematical calculations.

---

*The key question = what views and assumptions are encoded in talent decision systems?*

---

The key question becomes, "What views and assumptions are encoded in the talent decision systems?"

Other questions include:
Do we have any knowledge or insights into whose perspective/views of talent these frameworks are based?
What epistemological beliefs do the coders and designers hold?
Do the coders and designers think that talent is something an individual has?
Or do they believe that talent is something that an individual performs?
Or do coders and designers think another way about talent?

Knowledge of the assumptions is essential because the assumptions underpinning digitalised talent management strategies are embedded in specific talent decision systems. The views and assumptions of vendors become the basis of talent decisions. And let us remember that the who, what and how of talent decisions affect promotions, resource allocations and careers.

## Talent Decision Systems Emphasise Static Talent Meanings

Digitalised talent management relies on static talent meanings. But talent is dynamic, and rigid frameworks may not align with the organisation's changing needs. This can lead to strategic issues as vendors rarely fundamentally change their talent frameworks.

## Talent Decision Systems Emphasise Binary Decision-Making

Digitalised talent management strategies tend to emphasise binary decision-making because software code, by design, is reductionary. Emphasising binary decision-making is an outcome of using binary software code. Evaluations, judgments and talent scores are converted into "0s" or "1s." Get enough 1s, and that particular individual becomes "talent." Alternatively, receiving talent scores encoded as a 0 will hinder talent pool inclusion. In other words, using algorithms for talent decisions creates a situation whereby talent status is reduced to two outcomes: 1 = talent and 0 = not-talent.

*Talent decision systems emphasise reductionist binary outcomes whereby some humans are identified as talent and others are not.*

## A Few Words Before We Continue on Our Journey

Talent decisions start and end with strategy, and given the salience of talent decisions for strategy execution, we must reflect on the implications of negotiation processes presented in Part 5 for "strategy."

Reflecting on the implications of increasing digitalisation and technology-enabled decision-making enables us to appreciate the reciprocal and interconnected relationship between strategy and talent decisions.

The transition towards talent decision systems designed by vendors has resulted in a remarkable transformation of their role, propelling them to a prominent one in talent decisions. Vendors now bear increasing responsibility for creating and providing software and decision frameworks. This shift has led vendors to assume the dual role of both designers and drivers of talent decisions.

Opting for vendor-designed talent systems carries implications for various strategies:

– **Digitalisation strategies:** as key decision-makers prioritise vendor-designed talent decision systems, they are pursuing a technology-driven approach to digitalisation. A technology-driven approach involves key decision-makers seeking process designs embedded in software from external markets. This creates a situation whereby vendors may prescribe specific methods for executing processes. Vendors often embed pre-configured working methods into their software, encouraging process standardisation. While standardisation assists with compliance and control, it can also constrain flexibility, fluidity and context-specific requirements. The inability to respond to changing business needs and recognise contextual specifics means there is an increasing benefit in adopting an AND approach whereby organisations maintain both technology (externally designed) and business-driven (bespoke) approaches to digitalisation.

– **Talent strategies:** vendors, an external character, are increasingly powerful players and decision-makers because of the proliferation of vendor-designed frameworks. The rise of vendors is changing the face of talent decisions. Key decision-makers are, either by choice or by accident, increasingly outsourcing the thinking and doing for talent management resulting in talent-by-design approaches. Talent-by-design approaches entail formulating methods abstractly and sequentially. Formalised plans and policies outline a series of linear steps, wherein strategies are executed by progressing through step 1, step 2, step 3 and so forth. While this systematic and logical approach has merits, it can become rigid and inflexible when confronted with evolving circumstances.

– **Digitalised Talent Management Strategies:** prioritising or relying on vendor-designed systems, as noted above, gives rise to talent-by-design approaches to talent decisions. Pursuing talent-by-design methods (which vendors call "best practices") means that organisations cannot respond to changing business needs.

It is important to recognise that talent-by-design approaches are not strategic. Talent-by-design approaches involve an "imitation" strategy because key decision-makers have decided to implement and use the same frameworks as their partners and competitors. If organisations use the same frameworks, they essentially copy and imitate others. Imitating others is not, and cannot be, strategic. Using vendor-designed frameworks for talent meanings, identification and decision-making processes limits the ability to ensure talent decisions are aligned to and informed by the organisation's strategies. Transitioning to a talent-as-variety approach – in which ambiguity and diverse meanings and identification processes are allowed – is more indicative of a "strategic" way.

# Chapter 16
# Knowledge Implications

This point of our journey involves reflecting on how we have advanced our knowledge. Advancing our knowledge of key themes, key characters and different thinking is a core element of our journey. Advancing "knowledge" is a "somewhere" – a destination – in our (re)thinking journey. Advancing our knowledge is a key "why" you engaged with this book. I believe there is no limit to the human mind and that advancing knowledge about human decision-making helps workplace relations and broader society.

We reflect on the knowledge implications because I want you to think about your thinking – "What do you think?" – and the factors and variables that influence your thinking – "What do you think and why, why, why do you think that way?"

We benefit from also reflecting on the thoughts of others – "What do you think?" – and the factors and variables that have informed and influenced their thinking – "What do you think and why, why, why do you think that way?"

Let us reflect on our learnings.

## Talent Decisions are Complex

I am fascinated by and comfortable with complexity. I am aware, however, that many of my fellow #Teamhumans do not share my excitement. Regardless of your interest or comfort levels with complexity, talent decisions are and always will be complex.

Talent decisions are complex because talent is a socially constructed concept that exists only in the realm of ideas, and humans must negotiate a shared understanding of what constitutes talent. Individual biases, beliefs and values can influence the negotiation process, and the language and discourse surrounding talent can affect individual, team and organisational outcomes.

The COVID-19 pandemic has added another layer of complexity to talent decision-making as organisations must navigate a rapidly evolving and uncertain landscape while making strategic talent decisions. Multiple forces influence talent decisions, and it is crucial to make this point explicitly.

The colourful interconnected ropes picture on the book's cover seeks to represent the complexity of talent decisions. We cannot treat talent decisions as a bounded phenomenon. Talent decisions relate to other decisions and outcomes. Each talent decision influences decisions and outcomes outside talent management.

## Technology is a Key Character in Talent Decisions

Technology is a key character in talent decisions because talent management and technology are interrelated, and their relationship is reciprocal. Effective talent management requires technology for process execution, and technology captures and computes workforce and talent data, informing talent-based decisions and practices. Talent availability influences technology selection and use, and technology shapes workforce structures and compositions. A holistic approach to talent management incorporating technology is essential because it is a crucial factor in talent decisions. Technology has shaped jobs, careers and career aspirations throughout history and will continue to do so in the future.

## Talent Decisions are Always Subjective

Talent decisions are always subjective, and it is vital to acknowledge and openly discuss the biased nature of these decisions. It is important to emphasise that all talent decisions involve human subjectivity and biases, and decision-makers should know how biases influence their judgments.

The goal is not to eliminate bias. We can't eliminate bias. The goal, however, is to develop an awareness of prejudices by asking, "What do I think and why, why, why do I think that?" and "What do you think and why, why, why do you think that?"

## Talent Decisions are Always Human-Human Decisions

I will continue to argue that humans are always the leading character. Humans write the script, influence the scenes that play out, and determine how the story ends. In any story about talent decisions, humans always take centre stage. #TeamHumans will continue to play the lead role today and on a future day.

## Talent Decisions Start With Internalised Thoughts

Talent decisions begin with a thought, so understanding the human mind and brain is essential. The human brain interprets and makes sense of the world around us. Being responsible starts with recognising the crucial role that our brains and minds play in decision-making because talent decisions are the outcomes of actions, and our actions are the product of our thoughts, which exist only in the realm of our minds.

## Understand That Humans Don't Think the Same Way

Yes, I know that you know that humans do not think the same way. Stating "the obvious" is core to our (re)thinking journey. Making the point that not all humans think the same way is essential. I have learnt that common sense and shared understandings are not as "common" as we tend to believe.

It's important to acknowledge that humans don't think the same way regarding various aspects of life, including work, talent management and technology. Perceptions matter and can significantly impact our decision-making processes.

## Identify Whether Differences are Semantic Or Conceptual

Human perceptions differ. The key focus, therefore, is to understand whether human differences are semantic or conceptual. You have learnt that potatoes and talent decisions are connected. Semantic differences are a case of you say po-tah-toes and I say po-tat-oes but we agree that we are both referring to edible root vegetables. Conceptual differences, however, involve different thoughts and images. Conceptual differences may result in one human thinking of an edible root vegetable while another is imagining potatoes as a white carbohydrate. Another human may think of vodka because it is a product they associate with potatoes. It is essential to identify whether human differences are semantic (language-based) or conceptual (thinking-based). Ignoring conceptual differences can have significant consequences for talent decisions.

## Foundational Human Beliefs About Reality and Knowledge Differ

I may have introduced you to two new concepts. Ontology refers to the study of the nature of existence or reality, our viewpoints and understandings of reality, and questions about what sorts of things exist in the social world. Epistemology considers our different assumptions about knowledge creation and questions whether something is truth or opinion. Perceptions about reality and knowledge are separable into different ontological and epistemological teams.

Positivism asserts that reality is singular and fixed and that truth and knowledge are "out there" waiting to be discovered (think the *X-Files* TV series.)

Other perspectives, social constructionism and interpretivism, disagree. Advocates of this perspective believe that there are multiple realities and all notions of reality. All forms of knowledge are subjective and co-constructed (think the *Choose Your Own Adventure* book series.)

Whilst I've reduced ontological perspectives into simple categories that miss or ignore the nuances of ontology, I believe that highlighting the different perspectives helps us garner more knowledge about ourselves and our fellow humans.

## Talent Management is Not Human Resource Management

Talent Management and Human Resource Management is not the same. I have said it before and will repeat, "Human Resource Management is about doing the same thing to everyone. Talent management is about doing something to someone."

One of the fundamental differences between talent management and human resource management lies in their focus. While human resource management is concerned with The Workforce, talent management emphasises individual employees or a select group of individuals.

Another crucial distinction is the scope of activities and involvement of different humans. Human resource policies and practices apply to everyone in The Workforce regardless of their roles or talent levels. In contrast, talent management activities prioritise specific individuals or categories of individuals. Talent management practices tend to be exclusive, benefiting only a select group of individuals, whereas human resource practices are inclusive and apply to The Workforce.

## Talent Management is About Judging Value

*(Re)Thinking Talent Decisions* challenges the idea that talent management is a set of discrete practices and instead defines it as an activity where humans judge the value of other humans based on current and future strategic goals. This involves making subjective judgments about the value of individuals, which then inform decisions and resource allocations. I encourage decision-makers to engage in critical discussions about how value is judged and evaluated, and to reflect on whose judgments of value matter most. Ultimately, talent is always in the "eye of the beholder," and understanding this subjective nature of talent decisions is crucial to effective talent management.

## Talent Decisions are Founded On Internalised Thoughts About Value

The value we place on individuals when making talent decisions is based on what we perceive as valuable. To make sound talent decisions, we must be mindful of the assumptions and ideas underlying our views of talent. Understanding how we define and think about "value" and what we perceive as valuable or not valuable in others is essential for talent decisions.

## Talent Decisions Involve Various Characters

Presenting my ideas as a tale and a stage play helped to illuminate that talent decisions feature many characters. Each of the three presented character groups – humans, technology and vendors – plays a role in talent decisions.

We examined the different "human" categories to explicitly acknowledge that talking about human-to-human decision-making is complex because humans are not homogenous. Humans wear numerous "hats" including as an individual, a member of The Workforce, a member of a specific team (e.g., senior executive, HR, IT), different seniorities (senior executive versus line managers) and gender and cultural groups.

Humans also wear an external rather than an internal character hat, with numerous external parties interested in talent decisions. Technology vendors are interested in selling their software with their commercial interests informing talent meanings, regardless of the level of customisation. External vendors providing leadership capability and competency models are also commercially interested in talent decisions because they generate revenue when organisations "buy" evaluation frameworks.

Recognising the various characters and reflecting on their interests and goals is important. The "hat" an individual wears at a specific time informs and shapes their perspective. A character group's "stake" influences how specific talent meanings, practices and decision systems are accepted for "doing" talent management.

## Character Voices Are Not Equal

Our (re)thinking tale highlighted many times that not all voices are created equal. Some characters take centre stage, others campaign in the wings and others are excluded from the negotiation processes.

Accepted ways of thinking have implications for how we do talent management, and how we do talent management has implications for people's careers. Think about whose perspective has become the accepted way of thinking. Whose view is dismissed, and whose perspective are we missing?

## Strategy Represents the "Why" of Talent Decisions

I won't discuss details here because the previous chapter focused on strategy. However, let us remember the strategic implications and that the execution of strategies benefits from effective decision-making.

And when we talk about "strategy," we should reflect on the implications of talent decisions for the different strategies. You can sing my rephrased nursery rhyme:

Sharna and other humans
Sitting in a tree
T-H-I-N-K-I-N-G
First comes the organisational strategy
Then comes the talent management and digitalised strategies
Then comes digitalised talent management strategies as represented in policies and practices

## Talent is Always Contextual

Talent is always contextual. Societal, institutional, phenomenological, organisational, localised and individual factors influence how individuals think about talent. Talent can only be examined within a specific context, at a particular time, and from specific individual perspectives.

We should not assume that the meaning of talent is universal and spreads across organisations, industries, or countries. This is because specific contexts shape perceptions and beliefs about talent and can differ significantly depending on the environment in which they arise. As a result, talent decisions cannot be understood or discussed outside of their specific context. Recognising and accounting for the localised factors that influence how talent is perceived and evaluated in a particular setting is essential.

## Talent's Transferability

We must not assume that talent is transferrable. The transferability of talent is not automatic because talent is contextual.

## There are Many Ways to Think About "Talent"

Highlighting the vastly different ways humans think about talent is the core contribution of this book. Much of the scientific knowledge centres on key debates around whether talent is inherent or acquired, should focus on The Workforce (an inclusive approach) or a select group of someones (an exclusive approach) or emphasises particular individuals (subject view) or aspects of an individual (object view). The challenge is, however, that the scientific perspectives (including my four talent categories of (1) everyone, (2) specifically designated individuals, (3) specifically designated skills and capabilities, (4) specifically designated jobs, roles, or positions) largely fail to recognise the realities of how humans think about talent, talk about talent and how decision-makers identify talent.

There are infinite possible definitions of talent because talent meanings start with an internal thought. However, Part 4 of this book captured many ways we talk about talent inside science, popular culture, work-based contexts and everyday conversations (see Figure 16.1).

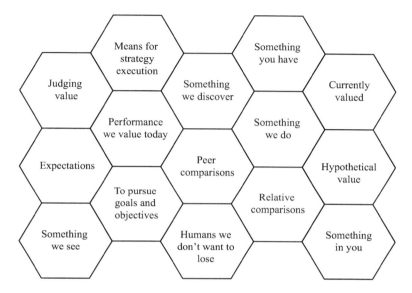

**Figure 16.1:** Talent categories.

## Think About Talent as a Verb Because We Value How Humans "Perform" Their Talent

A key outcome of this book is to get you to think about talent as a verb. Thinking about talent as a verb implies that talent is not just an innate ability or a static concept because we are interested in what an individual "does." Talent as a verb positions talent as a performative construct and recognises that we are interested in talent-in-action.

Talent, as a verb, recognises the reality of talent decisions whereby we judge whether or how individuals perform their talent. In workplace contexts, talent is primarily about how individuals perform their tasks and activities in accordance with the expectations of decision-makers. Talent evaluations judge how well individuals can complete their jobs, which must align with the preferences and goals of the evaluators. In other words, talent in the workplace is more about how decision-makers perceive individuals' talent performance. Talent assessments require individuals to conduct themselves and complete their tasks, activities and jobs per the evaluators' desires. Therefore, talent is a performative construct within the workplace.

## Think About Talent as A Series Of Observations

Talent decisions are based on a series of observations, which are particularly significant when we view talent as a verb – something we do. In this sense, we observe an individual's talent-in-action. Observations are salient when we think of talent as something we do because we are witnessing an individual's talent-in-action. We can observe how well they perform their tasks, how they approach problem-solving, how they collaborate with others and so on. These observations provide decision-makers with information to assess an individual's talent. As such, talent decisions can be based on observable actions and behaviours that indicate talent-in-action.

## It is Hard to Measure and Quantify Talent

Evaluating "talent" via numerical scores is part of many talent identification processes and a core functionality of talent decision systems. The willingness to recognise talent decisions' complex and subjective nature helps us question the ability to measure and quantify talent. I have long suspected the inability to reduce an individual's value to a number. I make this point via the following guiding principle:

> "Talent" is so complex and includes all the subtleties of life and organisations that it cannot be reduced to a single number, numerical digit, score, or measure. It is a rainbow, not black and white.

Seeking to measure and quantify talent may be flawed from the start because aspects of talent are hard to "put your finger on." Attributing scores to an individual's "potential" are always founded on the unknown. Judgements about potential are always theoretical. Talent scores, therefore, are based on an idealised view of an individual. Judging individuals and forecasting the possibility and probability of future outputs and performance is fraught. Who knows what the future looks like? Who knows what the future holds? Enacting talent decisions based on idealised reality may also limit responsible decision-making.

Talent scores emphasise past performance. And as we know from Finance, "past performance is not an indication of future performance." Are we then identifying talent based on outdated measures? (Especially when we realise talent frameworks are infrequently examined, validated, or updated.)

## Talent is a Team Sport

Talent scores rarely recognise the team-based nature of work. Technology and competency frameworks focus on an individual, but most work involves a broader system of interrelated tasks, activities, policies and processes. As documented in frameworks, superior performance fails to recognise that successful job, work and task execution is a team effort. Talent is a team sport.

## "Potential" is Always Hypothetical Value

The concept of talent is often discussed in terms of potential, which is future-oriented and based on subjective perceptions of value. Evaluating questions focus on whether an individual has the potential to become more valuable in the future. It isn't easy to define the characteristics required for potential. Potential is "hypothetical" because talent decisions based on potential are theoretical, speculative and subject to uncertainty.

Jordan B. Peterson, in presenting his eleventh of 12 Rules for Life in *Beyond Order*, reflects on the notion of potential, which is worth giving here:

> Whatever *potential* (original emphasis) might be . . . it does not follow the simple rules of material logic. Objects that play by the rules of the game we consider real (when we assume that what is real is also logical) can only be one thing at a time, and certainly not themselves and their opposite, simultaneously. Potential, however, is not like that. It is not categorisable in that manner . . . It is also not tangible, in the sense that the things we consider must be tangible. It does not even exist – except as *what could be* (original emphasis) exists. Perhaps it is best considered as the structure of reality, before reality manifests itself concretely in the present, where reality appears to most self-evidently exist. But creatures such as us do not contend with the present. It may therefore be that it is not the present that is most real – at least as far as our consciousness if concerned . . . left to our own devices, we turn our minds instead to investigating the future: *What could be?* (original emphasis) . . . That is the emergence of new being, new adventure, brought about by the conjunction of living consciousness with the great expanse of paradoxical possibility.

It's important to acknowledge the uncomfortable truth about potential: the realm of possibility is inherently uncertain, and outcomes are never guaranteed when investing in potential. While we may make cause-and-effect inferences, scientifically confirming or refuting them can be difficult. Establishing relationships between talent investments and outcomes is complex, as factors within and outside an individual's control influence outcomes.

The difficulty in establishing and articulating potential in material terms may be one of the reasons why most scientists talk about talent in terms of performance and potential. If talent and performance for the current day go together, then talent as hypothetical value for a future day is reaching out to hold their hands. Talent as the hypothetical value for a future day is asking to become part of the talent team. Talent as a hypothetical value for a future value follows closely behind. Although some scientists define talent management and talent according to potential, most imply that talent, performance AND potential are connected. Talent, performance and potential are inseparable. Reviewing the academic definitions presented above again illustrates the belief that you can't have one without the other; talent management focuses on performance and potential.

## Vendor-Designed Technology Plays A Key Role

The transition towards digitalised talent management and increasing automation can change the nature of decision-making. With digitalisation, key human characters can decide that technology is best placed to make talent decisions. Technology is frequently promoted as the solution to many human-people-talent-based problems associated with talent decisions (such as biased and ad hoc decisions). Technology is purported to be more objective, error-free and consistent in its decision-making capabilities than humans.

My research shows that digitalisation can change the "who" of talent decisions and further decrease certain human characters' role. Line managers can maintain a role. Line managers will continue to judge an individual's value. Line managers will maintain responsibility for inputting evaluating data into the talent system. HR's role, however, is more ambiguous. HR can continue to have a role in talent decisions if line managers seek their expertise and input. HR may assume a "justifying" role where they justify the outcomes of the automated processes to disgruntled individuals (if key humans decide to make talent decisions automatically).

There are other contexts where technology makes talent decisions. The extent to which automated decision-making becomes the norm is influenced by us – by you and me – and our perceptions of the value of technology. Humans decide to what extent technology transitions from a supporting to a leading role.

We can think of humans as providing the substance, while technology offers the shine.

## Identify What Shapes and Informs Talent Meanings

Asking, "What do you think talent means and why, why, why do you think that way?" has helped me understand why humans adopt and/or advocate for particular talent meanings. Over a decade's worth of questioning illuminates the importance of understanding Y.O.U. and the whys behind the Y.O.U.

Our (re)thinking tale highlighted some of the "whys" and learnt that meanings are informed and shaped by many factors, including movies, books, advertising, conversations with parents and teachers, sports and stereotypes. Talent decisions are about more than "work". Talent decisions are also societal decisions.

Congratulations, you have successfully increased your knowledge and thinking. We reflect on the implications of our (re)thinking talent decision tale for action next before concluding with some final words.

# Part 7: **Conclusion**

# Chapter 17
# Concluding Monologue

By presenting this book as a tale, offering thought-provoking questions, examples and analogies that connect complex ideas to familiar concepts, I hope to make the contexts "sticky." I want to create words that matter and inspire you to think more critically and deeply about all things talent and technology to improve decision-making. I want to improve human decision-making one decision at a time.

Now you may be asking, "Where to from here?" What can I do with my new knowledge?

Below are my thoughts about how you can continue advancing human decision-making in talent decisions and beyond.

## Action: Start With Y.O.U.

The importance of Y.O.U. (Your Own Understanding) in decision-making is highlighted, as our own experiences, beliefs and assumptions shape our decisions. Introspection is necessary to understand our thoughts, opinions, views, beliefs and values (see Figure 17.1).

Continually look inside yourself and ask, "What do I think and why, why, why do I think that?"

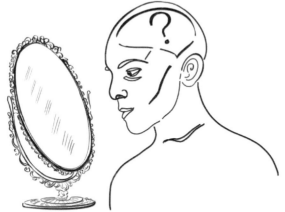

**Figure 17.1:** Start with Y.O.U. – Your Own Understanding.
Source: Copyright © Sharna Wiblen. All rights reserved.

## Action: Look in Before You Look Out

Understanding our thoughts is crucial to making responsible talent decisions. Self-reflection is encouraged before examining the thoughts of others. The tale of complexity, technology and subjectivity requires us to reflect on our thoughts and ask ourselves what we think.

A key action implication is to "Look in before you look out." Know what you think before engaging others. Think about your thinking.

## Action: Move from Y.O.U. to W.E.

Advancing human decision-making involves transitioning from Y.O.U. to W.E. Y.O.U. represents Your Own Understanding. W.E. focuses on Wider Exploration.

Examining the W.E. is vital because talent decisions do not end with a single Y.O.U. Talent decisions are a team sport. Remember to ask your fellow human counterparts, "What do you think and why, why, why do you think that way?" Advancing human decision-making requires a team effort.

Moving from Y.O.U. to W.E. helps us recognise that our decisions matter. Please know that your decisions affect you. Your decisions also affect others. *(Re)Thinking Talent Decisions* involves us all. Making better talent decisions is the job of us all. Recognise that your talent decisions and actions always do something to someone. Be mindful of the consequences and implications of your actions on your fellow someone's.

---

*(Re)thinking talent decisions starts with YOU. But talent decisions do not end with a single YOU. Talent decisions are a team sport.*

---

## Action: Learn About Your Ontology and Epistemology

Talking and writing about ontology and epistemology excites me because I think our different views of reality help account for our different views of talent. I hypothesise that some contentions stem from how we perceive the nature and structure of reality and knowledge. I hypothesise that members of #teampositivism are more inclined to talk about talent in terms of talent being discoverable. The notion that we all have talent and need to discover it (over time) implies that an individual's talent is fixed, and we can know the "truth" about talent. Talking about whether somebody has talent inside them also seems connected with this "fixed" view. Maybe, just maybe, positivists are staunch advocates of measuring and quantifying talent because they believe that knowledge is objective and measurable. Maybe, just maybe, positivists are more likely to talk about talent in binary terms – whether a human is or is not talented, has or doesn't have talent – because they like to confirm and reject hypotheses with "yes" and "no" answers part of their thinking. Are they more likely to advocate for an all-purpose talent meaning because they are comfortable viewing talent as "static?"[26]

## Action: Ask (Better) Questions

My first aim for this book is to incite questions. (Re)Thinking talent decisions involves asking questions. Be clear about the questions. Better questions underpin better answers. (Re)thinking talent decisions involves (re)asking questions. Ask whether this/that is the right question? Are these the right questions to be asking?

A secondary aim of this book is to encourage (re)asking and embrace the power of (re)framing. (Re)framing enables us to (re)question the benefits, challenges and obstacles. Reasking and reframing seek to address a component of decision-making identified by Nobel Laureate Daniel Kahneman: humans tend to supplement easier questions for harder ones without realising it.

The power of reframing or rephrasing questions is not lost on me. As a parent, I make daily enquiries about that day's school experiences. Many of these conversations start with an open enquiry, "I'd love to hear about your day." Open questions are more effective than the easier and more automatic, "How was your day?" Asking the latter question elicits a "good," "bad," "OK," "Huh?" or a shrug accompanied by a "dunno."

The older kids, well versed with mummy's enquiries, are more forthcoming with their chosen information. While my youngest sometimes responds with an "I don't want to talk about it," I will propose the need to talk about it because silence or abstaining from the conversation is not an option.

A short time may pass, but additional enquiries are always made. While essentially asking the same question, I adopt a different tack. My approach recognises that my questioning may have halted the conversation or encouraged a specific answer (e.g., an automatic or previous response). Trying another line of questioning is vital because my goal, my desired outcome, is to foster conversations and dialogue. My go-to exploratory question is, "Can you tell me more about that?"

You can think of yourself as a parent or as a medical practitioner. Medical practitioners only offer a "solution" after asking questions. Many of the questions which doctors ask are pivotal questions rephrased. They realise that a slight change in the language or framing can change patients' responses and answers.

Reasking and reframing also help humans to move away from their "action" bias. Humans love to "do." Humans potentially like to "do" more than they want to "think."

---

[26] I wonder, and wonder a lot, about whether increasing an individual's knowledge about how they view reality and knowledge would help humans learn more about themselves and that this knowledge would act as a "why" when asking about the assumptions/foundations/reasons for our thoughts (and why, why, why do you think that?).

I enjoy Joshua Fields Millburn from *The Minimalists*' following words because they highlight the propensity for us to seek "solutions" before comprehensively diagnosing the "problem":

> Most people want "solutions" because they're unwilling to dig down to the root of the problem. What if, instead of numbing the pain, you sidestepped the solutions and scrutinised the problem itself? If your desk chair is aflame, reading the *Fire Safety Manual* won't save you. The problem isn't a lack of instructions – the problem is your posterior is on fire.

I wonder if we seek "solutions" more than we ask questions. Will talent decisions and society benefit from us investing greater time and resources into asking diagnostic questions and prioritising "thinking" over "doing?"[27]

However, there are no right or wrong answers to the questions. Every decision-maker, technology and organisation are gloriously complex – what makes our world unique. While some ideas will apply to you, your team and your organisation, other ideas and discussions are less so. You can pick and choose but are encouraged to do so deliberately and intentionally. Use the non-applicable parts to improve your understanding (and empathy). Sometimes we don't know what we know or think about what we think until somebody asks us!

## Action: Make Responsible Talent Decisions

Talking, and on this occasion writing, about the complexity associated with #Teamhuman and #Teamtechnology sparks joy (kudos to Marie Kondo). The goal is to foster responsible talent management whereby decisions and actions are deliberate, intentional and informed.

Illustrating, illuminating and acknowledging Y.O.U. is the foundation of responsible decision-making. This book forms part of a broader program of speaking, writing and teaching whereby my desired outcome is to foster responsible decision-making. To be responsible means to devise and enact decisions and actions that are deliberate, intentional and informed.

- To be **deliberate** = undertake decisions and actions *with thought.*
- To be **intentional** = undertake decisions and actions *on purpose.*
- To be **informed** = undertake decisions and actions based *on knowledge.*

---

27 (Better) Questions underpin effective talent decisions. A key "where to from here" question is - if turning to vendors and using vendors designed systems are the answer, then what are the questions?

## Deliberate (With Thought)

Together we transition from conjecture and opinion to informed thoughts and perspectives. To do so, we are deliberate with "thinking." To be deliberate means to undertake decisions and actions "with thought." References to "deliberate" date back to the 1540s, with the word's etymology focusing on the mind – on activities that occur in our minds and heads. Being deliberate involves weighing ideas in their mind, giving careful consideration and/or discussing and examining reasons for or against them.

The short DrSharnaism to explain the notion of being deliberate is – "Know what you think and why, why, why you think that."

Being and acting deliberately means we allocate time, energy and attention to "thinking": thinking about Y.O.U. and thinking about W.E. (wider exploration), thinking about strategy, thinking about talent, thinking about technology and thinking about the world we want to live in.

## Intentional (On Purpose)

We transition from understanding our thoughts, what we think and why, why, why we think that to designing and enacting intentional decisions. Intentional decisions and actions are "on purpose." Decisions and actions are not accidental or the outcome of "going with the flow." Responsible decision-makers do not hand over their power, agency, or control. They participate in determining or shaping decisions and actions. Responsible decision-makers are "deciders," not "sliders."

---

*Responsible decision-makers are deciders, not sliders.*

---

The modus operandi of intentional decision-making involves investing in the design process – desired outcomes and the why, why, why of decisions and actions are predefined. You must always start with Y.O.U. – Your Own Understanding. Desired outcomes and the why, why, why of decisions and actions are founded on deliberate thought.

## Informed (Based on Knowledge)

Occurring alongside purposeful design processes are reflections about the extent to which decisions are based on knowledge. The goal is to transition from conjecture and opinion to informed thoughts and actions. Step 1 involves acknowledging where thoughts are founded upon what you think versus what you know. A second DrSharnaism to assist with the journey is to ask, "Do you think that, or do you know that?"

Basing decisions and actions on knowledge and insights reemphasises the salience of thinking. Thinking about what we think and whether our thinking is based on opinion – what we think – or knowledge – what we know and that we have evidence for? In this instance, evidence can be qualitative or quantitative data, sources of fact or observations relevant to the individual, team, or organisation.

---

*Responsible decision-making allows you to decipher between an "opinion" and a "perspective."*
*An opinion = "I think X."*
*A perspective = "I know X."*

---

Other forms of evidence include research, the empirical or scientifically valid information about the specific phenomena, topic, or subject. Scientists play a pivotal role in the latter, with many of their scientific insights underpinning or featured in the discussions and reflections included in this book.

Together, we can challenge the choices that have been created and explore other possibilities. We can engage in informed conversations that consider the complexity of talent and talent management. I do hope that this book will inspire you to undertake deliberate, intentional and informed decision-making.

## Action: Separate Thinking From The Results

Focusing on thinking enables humans to take responsibility for their decisions, regardless of the outcomes. Whether as anticipated, designed, or otherwise, the "result" or "outcome" happens after a carefully considered decision-making process.

*Thinking in Bets* is a fascinating book by Annie Duke, a renowned professional poker player turned decision strategist. One of the concepts that Duke delves into is the idea of "resulting," which is the tendency to judge a decision based on its outcome rather than the quality of the decision-making process itself. Duke explains that "resulting" is a dangerous cognitive trap that leads us to ignore valuable feedback and overestimate our abilities. Instead, Duke encourages us to focus on making the best possible decision given the information we have at the time rather than simply striving for a positive outcome. By embracing uncertainty and recognising the limitations of our knowledge, we can become better (and more responsible) decision-makers.

## Action: Pick and Use Your Words Wisely

Talk is often seen as "cheap." The things that really matter are decisions and actions. However, this assumption could not be further from the truth regarding talent decisions. Talent is often said to be an organisation's greatest asset, a source of competitive advantage and a crucial contributor to financial performance. But what about the way we talk about talent? Does it really matter how we define and describe talent? The answer is a resounding yes.

The meanings attributed to "talent" influence how decision-makers identify talent and the treatment of these individuals. In other words, how we talk about talent affects how we and others act. Like talent and technology, there is a reciprocal relationship between "talking" and "action." How we talk about talent every day shapes our perceptions and actions, both as individuals and as groups of individuals (The Workforce). We must be mindful of the language that we pick and use.

Talent decisions occur every day and I wholeheartedly agree with Brené Brown's words about the importance of considering the language humans use in their everyday lived experiences,

> How we, the collective, use language matters as much as, if not more than, arbitrary definitions that don't centre lived experiences. If research is going to serve people, it has to reflect their experiences.

My research and experiences show differences in how executives react depending on the language used. For example, I prefer to say, "We see the world differently" and talk in terms of different "perspectives" rather than the uncomfortable truth that humans are "biased" decision-makers. The first statement is more welcomed than the second statement which tends to elicit a negative or defensive "no I'm not" response. I also frame potential in terms of "hypothetical" value rather than "guessing," "betting," and "gambling," even though we are hoping that our investing in humans (rather than cards or horses) will "pay off" at a later date.

I was particularly interested in leaders' language and specific words during and post-COVID-19. The implied meanings underpinning internal messaging were of particular interest. I often wondered how leaders' talk during this immense uncertainty would influence whether The Workforce returned to work – work as a physical space as represented in an office or workplace. A multi-dimensional viewpoint on language acknowledges that leaders' language around work and talent impacts how individuals perceive their leaders' support.

By framing talent as an "investment" and choosing to retain The Workforce, leaders can make individuals feel like they have been embraced. Compare this verbal and (inferred) psychological contract to where leaders talked about talent as the organisation's most considerable "expense" or pursued a strategy of targeted or voluntary redundancies. Maybe, just maybe, executives that adopted this approach are more successful in having The Workforce come "back into the office." For the latter group, returning to "the office" may feel less like an experience of feeling valued and more like a reminder of being mistreated. It may reignite feelings of being dismissed or not appreciated.

It is not enough to acknowledge the importance of talent management. We must also be mindful of how we talk about talent. Strategy-as-discourse becomes a greater

...ority when decision-makers recognise languages' pivotal role in shaping human thought, behaviours and actions.

It's time to start paying attention to how you talk about talent. Your words matter and can make a difference in identifying, retaining and treating talent within your organisation. Talk is not cheap in this context; using the wrong words can be costly. So, think carefully about how you talk about talent because how we communicate our thoughts and ideas can elicit intended and unintended responses.

## Action: Learn How To "See"

What decision-makers "see" or "not see" influences talent decisions, promotions, access to development opportunities and careers. If talent decisions are based on seeing talent – what you see and do not see – then please learn how to "see." Learning how to "see" is particularly pertinent if you think you "Know talent when you see it" or think someone has the "X factor," because these judgments are affected by your "observing" skills and experience. Decision-makers must learn how to observe talent effectively.

I have long argued that executives must learn to generally and specifically observe talent-in-action. A heightened interest in ethnography arose after numerous executives noted that they "know talent when they see it." I then questioned if "we know talent when we see it" or are constantly judging an individual's talent-in-action or whether they performed their talent according to various measurements and expectations; who teaches decision-makers how to see?[28]

Anthropology and its research methodology of ethnography can help.[29] By developing skills in observation and research methodologies such as participant or non-participant observation, individuals can better understand how people complete tasks and interact in various contexts. This understanding is essential for deciding which tasks can be automated and which require human decision-making.

## Action: Revisit "The Endings"

Throughout our journey, we have seen how technology has transformed work, making decision-making easier and more convenient. However, we have also learnt the

---

[28] I teach executives how to "see." As an executive educator, my MBA and EMBA students learn the basics of ethnography and observation. Along with hearing about Sophie Goodman's expertise and experiences, students develop an understanding of the power of observing humans and interactions and the extent to which we judge others based on what we think we see. Armed with this insight, they know more about their thoughts and can make more responsible and effective decisions.

[29] Engaging with Sophie Goodman's chapter in *Digitalised Talent Management: Navigating the Human-Technology Interface* is a great place to start learning about ethnography because her insights relate to our (re)thinking tale.

complexity of talent decisions and humans' different understandings of knowledge. Moreover, as we consider the future of work, we must grapple with questions about the potential benefits and consequences of increasing digitalisation and automation.

We can think about how this tale ends in multiple ways because there is no clear conclusion. I offered three different "Endings."

### A Pre-defined Ending – Technology Will Have An "Impact"

Notwithstanding my inability to provide a neat conclusion, some humans adopt a different perspective. Positivists believe technology has immediate and direct consequences on work and is the principal character in the narrative of (re)thinking talent decisions. They advocate for objective knowledge and believe that projections about the consequences of technology presume that it automatically affects organisations that adopt it. Positivist assumptions are often sensationalised in media outlets and popular culture. Humans seem constantly attacked by robots or some form of artificial life. This narrative of humans versus robots influences how individuals view technology, especially AI innovations, in the workplace. According to positivists, there is a single "Ending." The Ending of our story is pre-determined. They can predict "The Ending" with confidence.

Our "Pre-defined Ending asserts that technology – in and of itself – will do things to other things.

### It Depends – Technology Can Influence, But Humans Decide How to Use Technology in the End

Another way of thinking believes technology is not the sole determinant of organisational outcomes and that its influence (rather than impact) depends on contextual factors. This perspective emphasises that technology is a tool, not the ultimate destination. Technology is not the "somewhere" of talent decisions. The Ending of the story of technology use is not pre-determined. How the story ends, well, "It Depends," because outcomes vary depending on how humans use technology and their decisions. Recognising that the relationship between technology and social factors is interconnected helps us approach talent decisions in ways that are mindful of the complex nature of talent decisions, strategy and outcomes.

Our "It Depends" Ending believes that human perceptions influence use patterns and outcomes.

## Infinite "It Depends" Endings – The interrelationship Between Humans and Technology Influences the Endings

I also introduced you to Social-material, a scientific theoretical perspective that acknowledges the complexity of technology and its simultaneous influence on social factors. The framework recognises the interrelationship between technology and humans, creating infinite possible outcomes for our tale. This perspective asserts that the ending of our (re)thinking tale continually evolves as technology and humans interact and change. Therefore, humans, myself included, are left to speculate about what the future might hold for the human-technology interface and talent decisions.

Our Infinite "It Depends" endings propose that human perceptions, experiences and material properties influence use patterns and outcomes.

This book proposes no definitive ending to the story of complexity, technology and subjectivity. Individuals' different perspectives and perceptions make it impossible to predict a single outcome. I encourage you all, my #Teamhuman counterparts, to consider the potential implications and effects of increasing digitalisation and automation. I also encourage you to imagine the impact (positivist) and influence (social constructionist and interpretivism) of technology-based decision-making within the context of "work." I also encourage you to think deeply about society's future and technology's role in shaping it.

Why? You ask. I will give you my three reasons why.

Why #1: Because humans make talent decisions and decide which "technology" to select, implement and use, or not use, in talent decisions in workplaces. But work-based talent decisions influence humans and humans are active members of society. Workplace talent decisions, therefore, affect organisations, communities, cultures and societies.

Why #2: Because highlighting the inherent complexity of the human-technology interface helps humans think about their thinking processes, everyday experiences and assumptions about what is possible and probable.

Why #3: Because humans are the main characters in all digitalisation tales. Humans design all technologies. Humans, therefore, can decide to "not design" or "release" certain technologies because of the unknown or potentially damaging consequences.

Together we must pay attention to the ever-changing technology landscape and dream about the potential good and bad implications for talent decisions.

## Action: Draw The World You Want To Create

Given human agency in all talent decisions and technology, I leave you with a final action. An action that involves "thinking" about the world as you would like to design it.

I encourage you to partake in a hands-on and creative exercise. The goal is to think about and draw the world you want to create. (We are bringing our thoughts into the material world.)

Start with a blank piece of paper. When designing, starting with a clean slate (as represented by the blank paper) is best.

Now, gather some drawing supplies and start drawing.

I am not going to give you any further specific directions. I am not telling you what to draw. Look and feel within yourself and transfer your thoughts onto the page.

However, I challenge you to use as many colours as possible. Include a kaleidoscope of talent colours as you compose your masterpiece. Don't limit yourself to a set of 12 colours. Use the most extensive colour range you can think of. A Google search shows that we humans can access massive colour sets. Imagine the possibilities, the options and the nuances if we considered 520 different colours when designing the world.

Designing from scratch is a powerful tool before all technological innovations start with an idea. All talent decisions begin with a thought. What's inside your mind and your imagination is powerful. So powerful that you can shape the world as we know it. So be mindful of what world you want to create. Recognise and appreciate the spectrum of human talents.

Together #Teamhuman can make the world a more colourful place.

Together #Teamhuman can make the world a better place.

#Teamhuman can make the world a better and more colourful place, one decision at a time.

Congratulations, my #Teamhuman counterparts. This is the end of our (re)thinking journey. Our journey started with telling you I want to encourage you to "think." This book is about thinking, exploring the power of our minds, how we perceive key concepts, and the implications of our "thinking" for humans and human-based decision-making. I wrote this book for you and me. I want to improve human decision-making, and I would be grateful if you could help me with this goal. We can improve together, one decision at a time. Again, thank you, my #Teamhuman counterparts, for making every day colourful.

# Endnotes

## Prologue

- **"Thinking" definition**: *Compact Oxford Dictionary, Thesaurus, and Wordpower Guide* (Oxford: Oxford University Press, 2001), 946.
- **"Thinking" definition**: Merriam-Webster Online Dictionary, https://www.merriam-webster.com/dictionary/thinking.
- **"Think" definition**: *Compact Oxford Dictionary, Thesaurus, and Wordpower Guide* (Oxford: Oxford University Press, 2001), 945.

## A Tale of Complexity, Technology, and Subjectivity

- **OECD's Dream Jobs report**: Anthony Mann, Vanessa Denis, Andreas Schleicher, Hamoon Ekhtiari, Tarralynn Forsyth, Elvin Liu and Nick Chambers, *Dream Jobs? Tennagers' Career Aspirations and the Future of Work* (2020), https://www.oecd.org/berlin/publikationen/Dream-Jobs.pdf.
- **". . . with specific technologies serving as enablers . . ."**: See Matt Beane and Wanda J. Orlikowski, "What Difference Does a Robot Make? The Material Enactment of Distributed Coordination," *Organization Science* 26, no. 6 (2015): 1553–1573. See doi:10.1287/orsc.2015.1004 for a discussion of digitalisation as an enabler.

## Introducing the Cast

- **Cognitive Bias Codex**: created by John Manoogian III and Buster Benson. Learn more about the Codex via designhacks.co.
- **Senior executives are losing sleep over talent issues**: as noted in a LinkedIn post by Bhushan Sethi, *Why CEO's are losing sleep over talent – and four ways to help them rest easier*, February 27, 2016, https://www.linkedin.com/pulse/why-ceos-losing-sleep-over-talent-four-ways-help-them-bhushan-sethi.
- **KPMG Keeping us up at night**: *Keeping Us Up at Night: The big issues facing business leaders in 2022*, https://assets.kpmg/content/dam/kpmg/au/pdf/2022/issues-facing-australian-leaders-2022-outlook.pdf.
- **Debating the suitability of HR**: see the following for a scientific discussion of HR's role in talent management: Thomas J. Calo, "Talent Management in the Era of the Aging Workforce: The Critical Role of Knowledge Transfer," *Public Personnel Management* 37, no. 4 (2008), 403–416; Marion Devine and Marcus Powell, "Talent management in the public sector," *360 The Ashridge Journal* (2008): 1–6.

- "... **talent identification includes online and offline data**": Talent identification is a two-stage process: Kristiina Mäkelä, Igmar Björkman and Mats Ehrnrooth, "How do MNCs establish their talent pools? Influences on individuals' likelihood of being labeled as talent," *Journal of World Business* 45, no. 2 (2010): 134–142.
- **The Center for Effective Organizations report**: Edward Lawler, Alec Levenson and John Boudreau, "HR Metrics and Analytics: Use and Impact," *Human Resource Planning* 27, no. 4 (2004): 27–35.
- "... **HR had fallen victim to unrealistic expectations**": David Brown, "eHR – victim of unrealistic expectations," *Canadian HR Reporter* 15, no. 5 (2002): 1; and "HR pulled in two directions at once," *Canadian HR Reporter* 17, no. 4 (2004): 1–2.
- "... **for executing specific data-based tasks in a specific order**": Wanda J. Orlikowski and Susan Scott, "The algorithm and the crowd: Considering the materiality of service innovation," *MIS Quarterly* 39, no. 1 (2015): 201–216.
- "**The HR and talent vendor space is experiencing rapid expansion**": https://www.shrm.org/resourcesandtools/hr-topics/technology/pages/josh-bersin-presents-hr-tech-2022.aspx.
- "**Billion-dollar valuations**": https://joshbersin.com/2021/07/hr-tech-is-white-hot-is-every-vendor-now-a-unicorn/.
- "**Alec Levenson delves into the benefits and limitations of competency models**": Alec Levenson, "Competencies in an Era of Digitalised Talent Management," in *Digitalised Talent Management: Navigating the Human-Technology Interface*, ed. Sharna Wiblen (New York: Routledge, 2021), 51–78.

## Talent Decisions in the Pursuit of Strategy

- "**Reflecting on the Future: What the Space Race . . .**": aspects of this example were initially published as a blog post, "What the Space Race is Illuminating about the shifting boundaries of talent," on SharnaWiblen.com, published October 25, 2021.
- **Merriam-Webster online dictionary defines strategy as**: https://www.merriam-webster.com/dictionary/strategy, accessed June 24, 2022.
- **Compact Oxford Dictionary, Thesaurus and Wordpower Guide** (Oxford: Oxford University Press, 2001), 896.
- "**ChatGPT answered "What is Strategy"**: accessed May 13, 2023.
- "**While posing "What is the definition of strategy?" to ChatGPT**": accessed May 13, 2023.
- **Strategy definition by Alfred Chandler**: Alfred Chandler, *Strategy and Structure: Chapters in the History of the American Industrial Enterprise* (MIT Press, reprint by BeardBooks, Washington, USA, 1969), 13,
- **Strategy definition by Henry Mintzberg**: Henry Mintzberg, "Patterns in Strategy Formulation," *Management Science* 24, no. 9 (1978): 934–948.

- **Strategy definition by Peter Drucker**: learn more about Peter Drucker and his business ideas in Peter Drucker, "The Theory of the Business," *Harvard Business Review* (September–October 1994): 95–104.
- **Strategy and Michael Porter**:
    - "Competitive strategy, and its core disciplines . . .": Michael Porter, *Competitive Strategy: Techniques for Analysing Industries and Competitors* (New York: Free Press, 2004), xiv.
    - "Staying flexible in strategic terms . . .": Michael Porter, *Competitive Strategy: Techniques for Analysing Industries and Competitors* (New York: Free Press, 2004), xv–xvi.
    - "Successful strategies require choice": Michael Porter, *Competitive Strategy: Techniques for Analysing Industries and Competitors* (New York: Free Press, 2004), xiv.
- **Meyers on "Strategy-as-practice . . . proposes . . ."**: Maria Christina Meyers, Marianna van Woerkom, Jaap Paawe and Nicky Dries, "HR managers' talent philosophies: prevalence and relationships with perceived talent management practices," *The International Journal of Human Resource Management* 31, no. 4 (2020): 562–588, doi:10.1080/09585192.2019.1579747. Quote references Paula Jarzabkowski, "Strategy as Practice: Recursiveness, Adaptation, and Practices-in-Use," *Organization Studies* 25, no. 4 (2004): 529–560, https://doi.org/10.1177/0170840604040675.
- **Beyond HR: The New Science of Human Capital**: by John Boudreau and Peter Ramstad (Boston: Harvard Business School Press, 2007).
    - Leaders should consider talent, 221.
    - "Talentship helps organizations identify . . .", 20.
    - To consider pivotal areas where . . ., 40.
    - Talentship connects organizational and talent decisions, 86 and 87.
- **Robert E. Lewis and Robert J. Heckman**: "Talent management: A critical review," *Human Resource Management Review* 16, no. 2 (2006): 139–154.
- **Building a Game Changing Talent Strategy**: by Douglas Ready, Linda Hill and Robert Thomas, *Harvard Business Review*, January–February 2014, https://hbr.org/2014/01/building-a-game-changing-talent-strategy.
- **Business-driven approach**: Sharna Wiblen, David Grant and Kristine Dery, "Transitioning to a New HRIS: The Reshaping of Human Resources and Information Technology Talent," *Journal of Electronic Commerce Research* 11, no. 4 (2010): 251–267.
- **Technology-driven approach**: Sharna Wiblen, David Grant and Kristine Dery, "Transitioning to a New HRIS: The Reshaping of Human Resources and Information Technology Talent," *Journal of Electronic Commerce Research* 11, no. 4 (2010): 251–267.
- **"In the past, key decision-makers . . ."**: see Samir Shrivastava and James B. Shaw, "Liberating HR Through Technology," *Human Resource Management* 42, no. 3 (2003): 201–222.

- **"Pathway 1 . . ."**: Peter Weill and Stephanie L. Woerner, "Is Your Company Ready for a Digital Future?", *MIT Sloan Management Review* 59, no. 2 (2018): 21–25.
- **iPhone homepage**: https://www.apple.com/au/iphone/switch/ accessed July 27, 2022.
- **Wikipedia List of Android smartphones**: https://en.wikipedia.org/wiki/List_of_Android_smartphones, accessed July 28, 2022.

## Talent Decisions in the Pursuit of Knowledge

- **Knowledge definition**: *Compact Oxford Dictionary, Thesaurus, and Wordpower Guide* (Oxford: Oxford University Press, 200), 499.
- **ChatGPT "What is Knowledge?"**: accessed June 6, 2023.
- **ChatGPT "What is the definition of knowledge"**: accessed June 6, 2023.
- **"For instance, in my PhD project . . ."**: Sharna Wiblen, "Talking about Talent: Conceptualising Talent Management through Discourse," Doctor of Philosophy Thesis, University of Sydney, 2015.
- **Michael Crotty and the tree description of positivism**: Michael Crotty, *The Foundation of Social Research: Meaning and Perspective in the Research Process* (Crows Nest: Allen and Unwin, 1998), 8.
- **Choose Your Own Adventure books**: the book I have and refer to is by R.A. Montgomery, *Journey Under the Sea* (Sydney: Scholastic, 1978).

## Our Tale End(ings)

- **"Those who belong to team positivism"**: see Janet H. Marler and Sandy Fisher, "An evidence-based review of e-HRM and strategic human resource management," *Human Resource Management Review* 23, no. 1 (2013): 18–36 for an overview of scientific studies that apply different epistemological frameworks. Also read Wanda J. Orlikowski and Susan Scott, "Sociomateriality: Challenging the Separation of Technology, Work and Organization," *The Academy of Management Annals* 2 (2008): 433–474 for greater details about the application of a technological determinism theoretical framework to organisation-wide and HR technology projects.
- **"The social constructionist framework . . ."**: the following papers apply the social constructionist perspective: Sharna Wiblen, "Talking about Talent: Conceptualising Talent Management through Discourse," Doctor of Philosophy Thesis, University of Sydney, 2015; Sharna Wiblen, David Grant and Kristine Dery "Transitioning to a New HRIS: The Reshaping of Human Resources and Information Technology Talent," *Journal of Electronic Commerce Research* 11, no. 4 (2010), 251–267; Sharna Wiblen, Kristine Dery and David Grant, "Do you see what I see?

The role of technology in talent identification," *Asia Pacific Journal of Human Resources* 50, no. 4 (2012): 421–438.
- **Janet H. Marler's and my paper applying social-material**: Sharna Wiblen and Janet H. Marler, "Digitalised talent management and automated talent decisions: the implications for HR professionals," *The International Journal of Human Resource Management* 32, no. 12 (2021): 2592–2621, doi:10.1080/09585192.2021.1886149.
- **". . . technology only becomes useful when people use it"**: Wanda J. Orlikowski and Susan Scott, "Sociomateriality: Challenging the Separation of Technology, Work and Organization," *The Academy of Management Annals* 2 (2008): 433–474.
- **". . . dynamics influence technology's use patterns."**: myself and colleagues refer to patterns of use in the context of interpretive schemes – such as the skills, knowledge and assumptions about the technology that the user brings to bear in the following two papers: Sharna Wiblen, Kristine Dery and David Grant, "Do you see what I see? The role of technology in talent identification," *Asia Pacific Journal of Human Resources* 50, no. 4 (2010): 421–438; Kristine Dery, Richard Hall and Nick Wailes, "ERPs as 'technologies-in-practice': social construction, materiality and the role of organisational factors," *New Technology, Work and Employment* 21, no. 3 (2006): 229–241.

## (Re)Thinking Talent Management

- **"In 2006, Robert E. Lewis and Robert J. Heckman . . ."**: Robert E. Lewis and Robert J. Heckman, "Talent management: A critical review," *Human Resource Management Review* 16, no. 2 (2006): 139–154.
- **"Scientists continue . . . with three dominate approaches . . ."**: see Chapter 2 of Anthony McDonnell and Sharna Wiblen, *Talent Management: A Research Overview* (New York: Routledge, 2021).

## (Re)Thinking Talent Meanings

- **Talent definition:** *Compact Oxford Dictionary, Thesaurus, and Wordpower Guide* (Oxford: Oxford University Press, 2001), 926.
    - **"A special natural ability or aptitude . . ."**: from Dictionary.com, accessed September 30, 2022.
    - **"A natural aptitude, an inner quality that emerges effortlessly"**: from Workable.com, accessed September 30, 2022.
    - "(someone who has) a natural ability . . .": from Cambridge Dictionary, https://dictionary.cambridge.org/dictionary/english/talent, accessed September 30, 2022.

- **ChatGPT directed to answer "What is talent?" and "What is the definition of talent?"**: on April 20, 2023. Answers generated by Robert Sisson. The footnote highlights that the responses generated differed between first-time users and somewhat trained users, with ChatGPT generating vastly different answers to these questions than others would receive because ChatGPT is being trained on my writing.
- **"The vast array of scientific definitions . . ."**: see Anthony McDonnell and Sharna Wiblen, *Talent Management: A Research Overview* (New York:Routledge, 2021).
- **"We define talent . . ."**: John Boudreau and Peter Ramstad, *Beyond HR: The New Science of Human Capital* (Boston: Harvard Business School Press, 2007), 2.
- **"Talent has been used broadly . . ."**: Hilligje Gerritdina Van Dijk, "Administration VS.Talent: The Administrative Context for Talent Management," *Journal of Public Administration* 44, no. 3.1 (2009): 520–530.
- **"From a human capital perspective . . ."**: Nicky Dries, "The psychology of talent management: A review and research agenda," *Human Resource Management Review* 23, no. 4 (2013): 272–285.
- **"Talent refers to systematically developed . . ."**: Sanne Nijs, Eva Gallardo-Gallardo, Nicky Dries and Luc Sels, "A multidisciplinary review into the definition, operationalization, and measurement of talent," *Journal of World Business* 49, no. 2 (2014): 180–191, https://doi.org/10.1016/j.jwb.2013.11.002.
- **"John Boudreau and I posed this question . . ."**: definitions noted in John Boudreau's "The Future of HR: Five Essential but Overlooked Questions" article published on aNewHR, February 26, 2020, https://anewhr.com/the-future-of-hr-five-essential-but-overlooked-questions/, accessed November 8, 2022.
- **"In February 2022, during the global pandemic . . ."**: Sharna Wiblen and Alec Levenson, *HR technology purchasing decisions: Who gets to decide how we act on talent?* Enterprise Effectiveness Network, Center for Effective Organizations, 2022, online February 24, 2022.

## (Re)Thinking Talent Categories

- **Subject versus object**: Nicky Dries published the subject and object talent perspectives in "The psychology of talent management: A review and research agenda," *Human Resource Management Review* 23, no. 4 (n.d.): 272–285.
- **"Everyone is talent versus specific individuals . . ."**: see Anthony McDonell and Sharna Wiblen, *Talent Management: A Research Overview* (New York: Routledge, n.d.).
- **Learn more about John Boudreau and Peter Ramstad's *Talentship***: via "Talentship and the New Paradigm for Human Resource Management: From Profes-

sional Practices to Strategic Talent Decision Science," *Human Resource Planning* 28, no. 2 (n.d.): 17–26; "Talentship, talent segmentation, and sustainability: A new HR decision science paradigm for a new strategy definition," *Human Resource Management* 44, no. 2 (n.d.): 129–136; and "Talentship and HR Measurement and Analysis: From ROI to Strategic Organizational Change," *Human Resource Planning* 29, no. 1 (n.d.): 25–33.
- **Maybelline's advertising campaign**: 1991 advertisement viewed via YouTube, https://www.youtube.com/watch?v=ZDO-2qce1oI, accessed September 2, 2022; Maybelline's Make It Happen 2016 tagline from https://www.mamamia.com.au/maybellines-new-tagline/, accessed September 2, 2022.
- **Discovering talent: The case of My Little Pony**: Brad Carrabine, *The Cutie Mark Crusaders*, Part of the My Little Pony Series published by The Five Mile Press (2014).
- **Stephen R. Covey and Cynthia Covey Haller**: *Live Life in Crescendo: Your Most Important Work is Always Ahead of You* (London: Simon & Schuster, 2022).
  - "As we work to uncover and utilise . . .": (2022), 27–28.
  - "It's important to discover your purpose . . .": (2022), 28–29.
  - ". . . It is essential to discover . . .": (2022), 240.
  - "I have always believed . . .": (2022), 240.
- **Scientific paper about boring people**: Wijnand A.P. Van Tilburg, Eric R. Igou and Mehr Panjwani, "Boring People: Stereotype Characteristics, Interpersonal Attributions, and Social Reactions," *Personality and Social Psychology Bulletin* (2022), 014616722210791, doi:10.1177/01461672221079104.
- **"My awareness of talent as something that you see . . ."**: arose from my PhD; see Sharna Wiblen, "Talking about Talent: Conceptualising Talent Management through Discourse," Doctor of Philosophy Thesis, University of Sydney, 2015.
- **"Do you see what I see? The role of technology in talent identification"**: Sharna Wiblen, Kristine Dery and David Grant, "Do you see what I see? The role of technology in talent identification," *Asia Pacific Journal of Human Resources* 50, no. 4 (2012): 421–438.
- **Wikipedia describes sports scouts**: https://en.wikipedia.org/wiki/Scout_(sport) accessed November 30, 2022.
- **Moneyball**: Michael Lewis, *Moneyball* (New York: W.W. Norton & Company, 2004):
  - Discovering talent for talent scout (2004), 37.
  - "You could see he shouldn't be out there" (2004), 166.
  - Focused on potential: (2004), 45.
  - Talent scouts as bouncers: (2004), 15.
  - "Good face": (2004), 7.
  - Past player experiences: (2004), 263.
  - Accurate assessment of players thoughts from Bill James: (2004), 68–69.

- "The system is the star": (2004), 59.
- Expose the views of insiders: (2004), 62.
- "We're blending what we see, but we aren't allowing . . .": (2004), 37.
- Statistics are an uncertain guide to future performance: (2004), 136.
- "What gets me really excited . . . warts . . .": (2004), 149.
- **"For example, Lucien Alzari notes . . .":** Lucien Alzarai, "A chief HR officer's perspective on talent management," *Journal of Organizational Effectiveness: People and Performance* 4, no. 4 (2017): 379–383, doi:10.1108/JOEPP-05-2017-0047.
- **Talent management definitions referring to performance**:
  - David Collings and Kamel Mellahi, "Strategic talent management: A review and research agenda," *Human Resource Management Review* 19, no. 4 (2009): 304–313.
  - Kristiina Mäkelä, Ingmar Björkman and Mats Ehrnrooth, "How do MNCs establish their talent pools? Influences on individuals' likelihood of being labeled as talent," *Journal of World Business* 45, no. 2 (2010): 134–142.
  - Anthony McDonnell, "Still Fighting the War for Talent? Bridging the Science Versus Practice Gap," *Journal of Business and Psychology* 26, no. 2 (2011): 169–173.
  - Eva Gallardo-Gallardo and Marian Thunnissen, "Standing on the shoulders of giants? A critical review of empirical talent management research," *Employee Relations* 38, no. 1 (2016): 31–56.
  - Sanne Nijs, Eva Gallardo-Gallardo, Nicky Dries and Luc Sels, "A multidisciplinary review into the definition, operationalization, and measurement of talent," *Journal of World Business* 49, no. 2 (2014): 180–191, https://doi.org/10.1016/j.jwb.2013.11.002.
  - Gunter Stahl, Ingmar Björkman, Elaine Farndale, Shad Morris, Jaap Paauwe, Philip Stiles, Jonathan Trveor and Patrick Wright, "Global Talent Management: How Leading Multinationals Build and Sustain Their Talent Pipeline," *INSEAD Working Papers Collection* 34 (2007): 1–36.
- **Talent management definition relates to potential**:
  - Gunter Stahl, Ingmar Björkman, Elaine Farndale, Shad Morris, Jaap Paauwe, Philip Stiles, Jonathan Trveor and Patrick Wright, "Global Talent Management: How Leading Multinationals Build and Sustain Their Talent Pipeline," *INSEAD Working Papers Collection* 34 (2007): 1–36.
  - John Boudreau and Peter Ramstad, *Beyond HR: The new science of human capital* (Boston MA: Harvard Business School Press, 2007), 2.
- **"Brené Brown highlights the inherent tension . . .":** and the requirement to "Be like everyone else, but Better," in *Atlas of the Heart: Mapping Meaningful Connection and the Language of Human Experience* (London: Vermilion, 2021), 20.
- **Talent decisions depend on relative performance**: Sanne Nijs, Eva Gallardo-Gallardo, Nicky Dries and Luc Sels, "A multidisciplinary review into the defini-

tion, operationalisation, and measurement of talent," *Journal of World Business* 49, no. 2 (2014): 180–191, https://doi.org/10.1016/j.jwb.2013.11.002.
- **Proxy performers**: Jerry Suls, René Martin and Ladd Wheeler, "Social Comparison: Why, With Whom, and With What Effect?," *Current Directions in Psychological Science* (2002): 159–163.
- **Shane Warne**: cricket statistics taken from his Wikipedia page, https://en.wikipedia.org/wiki/Shane_Warne, accessed February 20, 2023.
- **Stuart McGill**: information from his Wikipedia page .https://en.wikipedia.org/wiki/Stuart_MacGill, accessed February 20, 2023.
- **"When we develop expectations"**: Brené Brown, *Atlas of the Heart: Mapping Meaningful Connection and the Language of Human Experience* (London: Vermilion, 2021).
- **Performance Review meme**: I accessed the performance review meme from a reddit thread: https://www.reddit.com/r/LateStageCapitalism/comments/5dzlt8/performance_review_cant_let_the_peons_feel_good/, accessed February 20, 2023.
- **Brené Brown connection between expectations and the human mind**: *Atlas of the Heart: Mapping Meaningful Connection and the Language of Human Experience* (London: Vermilion, 2021), 43.
- **Brené Brown and Stealth expectations**: *Atlas of the Heart: Mapping Meaningful Connection and the Language of Human Experience* (London: Vermilion, 2021), 43–45.

# External Character's Talent Categories

- **Role of customers in defining talent**: you can find details of the role of customers in defining talent in Sharna Wiblen, "Talking about Talent: Conceptualising Talent Management through Discourse," Doctor of Philosophy Thesis, University of Sydney, 2015; and Sharna Wiblen and Anthony McDonnell, "Connecting 'talent' meanings and multi-level context: a discursive approach," *The International Journal of Human Resource Management* 31, no. 4 (2020): 474–510, doi:10.1080/09585192.2019.1629988.
- **"Not all voices . . ."**: Anthony McDonnell and Sharna Wiblen, *Talent Management: A Research Overview* (New York: Routledge, 2021), 35.
- **Lominger Leadership Architect**: learn more at https://www.kornferry.com/capabilities/leadership-professional-development/training-certification/korn-ferry-leadership-architect-certification.
- **9-Box**: Google "9-box" to learn about the diversity of perspectives (and acceptance of) the 9-box framework that evaluates an individual's performance and potential.
- **"My research shows that even when stakeholders . . ."**: see Sharna Wiblen, "Talking about Talent: Conceptualising Talent Management through Discourse,"

Doctor of Philosophy Thesis, University of Sydney, 2015; and Sharna Wiblen and Anthony McDonnell, "Connecting 'talent' meanings and multi-level context: a discursive approach," *The International Journal of Human Resource Management* 31, no. 4 (2020): 474–510.

## Negotiating Talent Meanings

- **All-purpose talent meanings and justice**: find discussions of the linkages between consistent talent definitions and justice in Jolyn Gelens, Joeri Hofmans, Nicky Dries and Roland Pepermans, "Talent management and organisational justice: employee reactions to high potential identification," *Human Resource Management Journal* 24, no. 2 (2014): 159–175, doi:10.1111/1748-8583.12029; Jerald Greenberg, *The quest for justice on the job: essays and experiments* (Thousand Oaks, CA: Sage Publications, 2002); Edward P. O'Connor and Marian Crowley-Henry, "Exploring the Relationship Between Exclusive Talent Management, Perceived Organizational Justice and Employee Engagement: Bridging the Literature," *Journal of Business Ethics* (2017): 1–15, doi:10.1007/s10551-017-3543-; and Nicky Cries, "The psychology of talent management: A review and research agenda," *Human Resource Management Review* 23, no. 4 (2013): 272–285.
- **"My teaching and research have brought light . . . "**: see Sharna Wiblen, "Talking about Talent: Conceptualising Talent Management through Discourse," Doctor of Philosophy Thesis, University of Sydney (2015); and Sharna Wiblen and Anthony McDonnell, "Connecting 'talent' meanings and multi-level context: a discursive approach," *The International Journal of Human Resource Management* 31, no. 4 (2020): 474–510; and Sharna Wiblen, David Grant and Kristine Dery, "Questioning the Value of a Consistent Approach to Talent Management: When One Best Way is not Enough," paper presented at the Academy of Management Conference, Vancouver, Canada, 2015.
- **"Most scientific . . . characters"**: any scientific paper that adopts David Collings and Kamel Mellahi's definition of talent management as proposed in the following paper advocates for an all-purpose talent meaning: "Strategic talent management: A review and research agenda," *Human Resource Management Review* 19, no. 4 (2009): 304–313. Specific scientific papers include Paul Iles, Xin Chuai and David Preece, "Talent Management and HRM in Multinational companies in Beijing: Definitions, differences and drivers," *Journal of World Business* 45, no. 2 (2010): 179–189; and Stefan Jooss, Ralf Burbach and Huub Ruël, "Examining talent pools as a core talent management practice in multinational corporations," *The International Journal of Human Resource Management* (2019): 1–32, doi:10.1080/09585192.2019.1579748.

- **"Multiple ways enables dexterity . . ."**: see Sharna Wiblen, David Grant and Kristine Dery, "Questioning the Value of a Consistent Approach to Talent Management: When One Best Way is not Enough," paper presented at the Academy of Management Conference, Vancouver, Canada, 2015.

## Negotiating Talent Identification

- **"The scene begins with the scientists . . ."**: any scientific paper that adopts David Collings and Kamel Mellahi's (2009) definition of talent management as proposed in the following paper advocates for an all-purpose talent meaning: "Strategic talent management: A review and research agenda," *Human Resource Management Review* 19, no. 4 (2009): 304–313. Specific scientific papers include Paul Iles, Xin Chuai and David Preece, "Talent Management and HRM in Multinational companies in Beijing: Definitions, differences and drivers," *Journal of World Business* 45, no. 2 (2010): 179–189; and Stefan Jooss, Ralf Burbach and Huub Ruël, "Examining talent pools as a core talent management practice in multinational corporations," *The International Journal of Human Resource Management* (2019): 1–32, doi:10.1080/09585192.2019.1579748.
- **"DTM include well-defined criteria . . ."**: see Sharna Wiblen and Janet H. Marler, "Digitalised talent management and automated talent decisions: the implications for HR professionals," *The International Journal of Human Resource Management* 32, no. 12 (2021): 2592–2621, doi:10.1080/09585192.2021.1886149; and Sharna Wiblen, "Digitalised Talent Management: An Introduction," in *Digitalised Talent Management: Navigating the Human-Technology Interface*, ed. Sharna Wiblen (New York: Routledge, 2021).
- **"They offer access to step-by-step . . ."**: algorithms that provide step-by-step electronically encoded instruction is a point made by Wanda J. Orlikowski and Susan Scott, "The algorithm and the crowd: Considering the materiality of service innovation," *MIS Quarterly* 39, no. 1 (2015): 201–216.
- **Algorithms as control mechanisms**: Katherine C. Kellogg, Melissa A. Valentine and Angèle Christin highlight the relationship between algorithms and control in "Algorithms at Work: The New Contested Terrain of Control," *Academy of Management Annals* 14, no. 1 (2020): 366–410, doi:10.5465/annals.2018.0174.
- **". . . my research shows that HR characters are not (always) a united team"**: see Sharna Wiblen and Janet H. Marler, "Digitalised talent management and automated talent decisions: the implications for HR professionals," *The International Journal of Human Resource Management* 32, no. 12 (2021): 2592–2621, doi:10.1080/09585192.2021.1886149; Sharna Wiblen, "Talking about Talent: Conceptualising Talent Management through Discourse," Doctor of Philosophy Thesis, University of Sydney (2015); and Sharna Wiblen and Anthony McDonnell, "Connecting 'talent' meanings and multi-level context: a discursive approach," *The International Jour-*

*nal of Human Resource Management* 31, no. 4 (2020): 474–510; and Sharna Wiblen, David Grant and Kristine Dery, "Questioning the Value of a Consistent Approach to Talent Management: When One Best Way is not Enough," paper presented at the Academy of Management Conference, Vancouver, Canada, 2015; Sharna Wiblen, "Talking about Talent: Conceptualising Talent Management through Discourse," Doctor of Philosophy Thesis, University of Sydney (2015); and Sharna Wiblen, Kristine Dery and David Grant, "Do you see what I see? The role of technology in talent identification," *Asia Pacific Journal of Human Resources* 50, no. 4 (2012): 421–438.

- **"My research also suggests some HR characters are open to a more flexible approach"**: see papers listed above.
- **Dr Cathy O'Neill and fairness and justice**: Cathy O'Neill, *Weapons of Math Destruction: How Big Data Increases Inequality and Threatens Democracy* (UK: Penguin Books, 2017): fairness quote, 95. Note about reviewing fairness, 207.

## Negotiating Talent Decision Systems

- **Some of my early HR technology work**: see Kristine Dery, David Grant and Sharna Wiblen, "Human Resource Information Systems: Replacing or Enhancing HRM," paper presented at the 15th World Congress of the International Industrial Relations Association IIRA, 2009, "The New World of Work, Organisations and Employment," Sydney, Australia; David Grant, Kristine Dery, Nick Wailes and Sharna Wiblen, "Human Resource Information Systems (HRIS): An Unrealised Potential," paper presented at the Annual CIPD Centres' Conference Nottingham, United Kingdom, 2009; Sharna Wiblen, David Grant and Kristine Dery, "Transitioning to a New HRIS: The Reshaping of Human Resources and Information Technology Talent," *Journal of Electronic Commerce Research* 11, no. 4 (2010): 251–267.
- **ManuOrg case study**: you can find details of the ManuOrg case study in Sharna Wiblen, David Grant, and Kristine Dery, "Transitioning to a New HRIS: The Reshaping of Human Resources and Information Technology Talent," *Journal of Electronic Commerce Research* 11, no. 4 (2010): 251–267.
- **"My research revealed that an Australian Professional Services Firm"**: see Sharna Wiblen, Kristine Dery and David Grant, "Do you see what I see? The role of technology in talent identification," *Asia Pacific Journal of Human Resources* 50, no. 4 (2012): 421–438; Sharna Wiblen and Janet H. Marle, "Digitalised talent management and automated talent decisions: the implications for HR professionals," *The International Journal of Human Resource Management* 32, no. 12 (2021): 2592–2621, doi:10.1080/09585192.2021.1886149.

## Strategic Implications

- **"Thorsten Grohsjean, Linus Dahlander, Ammon Salter, and Paola Criscuolo, in an *MIT Sloan Management Review* make a crucial point . . ."**: "Better Ways to Green-Light New Projects," *MIT Sloan Management Review* (2022), https://sloanreview.mit.edu/article/better-ways-to-green-light-new-projects/.

## Knowledge Implications

- **"The transferability of talent is not automatic . . ."**: Anthony McDonnell and I talk about the contextual nature of talent in Wiblen and McDonnell (2020, 477), "Connecting 'talent' meanings and multi-level context: a discursive approach," *The International Journal of Human Resource Management* 31, no. 4 (2020): 474–510;
- **Jordan B. Peterson:** in presenting his eleventh of 12 Rules for Life in *Beyond Order: 12 More Rules for Life* (New York: Penguin Books, 2021), 305–306.
- **"My research shows that digitalisation . . ."**: see Sharna Wiblen and Janet H. Marler, "Digitalised talent management and automated talent decisions: the implications for HR professionals," *The International Journal of Human Resource Management* 32, no. 12 (2021): 2592–2621, doi:10.1080/09585192.2021.1886149.

## Concluding Monologue

- **Ask (Better) Questions**: the power of reasking and reframing is discussed by Daniel Kahneman in *Thinking, Fast and Slow* (Sydney: Penguin Books, 2012).
- **Joshua Fields Milburn and the solutions are the problem**: quote from Joshua Fields Millburn blog post *You Cannot Fix Anything*, https://www.theminimalists.com/cannotfix/.
- **The etymology of deliberate**: learn about the etymology of "deliberate" via https://www.etymonline.com/word/deliberate, accessed 20 September 2022.
- **Separate thinking from results**: learn about "resulting" from Annie Duke, *Thinking in Bets: Making Smarter Decisions When You Don't Have All the Facts* (New York: Portfolio/Penguin, 2019).
- **Pick and use your words wisely and Brené Brown**: in Brené Brown, *Atlas of the Heart: Mapping Meaningful Connection and the Language of Human Experience* (London: Vermilion, 2021), 116.
- **Learn How to See**: learn about the fundamentals of anthropology, ethnography and observations and the connection to digitalised talent management in Sophie Goodman "Anthropology, Culture, and Ethnography's Value in Understanding Digitalised Talent Management," in *Digitalised Talent Management: Navigating*

*the Human-Technology Interface,* ed. Sharna Wiblen (New York: Routledge, 2021), 18–38.

- **520 Colours**: a Google search to enquire about the largest range of coloured pencils I could find showed a 520 colour pencil set: https://www.amazon.com.au/Coloured-Professional-Wax-Based-Sketching-Colouring/dp/B09V2M1S5Q/ref=asc_df_B09V2M1S5Q/?tag=googleshopdsk-22&linkCode=df0&hvadid=463598465987&hvpos=&hvnetw=g&hvrand=6235633231162340778&hvpone=&hvptwo=&hvqmt=&hvdev=c&hvdvcmdl=&hvlocint=&hvlocphy=9071884&hvtargid=pla-1661263095521&psc=1, accessed March 10, 2023.

# List of Figures

| | | |
|---|---|---|
| **Figure 2.1** | Start with Y.O.U. – Your Own Understanding —— | **15** |
| **Figure 10.1** | Overview of scientific talent categories —— | **113** |
| **Figure 10.2** | Talent categories —— | **114** |
| **Figure 10.3** | Talk about Talent as – Something in you —— | **116** |
| **Figure 11.1** | External characters interested in talent decisions —— | **151** |
| **Figure 16.1** | Talent categories —— | **213** |
| **Figure 17.1** | Start with Y.O.U. – Your Own Understanding —— | **219** |

# About the Author

**Sharna Wiblen** (PhD) is an author, an award-winning executive educator, a co-leader of the Enterprise Effectiveness Network, Senior Research Scientist at the Centre for Effective Organizations at USC's Marshall School of Business (USA), Assistant Professor at Sydney Business School, University of Wollongong (Australia) and a Research Fellow with Leeds Business School (UK).

Sharna is a respected authority in talent management, organisational effectiveness and the future of work. With a unique blend of academic expertise and over 15 years of industry experience, she is a leading voice in promoting responsible talent management strategies.

As a co-leader of the Enterprise Effectiveness Network (EEN), Sharna is at the forefront of brokering dialogue between academia and industry. Through this role, she facilitates collaborations, fosters knowledge exchange and helps organisations find systemic solutions to their talent and strategy execution challenges. Her ability to bridge the gap between theory and practice has garnered recognition as a trusted executive advisor and an effective and engaging speaker.

With a passion for uncovering the complexity of talent management, Sharna's research explores the boundaries between talent, organisational effectiveness and the influence of digitalisation. She delves into how organisations attribute value to individuals and mobilise their workforce to execute strategies successfully. Her work highlights humans' vital role in the digital transformation era, emphasising the need for inclusive and human-centric approaches to organisational design.

Sharna's academic rigour is complemented by her extensive industry experience as a management consultant, human resource and recruitment coordinator, and retail service manager. This diverse background enables her to bring real-world insights and practical relevance to her research and consulting endeavours. Her ability to effectively communicate with academics and practitioners ensures that her work resonates with diverse audiences and drives meaningful organisational change.

As an accomplished author, Sharna has published in esteemed journals and authored influential books, including *Talent Management: A Research Overview* and *Digitalised Talent Management: Navigating the Human-Technology Interface*. Her expertise extends to executive education, where she imparts her knowledge and passion for responsible talent management. Sharna's work continues to shape conversations, influence practices and inspire decision-makers to embrace strategic, informed and responsible talent management approaches in the face of evolving workplaces and technological advancements while recognising the power of humans and human decision-making.

## Contact

Sharna Wiblen is available for speaking, consulting, executive development and coaching.
Visit www.sharnawiblen.com to learn more.

# Index

#Teamhuman  15, 33, 59, 199, 207, 222, 228–229
#Teamtechnology  15, 33, 222

Actions  3, 9, 13, 15–16, 17, 18, 33, 35–37, 39–44, 48–49, 61, 63, 74, 79, 82, 87, 93, 95, 102, 113, 115, 125–126, 132, 134, 137, 139, 144, 148, 154, 157, 161, 170, 180, 187, 192, 199, 208, 214, 220, 222–226
Alec Levenson  27
Alfred Chandler  37
Ammon Salter  201
An admired CEO or business guru  166
Android  54–55
Annie Duke  224
Anthony McDonnell  96n15, 105n17, 112n18, 135, 152n24
Apple  54–55
Assumptions  10, 13, 15, 17, 40–41, 62–63, 66, 68, 70–72, 74, 76, 79, 82, 117, 123, 128, 137, 158, 202, 209–210, 219, 221n26, 227–228

Bias  3, 8, 13, 15–16, 17, 17n5, 18, 19, 21, 23, 122–123, 130–132, 142, 157, 201, 207–208, 216, 221, 225
Billy Beane  128–131, 131n19
BlackRock  48
Blue Origin  33–34
Brené Brown  140, 145, 147, 225

Cathy O'Neill  179
CEO  50, 126, 154, 164–166, 168, 178
ChatGPT  36, 59, 105, 105n16
Competencies  11, 26–27, 121, 155, 165, 167, 169, 175–176, 178, 211, 214
Competitive advantage  36–38, 85, 135, 225
Complexity  3–4, 8, 10–11, 13–14, 17–18, 21, 28, 36, 38, 42–44, 48, 53–59, 62, 63n9, 67, 69–70, 73–76, 81, 89, 98, 103, 105n16, 109, 111, 115, 117, 120, 125, 132, 138, 146–147, 157–158, 167–168, 170, 178–179, 181, 183, 189, 191, 193, 197, 207, 211, 214–215, 219–220, 222, 224, 227–228
Consultants  9, 37, 152–153
Context  4, 10, 18, 20, 22–23, 34, 40, 43, 46, 50–51, 55–57, 66–67, 69, 74–75, 88–90, 93, 102, 104, 105n16, 106n17, 108–109, 133, 142–143, 147, 149, 152, 163, 170, 173–174, 182–183, 187, 191, 204, 212, 226, 228

COVID 19 pandemic  4, 56, 83, 108, 207
Creating business plans  39
Culture  41, 55, 66, 68, 71–72, 74, 116, 121, 213, 227
Customers  54, 153
Customisation  25, 53–54, 156, 187
Cynthia Covey Haller  118

Daniel Kahneman  221
David Collings  135
David Grant  53n8, 69, 125–126, 186
Decision-makers  8–9, 18, 69, 139–140, 142, 145, 147, 226
Decision-making  3–4, 7–8, 10–14, 16, 18, 20, 22–24, 26, 33, 35, 41, 50, 52, 53n8, 57, 73–74, 81, 87, 89–90, 95, 97–98, 122, 137, 149, 154, 157–158, 163, 179–180, 183–184, 186, 192–193, 199–200, 202–205, 207–209, 211, 214, 216, 219–224, 226, 228–229
Digitalisation  4–5, 7–8, 10, 12, 20, 23, 25, 28, 33–34, 46, 49–51, 53–58, 63n9, 67, 69–70, 72–74, 83–84, 87, 89–90, 104, 109, 133, 155, 157, 175, 181, 186, 200, 204, 216, 227–228
– meanings and definitions  89
Digitalisation Strategies  49, 56, 200, 204
– business-driven approach  50–51, 54–55
– technology-driven approach  25, 50–55, 200, 204
Digitalised Talent Management  27, 90, 175
Digitalised Talent Management Strategies  56
Disability  16
Disney  35, 44
Disneyland  35
Douglas Ready  48

Efficiency  26, 28, 53, 179
Elaine Farndale  135
Emotions  12, 71, 84, 122, 130
Enterprise Resource Planning System  7, 23, 90, 184
Envision  48
Eva Gallardo-Gallardo  106, 135, 143
Experts, admired CEOs or business gurus  154

Fairness  94–95, 169, 179, 183, 192
Finance  24, 52, 164, 166, 185
Future of work  6, 20

Gender  16, 122
Google  34–35, 49, 54, 71, 88, 104, 108, 229
Günter Stahl  135

Henry Mintzberg  37
Hilligje Gerritdina Van Dijk  106
Human mind/brain  8, 10, 12, 64n10, 65, 93, 98, 103–104, 111, 145, 151, 157, 207–208
Human Resource Information System  7, 24, 90, 184, 189
Human Resource Management  21, 93–96, 139, 210
Human Resources  7, 9, 21–22, 24–26, 28, 43, 46–47, 52, 75n11, 90, 93–96, 108, 119–120, 125–126, 135, 139, 164, 166, 175–178, 184–187, 189, 192–193, 200, 210–211, 216
Humans  3, 5–6, 7, 8, 9, 10, 11, 12, 12n3, 13, 15–21, 22n6, 23–24, 27–28, 31, 33–34, 38–43, 45, 47, 49, 51, 53–54, 56–57, 59–65, 67, 69–76, 81–84, 87, 90–91, 93–94, 96–98, 101, 109–111, 113–122, 127–129, 131, 133, 139–141, 143, 145, 148, 151, 154, 157–158, 163, 169, 180, 182, 184, 186, 192, 199, 201, 203, 207–213, 216, 221, 221n26, 224–225, 226n28, 227–229
Humans mind/brain  12–13, 16, 19, 154, 208
Human-Technology interface  4–5, 6, 7, 10, 33, 57, 60, 72, 76, 199, 228

Information Technology  24, 52, 116, 164, 166, 184–185, 187, 189, 211
Ingmar Björkman  135

Jaap Paauwe  135
Janet H. Marler  75n11
Jeff Bezos  33
John Boudreau  46–48, 50, 106, 108, 112
Jonathan Trevor  135
Joshua Fields Millburn  222
Judgments  8–9, 10, 16–19, 22, 31, 41, 93, 96–97, 102, 105n16, 114–115, 119, 123–125, 127–129, 139–143, 145, 147, 155, 158, 173, 177, 191–192, 203, 208, 210, 213, 216, 224, 226, 226n28
Justice  94, 169, 179

Kaleidoscope of talent colours  103, 109, 151, 158, 181, 192, 229
Kamel Mellahi  135
Knowledge  13, 23–24, 26–27, 31, 38n7, 47–48, 51–52, 59–71, 64n10, 73–76, 90–91, 93, 98, 105, 108–109, 111–112, 118, 120, 154, 157–158, 165, 175, 185–187, 197, 199, 202, 207, 209, 212, 216, 219–220, 221n26, 222–224, 227
– Aboriginal  63n9, 67–68
– Artificial Intelligence  34, 90, 184
– definitions  59
– Epistemology  61–63, 66, 68, 76, 109, 209, 220
– indigenous  67
– Interpretivism  63–67, 109, 209, 228
– Ontology  61–63, 66, 68, 76, 109, 209, 220
– Positivism  63, 66, 70, 157, 209, 220, 227
– reality  13, 14n4, 17, 20, 22, 35, 62–64, 67–68, 76, 109, 126, 146–148, 157, 161, 180, 184, 209, 213–215, 220, 221n26
– Social constructionism  64–67, 70, 73–74, 109, 157, 209
– Socio-material  70, 75, 75n11
– Technological Determinism  70, 72
– truth  8, 10, 63–67, 70, 73, 97, 109, 118, 137, 157, 171, 180, 186, 209, 215, 220, 224–225
Knowledge implications  207
Kristiina Mäkelä  135
Kristine Dery  53n8, 125–126, 186

Language and discourse  3, 15, 40, 42–44, 48, 68, 103, 131, 136–137, 158, 207, 209, 221, 225–226
Leadership  11, 25–27, 37–38, 121–122, 155, 164–165, 167, 169, 175–176, 178, 211
Lego  35, 44
Linda Hill  48
Line managers  9, 20–21, 22, 28, 39, 125–126, 165, 177–178, 211, 216
LinkedIn  88
Linus Dahlander  201
Luc Sels  106, 135, 143
Lucien Alziari  133

Marian Thunnissen  135
Mats Ehrnrooth  22, 135
Maura Stevenson  48
Maya Angelou  85
MedVet  48
Michael Crotty  64
Michael Lewis  128
Michael Porter  37–38, 38n7, 39, 40, 46
Microsoft Teams  88
Moneyball  128–132
Motivation  19, 82

Nicky Dries  106, 135, 143

Observations  14, 60, 109, 125–128, 131, 214, 226, 226n28
Oracle  185, 189
Outcome  4–5, 13, 17, 19, 24, 26, 31, 33–36, 38, 40–41, 44–47, 51, 54, 58–59, 61, 65–67, 69–74, 76, 82–84, 87–88, 95, 97, 108–109, 113, 115–116, 120, 122, 127, 130–132, 131n19, 134, 136–141, 143, 146, 148, 157–158, 165, 168, 170–171, 173, 175, 179–180, 197, 199–200, 203, 207–208, 213, 215–216, 221–224, 227–228

Paola Criscuolo  201
Patrick Wright  135
Paul DePodesta  129–132
Perceptions  3, 9, 12, 14–15, 16, 17, 18, 19, 21–22, 22n6, 31, 38, 40–41, 43–44, 47, 63, 69–70, 76, 81, 89, 94, 96–97, 102, 104, 109, 115–116, 119, 121–129, 131–132, 136–137, 145–146, 151, 153–154, 157–158, 166, 180, 199, 209–210, 212–213, 215–216, 220, 225, 227–229
Performance Management  18, 21–22, 96, 120–121, 136, 146, 180
Perspectives  3, 10, 18, 20, 22, 38n7, 39–40, 43–44, 63, 66–67, 72–76, 81–83, 89, 93–94, 96, 96n15, 102, 111–114, 118, 124, 126, 148, 151, 153, 157–158, 161, 168, 171, 177, 179, 182, 184, 191–192, 209, 212, 223, 225, 228
Peter Drucker  37
Peter Ramstad  46, 48, 50, 106, 112
Philip Stiles  135
Process engineering  52, 55

Race and ethnicity  16
Reflection  14, 19, 88, 98, 101, 113, 124, 220
Reframing  221
Research  61
- methodology  61
- research questions  61
Responsible talent decisions  12–13, 14, 16, 21, 23–24, 33, 49, 51–52, 54, 82, 87, 89, 91, 109, 112, 138, 157, 180, 185, 199–201, 208, 214, 220, 222, 224, 226n28
Richard Branson  33
Robert E. Lewis  47–48, 95–96, 128
Robert J. Heckman  47–48, 95–96
Robert Thomas  48

Role of thoughts  3, 8–9, 10, 12–19, 12n3, 31, 38n7, 41–42, 48, 81, 87, 89, 91, 93, 102–104, 114, 124, 145, 154, 164, 168, 181, 191, 207–210, 219–220, 221n26, 223, 226, 226n28, 229

Sabermetrics  129
Sanne Nijs  106, 135, 143
SAP  185, 187, 189
Scientists  3, 5, 14, 60–64, 66, 72–76, 90, 96, 105, 111, 126, 139, 143, 152, 152n24, 165, 174–175, 201, 215, 224
Senior executives  9, 20, 178, 187
Shad Morris  135
Shane Warne  144
Sharna Wiblen  96, 108, 126, 152, 169, 181, 189, 225
Slack  88
Sophie Goodman  226n28, 226n29
Stephen R. Covey  118
Stereotypes  16–17, 121–123, 131–132, 216
Strategic implication  199
Strategy  3–4, 9–10, 20, 22, 24–25, 27, 31, 33–59, 38n7, 61, 67, 81, 91, 95, 97–98, 103–104, 108–109, 112, 114, 127, 132–136, 141, 148–149, 152, 154, 157–158, 163–164, 166–169, 171, 173–174, 176, 178, 181–182, 185–187, 190, 193, 197, 199–202, 204–205, 207, 210–212, 223, 225, 227
- meanings and definitions  36–37, 39
- strategy-as-expereince  40–41
- strategy-as-experience  40–41, 51
- strategy-as-practice  43
- Strategy-as-variety  40–44
- strategy-by-design  40, 46, 168
Stuart McGill  144
Subjectivity  8–9, 10, 11, 13–14, 16, 22, 28, 59, 61, 63–69, 64n10, 76, 93, 95–98, 105n16, 109, 114–115, 120, 125–126, 128, 130, 137–138, 145, 147, 157, 177, 180, 183, 192n25, 197, 208–210, 214–215, 220, 228
Susan Scott  74

Talent
- acquired  59, 68, 107, 111, 152, 212
- all-purpose talent meanings  169, 179, 185
- as an investment  225
- as something you have  17
- concept  3, 8, 13–14, 19, 27, 31, 36, 46, 59, 61, 64, 67–68, 81–82, 84, 102–104, 114, 128, 133–134, 136–137, 139–143, 139n21, 145, 158, 163, 178–179, 181, 191, 207, 213, 215

## Index

- consistency 169
- Definitions and meanings 26, 134, 166, 168–169, 171, 173, 177, 179, 182–183, 188, 191, 221
- everyone is talent 112
- exclusive 111–112, 152, 210, 212
- expectations 6, 24, 114, 124–125, 132, 136, 142, 145–148, 151, 153, 176, 213, 226
- inclusive 111, 152
- individuals 4, 9, 94, 102, 112, 114, 142, 152
- inherent 111
- jobs, roles, or positions 9, 112, 152, 212
- meanings and definitions 103–106, 108, 135, 143, 216
- negotiation of talent meanings 168
- negotiation 3, 10, 22, 83n12, 161, 163–165, 169, 173–174, 182–183, 191–192, 197, 204, 207, 211
- object 112
- performance 5, 18, 20–21, 22, 27, 40, 47–48, 95–96, 104, 105n16, 106–107, 112, 114, 120–121, 127, 129–130, 134–136, 141–146, 153–155, 169, 176–177, 180, 213–216, 225
- potential 7, 16, 19, 22, 25–26, 27, 50, 61, 69, 72, 82, 90, 96, 98, 105n16, 106–109, 114, 125–126, 128–129, 132, 135–138, 137n20, 144, 146–147, 153, 155–156, 169–170, 175, 180–182, 184–185, 192, 201, 214–216, 225, 227–228
- skills and capabilities 4, 6, 9, 26, 45, 103, 109, 112, 114, 118, 122, 148, 152, 158, 175, 212
- social construction 3, 10, 157, 207
- subject 112
- Talent and proxies 143–144, 180
- Talent and sport 105, 105n16, 108, 115–116, 127–128, 130–132, 180, 216
- Talent as a relative concept 139
- Talent as a time-based concept 134
- Talent as a Verb 43, 84, 124–125, 158, 213–214
- Talent as humans we don't want to lose 148, 158
- Talent as (hypothetical) value for a future day 136, 155
- Talent as performance 135
- Talent as relative to a decision-maker's undefined expectations 147
- Talent as relative to goals and objectives 142
- Talent as relative to peers 142–143, 155
- Talent as relative to performance 141
- Talent as something in you 115, 117–119, 158
- Talent as something that we do 123–124, 158, 202
- Talent as something that we see 125–127, 129, 131, 158
- Talent as something we currently value 134
- Talent as something we discover 117–118, 128, 158
- Talent as something you have 119, 121, 155, 158
- Talent decisions 3–4, 5, 8–28, 31, 33–34, 36, 38, 44, 46–49, 55–59, 61–62, 63n9, 67, 69–70, 73, 75n11, 79, 81–82, 87–91, 93–95, 97–98, 102–104, 109, 112–113, 115, 123–126, 132–134, 136–149, 137n20, 151, 153–158, 161, 163, 165, 169–171, 174–179, 182–184, 189, 191–193, 192n25, 197, 199–205, 207–216, 219–222, 222n27, 225–229
- Talent frameworks 7, 25–27, 37, 63, 68–70, 72–74, 75n11, 111–112, 115, 152, 155, 164–167, 178–180, 188, 190, 192, 201–202, 214, 228
- Talent Management 3–4, 5, 6, 7, 8, 9, 10, 11, 17, 20–21, 23, 26–27, 31, 33–34, 44–49, 55–58, 61, 63n9, 64n10, 67, 75n11, 76, 79, 85, 87, 93–98, 96n15, 103, 105, 109, 111, 114, 133–136, 139–141, 148–149, 152, 155, 157, 166–168, 174–175, 179, 182–189, 192–193, 199–202, 204, 207–212, 215–216, 222, 224–225
- integrated approach 182, 193
- meanings and definitions 95–96, 135
- retention 9, 96, 135, 141, 148, 173
- systematic approach 174–181, 192–193
- talent acquistion 9, 96, 119–120
- talent development 8–9, 22, 27, 36, 38, 46–47, 49, 55, 68, 79, 81, 93, 96–97, 105, 109, 111, 118–120, 135, 141, 153, 158, 173, 176, 188, 208, 226n28
- talent identification 9, 18, 21–22, 27, 45–46, 60, 64n10, 65, 74, 88, 93, 96–97, 104, 108, 111–113, 115, 125–126, 128–132, 135–136, 140, 144, 153, 161, 164, 171, 173–183, 185, 188, 191–193, 192n25, 197, 209, 212, 214, 225–226
- Talent mamnagement as a judgment-orientated activity 96
- talent retention 93, 141, 148, 225
- talent reviews 22
- Talent Management Strategy 33, 44, 56–57, 201, 204
- Talent pools 95–96, 122, 141, 148, 169, 193
- Talent scores 21, 146, 176, 180, 188, 192n25, 203, 214
- Talent scouts 128–129, 131–132
- Talent Strategies 200
- Talent systems 7, 12, 20–21, 26–27, 34, 179, 184–185, 189–190, 200, 204
- Talent-as-variety 170, 205

Talent-by-design 168, 174, 192, 204–205
Talent-in-action 124–131, 147, 158, 174, 180, 213–214, 226
Talentship 46–47, 112
Tata Group 48
Technology 4–5, 6, 7, 9–12, 14–15, 23–26, 28, 33–34, 37, 46, 49–60, 67–76, 75n11, 79, 87–91, 90n14, 97–98, 104, 120–122, 125, 138, 154, 156–157, 161, 165–167, 169, 175–178, 181, 183–189, 192–193, 197, 199–202, 204, 208–209, 211, 216, 219–220, 222–223, 225–229
 – algorithms 23–24, 26, 33, 57, 75, 90, 171, 175, 179, 184, 188, 192, 200–201, 203
 – artificial intelligence 6–7, 33, 73
 – automation 5–6, 7, 8, 10, 28, 33–34, 57, 69, 73, 75n11, 87–90, 175, 216, 226–228
 – best practices 26, 52, 204
 – blockchain 50, 90
 – cloud-based software 25
 – cloud-based 25, 188
 – data 4–5, 7, 10, 12, 17, 21–22, 24–26, 50, 53, 61, 66, 102, 111, 123, 130, 152, 175–176, 179–180, 183, 185–186, 189, 193, 208, 216, 224
 – history 5, 14n4, 23–24, 34–35, 40, 44, 49, 106n17, 187, 193, 208
 – implementation 6, 25, 50, 52–55, 71, 74, 166–167, 186–188
 – internet of things 90
 – machine learning 7, 33, 50, 73, 90
 – meanings and definitions 89
 – quantum computing 90
 – robots 69, 71–72, 227
 – social media 90
 – software-as-a-service 25, 52–53, 90, 188
 – standardisation 25–26, 28, 50, 53, 165, 175, 179, 204
 – Virtual and Augmented Reality 90
Technology frameworks 184
The Ending 69, 181, 192, 226–227

The Workforce 11, 18–19, 20, 21, 22, 22n6, 28, 34, 36, 38–46, 53, 57, 89, 94, 96–97, 103, 111–112, 132–134, 139–140, 152–153, 161, 171, 173–174, 191–192, 210–212, 225
Thorsten Grohsjean 201
Twitter 88

Unions 153, 165

Value 8–9, 10, 11, 12n3, 14–19, 21–22, 25–27, 31, 34, 36, 38–39, 46–47, 50–51, 54, 73, 82, 90, 93, 96–97, 102–104, 105n16, 107, 111, 113–115, 121–122, 124–126, 130–132, 134–137, 139–140, 143, 146, 148, 153–155, 158, 164, 166, 169, 171, 173–174, 176–178, 180–184, 187, 191–192, 199–200, 210, 213–216, 225
Vendor-designed systems 52, 185–186, 189, 193
Vendors 9, 11, 23–27, 28, 51–53, 53n8, 155, 165, 167, 169, 174–175, 178, 185–186, 188–190, 192–193, 199–202, 204, 211, 222n27
 – SuccessFactors 25
Virgin Galactic 33–34

Wanda Orlikowski 74
Work 4–5, 6, 7, 20, 25, 27, 34, 41–42, 44, 48, 53–56, 53n8, 59–60, 63, 69, 71–72, 79, 81–85, 83n12, 88–89, 93, 98, 101–102, 105, 107, 109, 111, 113, 118–119, 121–122, 125, 129, 133–134, 143, 154, 157, 166, 179, 186, 209, 213–216, 225–228
 – Work as a set of activities that you do 84
 – Work as an experience 84–85
 – Work as somewhere 83
WorkDay 189
Workforce differentiation 22, 47, 95, 139–141, 174, 181, 183, 192

Y.O.U. – Your Own Understanding 9, 11–13, 14, 19, 22n6, 36, 103, 134, 145–146, 149, 161,163, 173, 191, 216, 219–220, 222–223